ETHNIC EUROPE

EDITED BY ROLAND HSU

# Ethnic Europe

*Mobility, Identity, and Conflict in a Globalized World*

STANFORD UNIVERSITY PRESS

STANFORD, CALIFORNIA

Stanford University Press
Stanford, California

Chapter 3, "Ethnicity in Post–Cold War Europe, East and West,"
© by Rogers Brubaker.

Chapter 9, "Experiment Mars, Turkish Migration, and the Future of Europe:
Imaginative Ethnoscapes in Contemporary German Literature," © by Leslie
A. Adelson.

Library of Congress Cataloging-in-Publication Data
Ethnic Europe : mobility, identity, and conflict in a globalized world / edited
by Roland Hsu.
     p. cm.
  Includes bibliographical references and index.
  ISBN 978-0-8047-6946-4 (cloth : alk. paper)--ISBN 978-0-8047-6947-1
(pbk. : alk. paper)
  1. Ethnicity--Europe. 2. Group identity--Europe. 3. Minorities--Europe.
4. Immigrants--Europe. I. Hsu, Roland, 1961-
  D1056E837 2010
  305.80094--dc22                                    2009037162

Typeset by Bruce Lundquist in 10/14 Janson

# Contents

# Contributors

**Leslie A. Adelson** has been Professor of German Studies at Cornell University since 1996, where she is also a Graduate Field member of Jewish Studies, Feminist, Gender, and Sexuality Studies, and Comparative Literature. She teaches modern German literature with an emphasis on literature since 1945, and postcolonial theories of culture and history. Focal interests concern minorities and migrant cultures in postwar Germany, especially regarding Jews and Turks, and interdisciplinary and transnational approaches to German literature. Adelson's most recent book, *The Turkish Turn in Contemporary German Literature: Toward a New Critical Grammar of Migration*, appeared in 2005. Her first, *Crisis of Subjectivity* (1984), was the first scholarly monograph to deal with the literary prose of Botho Strauß. The Modern Language Association of America awarded her the Aldo and Jeanne Scaglione Prize for an Outstanding Scholarly Study in the Field of Germanic Languages and Literatures for *Making Bodies, Making History: Feminism and German Identity* (1994). Adelson held research fellowships from the Alexander von Humboldt Foundation in 1987 and 1992, and from the National Endowment for the Humanities in 2003. She has served on the editorial boards of professional journals such as *New German Critique, German Quarterly*, and the *Women in German Yearbook*, and held elected offices in the Modern Language Association. For her overall contributions to the field of postwar German cultural studies, Adelson received the German Academic Exchange Service (DAAD) Prize for Distinguished Scholarship in the Humanities in 1996. New projects revolve around the conceit of futurity in German literature in the twentieth and twenty-first centuries. Twice chair of Cornell University's Department of German Studies, Adelson currently directs Cornell University's interdisciplinary Institute for German Cultural Studies.

**Rogers Brubaker** has taught in the Department of Sociology at UCLA since 1991. Brubaker has written widely on social theory, immigration, citizenship, nationalism, and ethnicity. His first book explored the idea of rationality in the work of Max Weber, while his subsequent work analyzed European nationalism in historical and comparative perspective. *Citizenship and Nationhood in France and Germany* (1992) sought to explain the sharply differing ways in which citizenship has been defined vis-à-vis immigrants in France and Germany; *Nationalism Reframed: Nationhood and the National Question in the New Europe* (1996) compared contemporary East European nationalisms with those of the interwar period, both emerging after the breakup of multinational states into would-be nation-states. More recently, in a series of analytical essays, many of them collected in *Ethnicity Without Groups* (2004), Brubaker has critically engaged prevailing analytical stances in the study of ethnicity and nationalism and sought to develop alternative analytical resources. His most recent book, *Nationalist Politics and Everyday Ethnicity in a Transylvanian Town*, coauthored with Margit Feischmidt, Jon Fox, and Liana Grancea, was published by Princeton University Press in 2006.

**Salvador Cardús** completed his doctorate in economics and now teaches sociology in the Faculty of Political Science and Sociology at the Universitat Autònoma de Barcelona. During the academic year 1993–94 he was Visiting Fellow at Fitzwilliam College, Cambridge. In 2005, he was invited as a Visiting Reseacher at the Institute for European Studies at Cornell University. Cardús's main research areas are the sociology of religion, the media, and nationalism. His published works include *Plegar de viure* (1981); *Les enquestes a la joventut de Catalunya*, with J. Estruch (1984); *El calendari i la seva significació a la societat moderna* (1985); and, more recently, *Política de paper: Premsa i poder a Catalunya 1981–1992* (1995). He has collaborated in major jointly authored publications such as *La política cultural europea* (1990) and *Formas modernas de religión* (1994), and he is a regular contributor to national and international sociological journals. The author is also a practicing journalist. He established the bulletin *Crònica d'Ensenyament* (1987–88) and from 1989 to 1991 he was deputy editor of the Catalan daily *AVUI*. His signature appears regularly in various newspapers and journals. A selection of his journalism appeared in the volume *Algú sap cap a on anem?* (1992), and his reporting on major religious affairs was published in *Concili amb folre i* *manilles: L'Església catalana a través del seu concili* (1995). He has also worked in television, as a consultant for the series *Ciutadans* (1994), *Les coses com són* (1995), and *Vides privades* (1996–98), produced by Televisió de Catalunya.

**Carole Fink** earned a B.A. from Bard College and an M.A. and Ph.D. from Yale University, joining the faculty of the Ohio State University History Department in 1991. She previously taught at the University of North Carolina at Wilmington, the State University of New York at Binghamton, Canisius College, Albertus Magnus College, and Connecticut College. Professor Fink, a specialist in European international history and historiography, has published three books, one translation, seven edited volumes, and more than fifty articles and chapters. These works include *Defending the Rights of Others: The Great Powers, the Jews, and International Minority Protection, 1878–1938* (Cambridge University Press, 2004), which was awarded the George Louis Beer Prize of the American Historical Association for the best book in European international history; *Marc Bloch: A Life in History* (Cambridge University Press, 1989), which has been translated into six languages; *The Genoa Conference: European Diplomacy, 1921–22* (Chapel Hill, 1984; Syracuse University Press paperback edition, 1993), which was also awarded the George Louis Beer Prize; an introduction to and translation of Marc Bloch's *Memoirs of War, 1914–15* (Cornell University Press, 1980; Cambridge University Press, 1988); as well as collections of essays, including *German Nationalism and the European Response, 1890–1945*; *Genoa, Rapallo, and European Reconstruction in 1922*; *The Establishment of European Frontiers after the Two World Wars*; *1968: The World Transformed*; *Human Rights in Europe Since 1945*; *1956: European and Global Perspectives*; and *Ostpolitik, 1969–1974: European and Global Responses*. Fink has been a section editor of the AHA's *Guide to Historical Literature and Peace/Mir: An Anthology of Historical Perspectives to War*. In 2007, she received The Ohio State University's Distinguished Scholar award.

**Alec G. Hargreaves** is Ada Belle Winthrop-King Professor of French and Director of the Winthrop-King Institute for Contemporary French and Francophone Studies at Florida State University. Formerly Chair of the Department of European Studies at Loughborough University, UK, he has held visiting positions at the University of Warwick, Cornell University, the Université de Lyon II, and the École Pratique des Hautes Études. A specialist on political, cultural, and media aspects of postcolonial minorities in France, he is author and editor of numerous publications, including *Voices from the North African Immigrant Community in France: Immigration and Identity in Beur Fiction* (Berg, 1991; second edition, 1997); *Immigration, "Race" and Ethnicity in Contemporary France* (Routledge, 1995; second edition, titled *Multi-Ethnic France: Immigration, Politics, Culture and Society*, 2007); *Racism, Ethnicity and Politics in Contemporary Europe* (Edward Elgar, 1995); coedited, with Jeremy Leaman, *Post-Colonial Cultures in France* (Routledge, 1997); coedited, with Mark McKinney, *Minorités postcoloniales anglophones et francophones: études culturelles comparées* (L'Harmattan, 2004) and *Memory, Empire and Postcolonialism* (Lexington, 2005). He is a member of the editorial boards of *Expressions maghrébines, Francophone Postcolonial Studies, International Journal of Francophone Studies, Journal of European Studies,* and *Research in African Literatures.* The French government honored him in 2003, naming him a Chevalier dans l'Ordre des Palmes Académiques, and in 2006 with the Légion d'honneur.

**Roland Hsu** is Assistant Director of the Forum on Contemporary Europe at the Freeman Spogli Institute for International Studies, and Lecturer in the Introduction to Humanities Program at Stanford University. He earned a B.A. at the University of California at Berkeley, and an M.A. and Ph.D. in history at the University of Chicago. His research and teaching explore the relationship between politics, art, and memory. Before coming to Stanford, Hsu was Assistant Professor of Modern European History at the University of Idaho, and Senior Associate Director of Undergraduate Advising and Research at Stanford, as well as Academic Advisor in the College of the University of Chicago. At Chicago, he also served as Assistant Director of the University Writing Programs. Hsu wrote his dissertation on modern European intellectual and cultural history, at the University of Chicago. His most recent work on post-Revolutionary France reconsiders the use of the analytic category of memory in historical interpretation.

**Kader Konuk** is Assistant Professor of German Studies and Comparative Literature at the University of Michigan. She is currently completing a book manuscript entitled *East West Mimesis: German-Jewish Exile and Secular*

*Humanism in Turkey.* The manuscript follows the plight of German-Jewish humanists who escaped Nazi persecution by seeking exile in a Muslim-dominated society. Konuk is the author of *Identitäten im Prozeß: Literatur von Autorinnen aus und in der Türkei in deutscher, englischer und türkischer Sprache* (Blaue Eule, 2001), a comparative investigation into novels by Sevgi Özdamar, Güneli Gün, and Latife Tekin. She is also the coeditor, with Cathy Gelbin and Peggy Piesche, of *AufBrüche: Kulturelle Produktionen von Migrantinnen, Schwarzen und jüdischen Frauen in Deutschland* (Ulrike Helmer, 1999). Konuk was awarded a fellowship by the National Endowment for the Humanities in 2007. Other fellowships were granted by the Institute for Advanced Studies Berlin, the Humboldt Foundation, the Center for Literary and Cultural Research in Berlin, the German Research Council in cooperation with the University of Paderborn, and the Research School of Humanities at the Australian National University in Canberra.

**Pavle Levi** is Assistant Professor of Film Studies in the Department of Art and Art History at Stanford University. He is the author of *Disintegration in Frames* (Stanford University Press, 2007), a study of aesthetics and ideology in the Yugoslav and post-Yugoslav cinema; and the editor of *Filosofska igračka* (Radio B92/Reč, 2004), a volume of Annette Michelson's selected writings on film and modernist art. Levi has published essays on East European cinemas, avant-garde art and film, and critique of ideology in the media.

**Saskia Sassen** is the Robert Lynd Professor of Sociology at Columbia University and a member of the newly established Committee on Global Thought, after a decade at the University of Chicago. She is also a Centennial Visiting Professor at the London School of Economics. Her new books are *Territory, Authority, Rights: From Medieval to Global Assemblages* (Princeton University Press, 2008) and *A Sociology of Globalization* (Norton, 2007). Other recent books are the third fully updated edition of *Cities in a World Economy* (Sage, 2006), the edited *Deciphering the Global* (Routledge, 2007), and the coedited *Digital Formations: New Architectures for Global Order* (Princeton University Press, 2005). She has just completed a five-year project for UNESCO on sustainable human settlement, published as one of the volumes of the *Encyclopedia of Life Support Systems* (Oxford, UK: EOLSS). She is a member of the Council on Foreign Relations, a member of the National

Academy of Sciences Panel on Cities, and was Chair of the Information Technology and International Cooperation Committee of the Social Science Research Council (USA). She has written for *The Guardian*, the *New York Times*, *Le Monde Diplomatique*, the *International Herald Tribune*, *Newsweek International*, *Vanguardia*, *Clarin*, the *Financial Times*, OpenDemocracy.net, and HuffingtonPost.com, among others. Her website is http://www.columbia.edu/sjs2/.

**Bassam Tibi** is Professor of International Relations and Director of the Center of International Affairs at the University of Göttingen, A. D. White Professor at Large at Cornell University, and currently Senior Research Fellow at Yale University. He received his academic training in social science, philosophy, and history at the Goethe University of Frankfurt, where he received his first Ph.D. in 1971. After teaching in Frankfurt and Heidelberg, Tibi was appointed Professor of International Relations at the University of Göttingen in 1973. In 1988 he was appointed by royal resolution Professor of Comparative Politics (Chair of Stein Rokkan) at the University of Bergen, Norway. Professor Tibi has held various visiting professorships, inter alia, in the United States (Harvard, Princeton, Berkeley, and Ann Arbor), Turkey, Sudan, Cameroon, and recently in Switzerland, Indonesia, and Singapore. On leave from Göttingen and Cornell, he spent the academic year 2004–5 first as a Visiting Scholar at Harvard University and then as a Senior Research Fellow at the Asia Research Center/National University of Singapore. Tibi was a Harvard Bosch Fellow from 1998 to 2000. His articles and essays have been published in leading journals such as *International Journal of Middle Eastern Studies*, *Millennium*, *The Fletcher Forum*, *Religion-Staat-Gesellschaft*, *Human Rights Quarterly*, and *Middle East Journal*, and in encyclopedias such as *The Oxford Encyclopedia of Modern Islam*, *Routledge Encyclopedia of Government and Politics*, and *Encyclopedia of Democracy*. His most recent books in English are *The Challenge of Fundamentalism* (University of California Press, updated edition, 2002), *Islam Between Culture and Politics* (Palgrave, expanded new edition, 2005), *Political Islam, World Politics and Europe* (Routledge, 2008), and *Islam's Predicament with Modernity* (Routledge, 2009). In 1995, German President Roman Herzog awarded him the Medal of the State/First Class. In 2003, he received the annual prize of the Swiss Foundation for European Awareness.

**Želimir Žilnik** was born in Niš, Serbia, in 1942, and is currently based in Novi Sad, Serbia. From the late 1960s, his socially engaged films and documentaries in former Yugoslavia and his unique visual style earned him critical accolades (*The Unemployed* [1968], Best Documentary at the Oberhausen festival, 1968; *Early Works* [1969], Best Film at the Berlin Film Festival), but also censorship in the 1970s for his unflinching criticism of the government apparatus. Low budget filmmaking and challenging political themes mark Žilnik's prolific career, which includes over forty feature and documentary films and shorts. Since the 1980s, he has been developing his unique docudrama language, which he used throughout the 1990s to reflect on political tensions, including EU sanctions, the NATO bombings, and Milošević's regime. His power to observe and unleash compelling narratives out of the lives of ordinary people is the common thread throughout his documentary and docudrama work, including *Tito's Second Time Amongst the Serbs* (1994). More recently, his focus has shifted beyond the divided Balkans to question their relationship with the tightening controls of European borders, as he has delved into the heart of issues of refugees and migrants in *Fortress Europe* (2000), *Kenedi Goes Back Home* (2003), *Kenedi: Lost and Found* (2005), and the most recent of the trilogy, *Kenedi Is Getting Married* (2007).

## Acknowledgments

I am delighted to acknowledge those who inspired the best of this work. First thanks go to Amir Eshel, whose vision for a high-level, deep-impact conference on ethnicity in today's Europe launched the project that ultimately developed into this book. His leadership of the Forum on Contemporary Europe at Stanford University's Freeman Spogli Institute for International Studies, his friendship, and his wise thoughts on all stages of this book are a continuing source of encouragement to me. I also thank my student research interns, Amazia Zargarian and Jonathan Jecker-Eshel, for their dedicated work. I hope that their work on this project will inspire them to pursue their own research. I wish to thank the Freeman Spogli Institute for International Studies for support to develop and complete this book, including support from the Mentored Undergraduate Research program to enable me to hire Amazia Zargarian and to help him develop his interest in such research and publication. I also wish to thank my editor at Stanford University Press, and the anonymous readers for their reviews and suggestions for the manuscript. Special thanks go to Joan Ramon Resina for his generous assistance on the first draft of the essay by Salvador Cardús, to Laura Seaman at the Forum on Contemporary Europe, and to Clare Cordero at Clarity Info for her superb editing of the entire manuscript. Finally, my great thanks to the contributors to this volume, for their patience and openness to my requests for revisions, and for their generosity in offering expertise with their essays, and with comments to improve my own. To all these colleagues and friends this work owes its strengths; any remaining shortcomings in the text are my own.

.   .   .

This book is dedicated to Julie Noblitt, who brings to life creativity and intellect.

R H

ETHNIC EUROPE

# CHAPTER ONE

# The Ethnic Question

*Premodern Identity for a Postmodern Europe?*

ROLAND HSU

In periods of European Union expansion and economic contraction, European leaders have been pressed to define the basis for membership and for accommodating the free movement of citizens. With the lowering of Europe's internal borders,[1] the member nations have raised the question of whether a European passport is sufficient to integrate mobile populations into local communities. Addressing the European Parliament on the eve of the 1994 vote on the Czech Republic accession to the European Union, Vaclav Havel, then president of the Czech Republic, selected particular civic values to define the new Europe to which all citizens would subscribe:

> The European Union is based on a large set of values, with roots in antiquity and in Christianity, which over 2,000 years evolved into what we recognize today as the foundations of modern democracy, the rule of law and civil society. This set of values has its own clear moral foundation and its obvious metaphysical roots, whether modern man admits it or not.[2]

Havel's claim that Greco-Roman and Christian values define what it means to be European can be read as a prescription for policy, and even sociability. In the increasingly multicultural Europe his definition has been repeated, but it has also been challenged: scholars, policy makers, and ethnic community representatives debate the most effective response to increasing heterogeneity and social conflict. For those who endorse, and also for those who reject Havel's idea of binding moral roots, this new collection on ethnicity in globalized Europe reveals surprising positions.

The scale and quality of change since Havel's 1994 speech challenges confidence that we know the principles to socialize new Europe. During 1995–2005, immigration into the European Union grew at more than double the annual rate of the previous decade.[3] Within the overall population growth, employment statistics, specifically for residents of very recent immigrant origin, are difficult to aggregate, but in terms of accessing professional positions, the numbers show a steep downward trend.[4] As immigration continues to grow, the lagging employment statistics offer one kind of evidence that recent immigrants face disproportionate difficulty accessing economic benefits beyond state welfare and unemployment provisions.[5] In this constituency, the rising entry rate and falling number of fully employed raise questions about how newer ethnic communities integrate into local community, and also about how they participate in the Union's system of expanding regional mobility. Once within the European Union, does the failure of particular groups to gain professional employment constrain access to economic and educational mobility? What impact does the lack of mobility have on ethnic and civic identity?

This collection offers new ways to see how thinking ethnically, even in sympathy with minority rights, may be creating a condition that constrains the European Union's grand promise of a European community. While Europe's open internal borders offer the promise of professional and social mobility, the region is following two tracks, in one direction for mobile citizens and in another for immigrants who arrive from increasingly distant origins and who do not integrate in the flow of students and advanced professionals able to relocate around Europe. In one tightly integrated volume, this collection gives the reader the unique and exciting combination of social science and humanist answers to these questions of globalized Europe. The essays, written by some of our most influential authors and analysts, take us into Europe's fast-growing communities, sweeping us from the global to the local. The collection moves along as if descending from the high vantage point of generalized views of mass-scale diasporas, down into the details of neighborhoods, borderlands, and the arts and literature spawned by the creative mixing of ethnic cultures. We begin by forming a theoretical basis for discussion.

## Using Ethnicity

Beyond lack of integration, increasingly intense and at times violent conflict raises questions about ethnic theory and policy. When we use ethnic categories, do we protect or rather divide and marginalize an identity? In the East, such questions spring from states founded on ethnic ties: will European Union and international community safeguards of ethnic Balkan enclaves produce normalized relations after massacres and ethnic cleansing? Does European and U.S. recognition of Albanian Kosovo validate claims for Flanders, Scottish, and Corsican independence and Basque ethnic heritage? Does litigation in the name of Roma—as opposed to human—rights impose on Italy and Croatia a mandate for effective policies of integration, or segregation?[6] In the West, concern stems from the contrary tradition of suppressing the politics of ethnic difference: the widespread riots in France in 2005 and 2007 by urban youths of mainly North and West African descent against police forces raise questions about the relevance and enforcement of the French non-ethnic, secular, republican model. In the United Kingdom, the tradition of multiculturalism, while distinct from French republicanism, is aimed for a similar goal of creating a common community beyond ethnic difference.[7] Yet the recent trials of suspects in the 2005 London transit bombings, ending in several court dismissals, have done little to resolve confusion about government policies to recognize local Imams as representatives of British Islamic communities.[8] With eroding confidence in national or local religious leaders to explain the violence, analysts assert contradictory explanations linking or distinguishing violence, ethnic communities, and policies of multiculturalism. Government prosecutors, media outlets, and self-proclaimed Islamic community leaders each speak for increasingly suspected UK Muslim communities, alternately claiming that the London public was targeted by those protesting UK troops sent to Iraq, or rather by domestic Islamic fundamentalist terrorist cells waging a campaign for community Shari'a law within larger UK society.[9]

In the French case, the violence of 2005 and 2007 has ruptured confidence in the balance traditionally struck between public security and ethnic tolerance.[10] France's official response was aimed more to excise rather than reintegrate the protesters. If there are identity-based messages from the protestors, their shared grievance has been effectively characterized as little more than the urge to vandalize. In 2005, against a backdrop of successive nights of media images of attacks on security police and private property, then interior minister Nicolas Sarkozy announced the imposition of "zero tolerance" for those he termed *"racaille"* [scum].[11] The descriptor was deployed to shape public opinion, and by and large had its intended effect. The Interior Ministry was given responsibility to marshal the response, when the prime minister, Dominique de Villepin, initiated a meeting of the government (Conseil des Ministres) to declare a national state of emergency. The declaration of emergency invoked a law dating from the 1954–62 War of Algerian Independence, and applied only previously against ethnic uprisings in French Algeria and New Caledonia for searches, detainments, house arrests, and press censorship without court warrant. Today we can note the irony of invoking a law originally written to suppress ethnic independence in order to put down what the government insisted was mainly vandalism; but at the time, fear of violence overwhelmed such insight into the government's awareness of the importance of the protestors' ethnic identity.

Based on the ministry's own records, the violence likely did not catch the government by complete surprise. As was reported in early July 2004, before the first episodes of riots, the French Interior Ministry had been presented with a report as early as June 2004 which documented nearly two million citizens living in districts of social alienation, racial discrimination, and poor community policing.[12] The document raised an alert that youth unemployment in what journalists have long referred to as *quartiers chauds* [troubled neighborhoods] surpassed 50 percent. Although a 1978 law has to a large extent impeded ethnic-based surveys, the report nevertheless acknowledges what most already understood: that the majority of the unemployed and disenfranchised youth were French-born whose parents or grandparents were of African descent.[13]

French researchers continue to struggle with constraints limiting ethnic data gathering. Social scientists characterize the problem of ethnic identity in France as a challenge to make visible the social phenomenon that is lived but officially kept invisible.[14] A recent book from the School for Advanced Study of the Social Sciences (EHESS) documents what seems to be renewed self-identification among French of Caribbean and African descent of a newly reconsidered common "black" identity.[15] The shared identity is not easily created. Post-war labor migrations from the French Caribbean and Francophone African diasporas formed mainly separate communities in France, but their children may be forming bonds.[16] While state-sponsored surveys still cannot collect data on ethnic family heritage, the youngest generation of French families from the Caribbean and the sub-Saharan Africa are creating an ethnic identity one step beyond even family heritage. The most recent generation of children of immigrants from the French Caribbean and from French sub-Saharan Africa are identifying as a community of "black" French.

*Ethnicity—Postwar and Today*

Postwar era immigration, from the 1950s European reconstruction through the 1960s and 1970s decolonization, is best defined as postcolonial migration.[17] As part of the extensive rebuilding of postwar Europe, European governments targeted particular nationalities in and around the greater Mediterranean region to attract an immigrant labor force. Throughout the 1950s and early 1960s, continued immigrant labor programs brought workers and their families, as well as the development of communities—planned and unplanned—that became neighborhoods for immigrants who essentially moved from countries that had been colonial periphery regions to the outskirts of cities in what had been the imperial metropole.[18] The new residents' education, language, and collective memory had been significantly shaped by colonial administrations, and that background gave them some familiarity with the host societies. Since 1990, however, and based on projections in this collection, we have entered a period, for lack of a better name, of post-postcolonial diaspora.

The peoples emigrating to Europe are increasingly coming from lands without characteristic European colonial heritage.[19] While few countries of origin have no instance of European intervention, the new arrivals are adding rapidly growing numbers of émigrés of global diasporas from Iraq, Iran, Afghanistan, Egypt, Syria, and Israel, as well as the Indonesian archipelago, the Philippines, and sub-Saharan and East Africa. This most recent demographic trend takes Europe, and the larger transatlantic West, into an era not well served by existing models of how individuals integrate and communities differentiate.[20]

In this collection, nine prominent authors substantiate this shift. The essays offer extended arguments on microhistories and long-term trends. In combination they create an unusual and productive dialogue between humanist cultural studies and social scientist modeling to confront assumptions and clarify recent trends of immigrant origin, European identity, and policies of tolerance.[21] It is clearest to begin the collection with the most basic question: How and why are some included and others excluded as members of new Europe? In Part One, three essays by Saskia Sassen (sociology/global thought, Columbia University), Rogers Brubaker (sociology, UCLA), and Salvador Cardús (sociology, Universitat Autònoma de Barcelona) refine the value of ethnicity as a category for understanding European social membership. Sassen highlights the way expanding Europe is also globalizing Europe, and reveals the implications of the overlapping local, national, supranational, and global domains for establishing who determines citizenship—or more broadly, membership—and in which constituency. As new immigrants enter the European Union, they relate simultaneously with traditional communities, voluntary organizations, and national governments but also with the increasingly robust European Union institutions, and now with global corporations. For example, a Hindu immigrant from Bangalore, India, to London, England, may join greater London in an established neighborhood of postcolonial émigrés but also may seek access to British cultural clubs (such as social, sports, and leisure membership organizations), attempt to run for electoral office, appeal to European Union labor protections, and find employment in a private multinational corporation that limits its responsibility to European labor laws. While in one domain the ethnic immigrant may be alien, new Europe in Sassen's model offers concentric spheres of membership that demand fresh study.

Brubaker offers an elegant model of ethnicity as an identity socially organized and politically expressed. In his model, if we are to understand ethnic

identity in its European context, we must treat separately the two realms—
the social and the political—to clarify the special interplay between today's
flows of immigration, separatist movements in the East and West, and the
dynamic state formation in Europe's eastern reaches. In today's Europe, immigrants affirm an ethnic affinity and heritage by joining social groups, and
this ethnicity may or may not coincide with the territorial ethnicity defended
by the nation. European ethnicities, in this model, are the result of the relationship between populations that are mobile, or that can mobilize, and
state ambitions. A most intriguing implication of Brubaker's insight is that
in Western Europe the weakening of the state may offer a means of satisfying demands for ethno-national self-determination. In several cases, including Belgium, Spain, and the United Kingdom, membership in the European
Union may enable states to devolve power to ethno-regions, to satisfy demands and also maintain institutions that can mediate disputes. In addition,
Brubaker's sociopolitical model of ethnic identity enables him to argue that
for Eastern Europe the concern over the instability caused by the breakup
of the ethno-Hungarian empire is to some extent answered by the accession
of Hungary, Slovakia, and Romania to the European Union. Now under a
bureaucratic apparatus legislated by a parliament in Strasbourg and an execu-
tive commission in Brussels, these communities with historical ethnic ties are
once again under a single administrative structure.

Facing the global and regional models of Sassen and Brubaker, Cardús
warns of the risk we run when we assume that ethnicity describes an organic
condition. Although he acknowledges that ethnographers have replaced the
biological category of race with the idea of cultural ethnicity, he nevertheless
detects an area of concern, where theories of European society contain the
assumption that mobile groups carry their ethnic qualities from one community to the next, as if cultural attributes are static, genetically coded, and
unaffected by social relations. Cardús's essay is best compared with those of
Sassen and Brubaker by interchanging the variables in the three models. Sassen makes the communities and domains (neighborhood, nation, employer)
relative, and Brubaker makes the relationship between individuals and institutions (national versus supranational ethnic politics) variable: Cardús
argues that even if domains and national relations hardly change, Europe's
increasingly mobile individuals alter the surface of their cultural attributes—
their manners, folk customs, and religious observance—to negotiate their

group membership. All three theorists, in this way, see today's Europe as a kind of laboratory of belonging, in which the institutions that include, the individuals who join, and the relating of the two are all transforming along with the expanding and globalizing society.

In Part Two, essays by Alec Hargreaves (French, Florida State University) and Pavle Levi (art and art history, Stanford University) with Želimir Žilnik (filmmaker, Serbia) reveal the way ethnicity nevertheless continues to be used to divide society, and to marginalize and alienate minorities. Hargreaves brings to light the consequences of the French government's history of obscuring ethnically coded survey data. By statutorily blocking the collecting in surveys of identifying ethnic detail, the French state continues its traditional commitment to its model of civic republican citizenship. However, Hargreaves also reveals how state media, housing, and employment agencies consistently perpetuate and accentuate ethnic profiling and stereotypes, often in clumsy projects to overcome discrimination and grievances that are not officially recognized. The result in France has been a tightening spiral of ethnic grievance, official denial, state-sponsored positive action policy, and the muting of research that could address minority grievance. Blocking social scientists from studying ethnic data cripples their efforts to document conditions, give voice to minority groups, and offer systematic analysis that could serve as the basis for improved state policy. As noted earlier in this essay, the republican model of citizenship, and the policy dictated to defend it from modern research detail, appears increasingly at odds with the rise of newly forming ethnic identities especially among younger generations of Francophone Caribbean and West African descent.

Levi focuses on the Balkan lands and what they reveal of Europe's tense internal relations. In sharp contrast to the European Union promise of the free flow of citizens between member states, this essay shines light on the shadow regions of border lands, and on a major artist's career spent documenting the experience of Europe's internal undocumented immigrants. Levi interviews and annotates the comments by one of Europe's leading filmmakers, Želimir Žilnik, whose films date from and depict the years of the most robust European Union expansion and internal immigration, from the 1960s to the present. Žilnik's recent films document the conditions and testimonies of those who attempt to cross without papers or sufficient economic resources from Moldova, Montenegro, Croatia, Slovenia, and Serbia into Italy, Austria, and the Czech Republic. Immigrants, local police, and border town residents each caricature one another as ethnic aliens: they agree, however, that the European Union Schengen agreement, promoted as a safeguard for citizen mobility, seems to them principally a means of facilitating the free flow of organized crime. Levi uses the interview with Žilnik to articulate in words what the filmmaker attempts in visual style: a manifesto on the ability of art and film to influence the creation of European transnational, multiethnic border cultures.

In Part Three, four essays by Bassam Tibi (international relations/ professor at large, University of Göttingen/Cornell University), Kader Konuk (Germanic/comparative literature, Michigan State University), Leslie Adelson (German studies, Cornell University), and Carole Fink (history, Ohio State University), build on this collection's theory and critique to propose four bold models of ethnicity as a promising tie for socializing Europe. Tibi begins with criticism of European multiculturalism, which, he argues, inadvertently enables European Islamist fundamentalism. He levels this critique in an attempt to challenge his fellow Muslim immigrants to embrace traditional European civic values (which he dates neither from antiquity nor the Christian era but rather from the French Revolution) as the foundation, not for multiculturalism but for a cultural pluralism that fosters social integration. In terms reminiscent of Havel's 1994 speech, but marked at an updated milestone of 1789, the result would replace Islamist fundamentalism with a Euro-Islam capable of Euro-integration.

Konuk sets Tibi's insight on European-Muslim ethnicity into the history of European-Turkish relations. Those readers questioning Turkey's European Union candidacy will find that the two essays shift the common critique of Turkish policy towards a more pressing question of Europe's social capacity to integrate prospective Turkish–European Union citizens. Konuk reveals the fate of European Jews who immigrated to Turkey during the 1930s, hired by Turkish universities as part of the Turkish modernization-Europeanization campaign, but never fully accepted as Turkish citizens. Just as this history reveals the fate of German Jews in Turkey, the essay reminds us to review Turkish experience in Germany. In the context of contemporary anxiety over Turkey's potential candidacy into the European Union, we are reminded of the history of difficulty both in Turkey and in Germany of integrating Turkish Germans and German Turks.

Adelson sustains the focus on German-Turkish relations and experiments with a comparison of literary poetics to find what may ultimately be a humanist recipe for the future of European ethnic relations. One may argue that Germany and Turkey, beyond the history of immigration that links them, also share the distinction of being the most unlikely models for a peaceful, enlarged, and cohesive Europe. Both German and Turkish histories include imperial expansionist campaigns and atrocities that warrant contrition, as well as suspicion from neighbors who face joining with them in a greater Europe. Modern German and Turkish literature has characteristically dwelled on their pasts, and perhaps understandably has offered little in the way of new cultural identity for societies that face the daunting task of reconciling historical legacies with the modern project of a peaceful, supranational Europe. Adelson, however, takes a bold step to relate (heretofore considered disparate) emphases on futurism in works by the German artist Alexander Kluge and those of the Turkish poets Berkan Karpat and Zafer Şenocak, to turn new attention to the possibility that German and Turkish literary artists may best describe and inspire models of a new ethnos and unprecedented sociability for Europe.

Fink addresses the question of the fate of Jews in expanding Europe. She perceives the globalization of Europe that Sassen first remarks on in this collection; but she notes the challenges that such expansion creates for European peoples seeking to build internal cohesion over and beyond their regional disparity, and to build foreign relations based on a coherent European position. European Jewry, plagued by the legacy of anti-Semitism in the West and by the revival of such ethnic bias in the new member states of the East, as well as divided by multiple ethnicities of Sephardic and Ashkenazi culture, generational change, and tension over models of community education, seems an unlikely cultural amalgam for integrating Europe. However, Fink argues in this concluding essay that Europe's Jews, while they are rebuilding relations across Europe's internal borders, and because they are, in Europe, the people most thoroughly connected with the greater Middle East, should be understood as a community integral in Europe's effort to deepen its internal cohesion and extend its global reach.

This volume on ethnicity in today's Europe was developed from the conference held at Stanford University in fall 2007 on the same subject, sponsored by the Forum on Contemporary Europe at the Stanford University Freeman Spogli Institute for International Studies, and by the Stanford Humanities Center. As part of the forum's series of programs studying European Union expansion, the conference brought together scholars from Europe and the United States to investigate the ethnic component of the way we understand social integration. Based on the strength of the papers, and the cross-disciplinary discussion, it was clear that we would greatly benefit from inviting the participants to consider the reactions to their research and write new papers for this collection. Throughout the process of revising contributions, we have remarked on the importance of this collection to provide new research and revised models for explaining how states differentiate membership and, simultaneously, communities socialize in rapidly changing Europe.

NOTES

1. Internal border controls were removed between participating member nations of the European Union by the so-called Schengen agreement drafted in 1985 and ratified by convention in 1995. The text prologue includes several caveats: "The practicalities of free movement within an area without internal border controls were first set out by the Schengen Agreement in 1985 and the subsequent Schengen Convention in 1995 that abolished controls on internal borders between the signatory countries. The Amsterdam Treaty on the European Union, which came into force on 1 May 1999, incorporated the set of measures adopted under the Schengen umbrella into the Union's legal and institutional framework. These measures are now fully accepted by 13 EU Member States (with the exception of the United Kingdom and Ireland), as well as other countries external to the Union (Norway and Iceland). New applicants to the Union will have to fulfil these same requirements. The Schengen principles of free circulation of people are backed by improved and still developing security measures to ensure that the EU's internal security is not threatened."

The official text of the agreement is located at: http://ec.europa.eu/justice_home/fsj/freetravel/frontiers/fsj_freetravel_schengen_en.htm

2. Vaclav Havel, *Speech to the European Parliament*, Strasbourg, March 8, 1994, calling for, among multiple items, a charter for Europe. He insisted that "the most important task facing the European Union today is coming up with a new and genuinely clear reflection on what might be called European identity, a new and genuinely clear articulation of European responsibility, an intensified interest in the very meaning of European integration in all its wider implications for the contemporary world, and the re-creation of its ethos or, if you like, its charisma."

3. European Commission, Eurostat: *Non-national Populations in the EU Member States—Issue Number 8/2006*. This issue offers comprehensive data on "the size,

composition and change of the non-national population in EU member states starting from 1990. This overview is based on data supplied by countries within the framework of the joint Eurostat-UNECE-UNSD-ILO-CoE Questionnaire on international migration statistics."

See also *Population in Europe 2005: First Results—Issue Number 16/2006.* "The SiF presents the main demographic trends in Europe in 2005. Population in the European Union has grown to more than 463 million, mainly thanks to the contribution by migration."

4. European Commission, Eurostat: *The Social Situation in the European Union 2004.* This ambitious survey is described as follows: "The Social Situation Report—published annually since 2000—provides a prospective overview of the social dimension in the European Union as a background to social policy development and contributes to the monitoring of developments in the social field across Member States. Furthermore, it establishes links to other Commission publications such as Employment in Europe, Industrial Relations in Europe and the Gender Equality Report. One special characteristic of this report is that it combines harmonised quantitative information with survey data on public opinion. In this way it acts as a reference document, with the perceptions and attitudes of people living in Europe added to the overall portrait of the social situation. This year the report seeks to portray the social dimension of the enlarged Union, looking at both developing social trends and emerging policy challenges."

For historical comparison, see Richard Rogers, ed., *Guests Come to Stay: The Effects of European Labor Migration on Sending and Receiving Countries.*

5. Among the studies with anecdote, policy, and theory, the most systematic analyses are: Ryszard Cholewinski, *Irregular Migrants, Access to Minimum Social Rights: Study on Obstacles to Effective Access of Irregular Migrants to Minimum Social Rights*; Gráinne de Búrca and Bruno de Witte, eds., *Social Rights in Europe*; and Joanna Apap, *The Rights of Immigrant Workers in the European Union: An Evaluation of the EU Public Policy Process and the Legal Status of Labour Immigrants from the Maghreb Countries in the New Receiving States.*

6. Multiple cases are being pressed on behalf of Roma rights in the European Court of Human Rights (ECHR), pitting advocates of integration in schooling, housing, and employment against those who defend policies of separation and special programs. See for instance: European Roma Rights Centre, "In Extraordinary Move, European Court of Human Rights Agrees to Hear Appeal in Recent School Discrimination Case Against Croatia," January 7, 2009, http://www.errc.org/cikk. php?cikk=3002. The original ECHR Grand Chamber Judgment of *Oršuš and Others v. Croatia* rendered July 17, 2008, is available at ECHR original application no. 15766/03.

7. Tariq Modood, Anna Triandafyllidou, and Ricard Zapata-Barrero, eds., *Multiculturalism, Muslims and Citizenship: A European Approach.*

8. The most recent trial of three suspects ended in August 2008 without a ver-

dict, producing many speculative interpretations. The basic version begins with John F. Burns, "Britain: London Bombing Trial Ends Without Verdict," *New York Times*, August 2, 2008.

9. Michael Evans, "MI5 Analyst Admits Link Between Terrorist Bombings and Iraq War," *The TimesOnline*, July 28, 2005; Simon Hughes, "Britain's Youngest Terrorist: Britain's youngest Al-Qaeda Terrorist Was Put Behind Bars Last Night," *The Sun*, August 19, 2008.

10. I give special thanks to Alec Hargreaves for his generous consultation on the historical and contemporary details of French government and social science engagement with ethnic communities.

11. The statement by Nicolas Sarkozy has provoked myriad responses. For an analysis of the outburst in the context of larger political maneuvers, see David Reiff, "Battle over the Banlieues," *New York Times Magazine*, April 15, 2007.

12. Amelia Gentleman, "Almost 2M Living in France's Angry Ghettos," *The Guardian*, July 6, 2004; Piotr Smolar, "Les RG s'alarment d'un <<repli comunautaire>> dans les banlieues," *Le Monde*, July 6, 2004.

See also the High Authority to Fight Discrimination and to Promote Equality (HALDE), an independent government body created by a law of December 2004 as part of the Interior Ministry's acknowledgment and response to racism and anti-Semitism in French society. For reports on the aftermath, see: Anna Mulrine, "After the Flames," *US News and World Report*, November 21, 2005, 35–37; and Kenneth J. Meier and Daniel P. Hawes, "Ethnic Conflict in France: A Case for Representative Bureaucracy?" *American Review of Public Administration* 39(3): 269–285.

13. For analysis of the constraints on ethnic surveys, see esp. Alec Hargreaves, *Multi-Ethnic France: Immigration, Politics, Culture and Society*, and his contribution in this collection, "Veiled Truths: Discourses of Ethnicity in Contemporary France."

14. Recent high-profile conferences focus on the challenge of overcoming what is framed as the issue of visibility. A most prominent example is "Representing Minorities: Visibility, Recognition, Political Representation," in *Colloque international: Représenter les minorités: Visibilité, reconnaissance et politique des représentations: Repenser la question des minorités non blanches. Une analyse comparative internationale des régimes de visibilité dans le recensement et dans les médias*, Paris, March 19, 2007, sponsored by CADIS (EHESS—CNRS), l'Ecole des Hautes Etudes en Sciences Sociales (EHESS), L'Institut National de l'Audiovisuel (INA).

15. N'Diaye Pap, *La condition noire: Essai sur une minorité française*.

16. Michael Kimmelman, "For Blacks in France, Obama's Rise Is Reason to Rejoice, and to Hope," *New York Times*, June 17, 2008, B1.

17. Two influential studies among analyses of the immigration to Europe during this era are: Eric J. Hobsbawm, *The Age of Empire, 1875–1914*; and Albert Memmi, *The Colonizer and the Colonized*, trans. Howard Greenfield.

18. Multiple case studies based on primary interviews are available in Jane

Kramer, *Unsettling Europe*. The impact of colonial projects and decolonization on European—especially French—culture is interpreted in Kristin Ross, *Fast Cars, Clean Bodies: Decolonization and the Reordering of French Culture*.

19. The scope of the new immigration trend is outlined in Anna Triandafyllidou and Ruby Gropas, eds., *European Immigration: A Sourcebook*; and Salvatore Engel-Di Mauro, ed., *The European's Burden: Global Imperialism in EU Expansion*. Several interpretative models are put forward in: Dipesh Chakrabarty, *Provincializing Europe: Postcolonial Thought and Historical Difference*; and Herman Lebovics, *Bringing the Empire Back Home: France in the Global Age*.

20. A most recent study gives current data in James Raymer and Frans Willekens, eds., *International Migration in Europe: Data, Models and Estimates*. The implications of this demographic swing are considered in: Etienne Balibar, *We, the People of Europe? Reflections on Transnational Citizenship*, trans. James Swenson, and should be compared with inter-European immigration studies, such as Anna Triandafyllidou, ed., *Contemporary Polish Migration in Europe: Complex Patterns of Movement and Settlement*.

21. Of the studies of ethnic identity in modern Europe, the several most influential works include: Saskia Sassen, *Guests and Aliens*; Rogers Brubaker, *Citizenship and Nationhood in France and Germany* (esp. 148–164, 168–178, and 179–189); and Eric Hobsbawm, *Nations and Nationalism since 1780*. The latter two have principle excerpts collected in: John Hutchinson and Anthony D. Smith, *Ethnicity*. Additionally, the following were influential in the writing of this introduction and deserve attention from those interested in the development of the scholarly literature on ethnicity in modern Europe: Joan Wallach Scott, *The Politics of the Veil*; Brubaker, *Nationalism Reframed: Nationhood and the National Question in the New Europe* (esp. introduction and chapter 3); Brubaker, "Migrations of Ethnic Unmixing in the 'New Europe,'" *International Migration Review* 32(4) (Winter 1998): 1047–1065; Alec G. Hargreaves and Jeremy Leaman, eds., *Racism, Ethnicity and Politics in Contemporary Europe*; Hargreaves, *Immigration, "Race," and Ethnicity in Contemporary France*; Hargreaves, *Multi-Ethnic France: Immigration, Politics, Culture and Society*; Jacqueline Andall, ed., *Gender and Ethnicity in Contemporary Europe*; Frank Bovenkerk, Robert Miles, and Gilles Verbunt, "Comparative Studies of Migration and Exclusion on the Grounds of 'Race' and Ethnic Background in Western Europe: A Critical Appraisal," *International Migration Review* 25(2): 375–391; Sheila Allen and Marie Macey, "Race and Ethnicity in the European Context," *British Journal of Sociology* 41(3) (September 1990): 375–393; Ruud Koopmans, *Contested Citizenship: Immigration and Cultural Diversity in Europe* (esp. 1–25 and chapter 4, "Minority Group Demands and the Challenge of Islam"); Montserrat Guibernau and John Rex, eds., *The Ethnicity Reader: Nationalism, Multiculturalism, and Migration*; and Judith G. Kelley, *Ethnic Politics in Europe: The Power of Norms and Incentives*.

WORKS CITED

Allen, Sheila, and Marie Macey. "Race and Ethnicity in the European Context." *British Journal of Sociology* 41(3) (1990): 375–393.

Andall, Jacqueline, ed. *Gender and Ethnicity in Contemporary Europe.* Oxford: Oxford University Press, 2003.

Apap, Joanna. *The Rights of Immigrant Workers in the European Union: An Evaluation of the EU Public Policy Process and the Legal Status of Labour Immigrants from the Maghreb Countries in the New Receiving States.* The Hague: Kluwer Law International, 2002.

Balibar, Etienne. *We, the People of Europe? Reflections on Transnational Citizenship,* trans. James Swenson. Princeton, NJ: Princeton University Press, 2004.

Bovenkerk, Frank, Robert Miles, and Gilles Verbunt. "Comparative Studies of Migration and Exclusion on the Grounds of 'Race' and Ethnic Background in Western Europe: A Critical Appraisal." *International Migration Review* 25(2) (Summer 1991): 375–391.

Brubaker, Rogers. *Citizenship and Nationhood in France and Germany.* Cambridge, MA: Harvard University Press, 1992.

———. "Migrations of Ethnic Unmixing in the 'New Europe'." *International Migration Review* 32(4) (1998): 1047–1065.

———. *Nationalism Reframed: Nationhood and the National Question in the New Europe.* Cambridge: Cambridge University Press, 1996.

Búrca, Gráinne de, and Bruno de Witte, eds. *Social Rights in Europe.* Oxford: Oxford University Press, 2005.

Burns, John F. "Britain: London Bombing Trial Ends Without Verdict." *New York Times,* August 2, 2008.

Centre d'Analyse et d'Intervention Sociologiques (CADIS), l'Ecole des Hautes Etudes en Sciences Sociales (EHESS), and L'Institut National de l'Audiovisuel (INA). *Colloque international: Représenter les minorités: Visibilité, reconnaissance et politique des représentations* [International Symposium: Representing Minorities: Visibility, Recognition, Political Representation]: *Repenser la question des minorités non blanches. Une analyse comparative internationale des régimes de visibilité dans le recensement et dans les médias.* Paris, March 19, 2007.

Chakrabarty, Dipesh. *Provincializing Europe: Postcolonial Thought and Historical Difference.* Princeton, NJ: Princeton University Press, 2008.

Cholewinski, Ryszard. *Irregular Migrants, Access to Minimum Social Rights: Study on Obstacles to Effective Access of Irregular Migrants to Minimum Social Rights.* Strasbourg: Council of Europe; Croton-on-Hudson, NY: Manhattan Publications, 2005.

Engel-Di Mauro, Salvatore, ed. *The European's Burden: Global Imperialism in EU Expansion.* New York: Peter Lang, 2006.

European Commission. Eurostat. *Non-national Populations in the EU Member States—Issue Number 8/2006.* http://epp.eurostat.ec.europa.eu/portal/page?_pageid=1073,46587259&_dad=portal&_schema=PORTAL&p_product_code=KS-NK-06-008

European Commission. Eurostat. *Population in Europe 2005: First Results—Issue Number 16/2006*. http://epp.eurostat.ec.europa.eu/portal/page?_pageid= 1073,46587259&_dad=portal&_schema=PORTAL&p_product_code=KS -NK-06-016

European Commission. Eurostat. *The Social Situation in the European Union 2004— Catalog Number: KE-AG-04-001-EN-C*. http://ec.europa.eu/ employment_social/publications/2004/keapo4001_en.html

European Court of Human Rights (ECHR). Grand Chamber Judgment of *Oršuš and Others v. Croatia* original application no. 15766/03. Rendered July 17, 2008.

European Roma Rights Centre. "In Extraordinary Move, European Court of Human Rights Agrees to Hear Appeal in Recent School Discrimination Case Against Croatia." January 7, 2009. http://www.errc.org/cikk.php?cikk=3002

Evans, Michael. "MI5 Analyst Admits Link Between Terrorist Bombings and Iraq War." *The TimesOnline*, July 28, 2005.

Gentleman, Amelia. "Almost 2M Living in France's Angry Ghettos." *The Guardian*, July 6, 2004.

Guibernau, Montserrat, and John Rex, eds. *The Ethnicity Reader: Nationalism, Multiculturalism, and Migration*. Cambridge: Polity Press, 1997.

Hargreaves, Alec G. *Immigration, "Race," and Ethnicity in Contemporary France*. London: Routledge, 1995.

———. *Multi-Ethnic France: Immigration, Politics, Culture and Society*. London: Routledge, 2007.

———, and Jeremy Leaman, eds. *Racism, Ethnicity and Politics in Contemporary Europe*. Aldershot: Edward Elgar, 1995.

Havel, Vaclav. *Speech to the European Parliament*. Strasbourg, March 8, 1994. http:// www.vaclavhavel.cz/index.php?sec=3&id=1&kat=2&from=122

High Authority to Fight Discrimination and to Promote Equality (HALDE). http://www.halde.fr/About-the-HALDE.html?page=article_en

Hobsbawm, Eric J. *The Age of Empire, 1875–1914*. New York: Vintage, 1987.

———. *Nations and Nationalism since 1780*. Cambridge: Cambridge University Press, 1990.

Hughes, Simon. "Britain's Youngest Terrorist: Britain's Youngest Al-Qaeda Terrorist Was Put Behind Bars Last Night." *The Sun*, August 19, 2008.

Hutchinson, John, and Anthony D. Smith. *Ethnicity*. Oxford: Oxford University Press, 1996.

Kelley, Judith G. *Ethnic Politics in Europe: The Power of Norms and Incentives*. Princeton, NJ: Princeton University Press, 2004.

Kimmelman, Michael. "For Blacks in France, Obama's Rise Is Reason to Rejoice, and to Hope." *New York Times*, June 17, 2008, B1.

Koopmans, Ruud. *Contested Citizenship: Immigration and Cultural Diversity in Europe*. Minneapolis: University of Minnesota Press, 2005.

Kramer, Jane. *Unsettling Europe*. New York: Random House, 1980.

Lebovics, Herman. *Bringing the Empire Back Home: France in the Global Age*. Durham, NC: Duke University Press, 2004.

Meier, Kenneth J., and Daniel P. Hawes. "Ethnic Conflict in France: A Case for Representative Bureaucracy?" *American Review of Public Administration* 39(3) (2009):269–285. http://arp.sagepub.com/cgi/reprint/39/3/269, doi: 10.1177/0275074008317844 (accessed April 6, 2009).

Memmi, Albert. *The Colonizer and the Colonized*, trans. Howard Greenfield. New York: Orion Press, 1965.

Modood, Tariq, Anna Triandafyllidou, and Ricard Zapata-Barrero, eds. *Multiculturalism, Muslims and Citizenship: A European Approach*. New York: Routledge, 2006.

Mulrine, Anna. "After the Flames." *US News and World Report*, November 21, 2005, 35–37.

Pap, N'Diaye. *La condition noire: Essai sur une minorité française*. Paris: Calmann-Lévy, 2008.

Raymer, James, and Frans Willekens, eds. *International Migration in Europe: Data, Models and Estimates*. Chichester, UK; Hoboken, NJ: John Wiley & Sons, 2008.

Reiff, David. "Battle over the Banlieues." *New York Times Magazine*, April 15, 2007.

Rogers, Richard, ed. *Guests Come to Stay: The Effects of European Labor Migration on Sending and Receiving Countries*. Boulder, CO: Westview Press, 1985.

Ross, Kristin. *Fast Cars, Clean Bodies: Decolonization and the Reordering of French Culture*. Cambridge, MA: MIT Press, 1995.

Sassen, Saskia. *Guests and Aliens*. New York: New Press, 1999.

Schengen Convention. http://ec.europa.eu/justice_home/fsj/freetravel/schengen/fsj_freetravel_schengen_en.htm

Scott, Joan Wallach. *The Politics of the Veil*. Princeton, NJ: Princeton University Press, 2007.

Smolar, Piotr. "Les RG s'alarment d'un <<repli comunautaire>> dans les banlieues." *Le Monde*, July 6, 2004.

Triandafyllidou, Anna, ed. *Contemporary Polish Migration in Europe: Complex Patterns of Movement and Settlement*. Lewiston, NY: Edwin Mellen Press, 2006.

———, and Ruby Gropas, eds. *European Immigration: A Sourcebook*. London: Ashgate, 2007.

PART ONE **The Ethnic Question**

# CHAPTER TWO

# Membership and Its Politics

SASKIA SASSEN

The growth of anti-immigrant sentiment in Europe is pushing towards the renationalizing of particular features of membership politics (Giugni and Passy 2006; White 1999; Vertovec and Peach 1997; Weil 2008; Body-Gendrot and Wihtol de Wenden 2007). Yet, this renationalizing of membership, even when ideologically strong, is institutionally weak given the increased formalization of the European Union (EU) level. And although the EU level is still thin compared to that of the national state, it is beginning to alter the underlying conditions which have fed the articulation between citizenship and the national state (Baubock 2006). The institutional development of the European Union and the strengthening of the European Court of Human Rights push the question of political membership towards a kind of European universalism (Jacobson and Ruffer 2006; Rubenstein and Adler 2000). The denationalizing represented by the EU is fed by the emergence of multiple actors, groups, and communities increasingly keen on broader notions of political membership and unwilling automatically to identify with a national state (Soysal 1997; Tunstall 2006).

**21**

These transformations in the EU raise questions about the actual meaning of that renationalizing of membership. Is it an ideational event that can exist even as the institutional settings of membership are becoming partly denationalized? Can growing discrimination against the alien coexist with a strengthening of the right to have rights, notably through the decisions of the European Court of Human Rights confirming rights of immigrants that the national legislatures had tried to withdraw? And can the ideological renationalizing of citizenship coexist with the Europeanizing of membership and multiple transnationalisms for identity politics? These changes raise questions about the assertion in most of the pertinent scholarship that citizenship has a necessary connection to the national state. Many of the changes in citizenship and alienage may not yet be formalized and some may never become fully formalized. But they may nonetheless be consequential for some of the issues that concern us in this collection, notably the question of immigration and ethnicity in today's Europe.

Addressing the question of citizenship and alienage against these transformations entails a specific stance. It is quite possible to posit that at the most abstract or formal level not much has changed over the last century in the essential features of both institutions. The theoretical ground from which I address the issue is that of their historicity and their embeddedness in projects of national state construction in the past and partial deconstruction in the present, notably the strengthening of the European Union and of the European Court of Human Rights. The purely formal features of citizenship and alienage easily obscure some of the microtransformations I am after here. Citizenship and alienage; each have been constructed in elaborate and formal ways. And each has evolved historically as a tightly packaged bundle of what were in fact often rather diverse elements. The dynamics at work today are destabilizing these bundlings and thereby making legible the fact itself of this bundling of diverse elements and its particularity. Social constructions that mark individuals and groups, such as race and ethnicity, may well become destabilized by these developments.

## Citizenship and Nationality

In its narrowest definition citizenship describes the legal relationship between the individual and the polity. This relationship can in principle assume many forms, in good part depending on the definition of the polity. In Europe the polity was originally the city, both in ancient and in medieval times. But it is the evolution of polities along the lines of state formation that gave citizenship in the West its full institutionalized and formalized character and that made nationality a key component of citizenship.

Yet the major transformations of the last two decades have once again brought conditions for a change in the institution of citizenship and its relation to nationality, and they have brought about changes in the legal content of nationality. Mostly minor formal and nonformal changes are beginning to dilute the European historical tradition (Baubock et al. 2007; Weil 1996; Wihtol de Wenden 1988). More generally, the long-lasting resistance of the modern state to dual or multiple nationality is shifting towards a selective acceptance. According to some legal scholars (Spiro 2008; Rubenstein and Adler 2000), in the future dual and multiple nationality will become the norm. Today, more people than ever before have dual nationality (Spiro 2008). Insofar as the importance of nationality is a function of the central role of states in the international system, it is quite possible that a decline in the importance of this role and a proliferation of other actors will affect the value of nationality. In this context, the incipient development of EU citizenship, even though as yet too thin to be a strong competitor to nation-based citizenship, may well signal a foundational, even if partial, change in the relationship between citizenship and the national state.

Placed in a larger historical trajectory, these transformations can be seen as possibly giving citizenship yet another set of features as it continues to respond to the conditions within which it is embedded (Sassen 1996, chapter 2; Sassen 2008, chapter 6; Sadiq 2007). The nationalizing of the institution, which took place over the last several centuries, may today give way to a partial denationalizing. A fundamental dynamic in this regard is the growing articulation of national economies with the global economy and the associated pressures on states to be competitive. Many of the economic and social policies associated with corporate economic globalization have reduced the interactions of states and citizens. For instance, the privatizing of state services—from prisons to welfare functions—means the citizen has far less to do with the state and much more with a private sector delivery operation. Crucial to current notions of the "competitive state" is state withdrawal from various spheres of citizenship entitlements, with the possibility of a corresponding dilution of loyalty to the state.

Citizens' loyalty may in turn be less crucial to the state today than it was at a time of people-intensive and frequent warfare, with its need for loyal citizen-soldiers (Turner 2000). Citizen-soldiers can today be replaced by full-time professional soldiers, and even contract "soldiers." Most importantly, warfare among highly developed countries has become less significant partly due to economic globalization. Global firms and global markets do not want the rich countries to fight wars among themselves, even as they engage in military operations in poor countries with valuable unexploited resources. The "international" project of powerful states today is radically different from what it was in the nineteenth and first half of the twentieth centuries. Today war is increasingly geared towards capturing resources and fighting potential enemies of the status quo in the less developed world, rather than capturing territory from one's neighbor in the highly developed world.

Many of the dynamics that built economies, polities, and societies in the nineteenth and twentieth centuries contained an articulation between the national scale and the growth of entitlements for citizens. During industrialization, class formation, class struggles, and the advantages of both employers and workers tended to scale at the national level and became identified with state-produced legislation and regulations, entitlements, and obligations. The state came to be seen as a key to ensuring the well-being of significant portions of both the working class and the bourgeoisie. The development of welfare states in the twentieth century became a crucial institutional domain for granting entitlements to the poor and the disadvantaged. Today, the growing weight given to notions of the competitiveness of states puts pressure on states to cut down on these entitlements. This in turn weakens the reciprocal relationship between the poor, and the vulnerable generally, and the state (for example, Munger 2002). Finally, the growth of unemployment and the fact that many of the young are developing weak ties to the labor market, once thought of as a crucial mechanism for the socialization of young adults, will further weaken the loyalty and sense of reciprocity between these future adults and the state (Roulleau-Berger 2003). This is then also fertile ground for disadvantaged citizens and the expanded numbers of middle-class citizens who are losing economic and social ground to turn their fears against immigrants.

These trends are destabilizing the meaning of citizenship as it was forged in the nineteenth and much of the twentieth centuries. Economic policies and technical developments we associate with economic globalization have strengthened the importance of cross-border dynamics and reduced that of borders for a growing range of activities and actors, though by no means for all. The expanded domain of markets has brought into question the foundations of the welfare state. T. H. Marshall (1977) and many others saw and continue to see the welfare state as an important ingredient of social citizenship. Today the assumptions of the dominant model of Marshallian citizenship have been severely diluted under the impact of globalization and the ascendance of the market as the preferred mechanism for addressing these social issues. For many critics, the reliance on markets to solve political and social problems is a savage attack on the principles of citizenship. Thus Peter Saunders (1993) argues that the citizenship inscribed in the institutions of the welfare state "is a buffer against the vagaries of the market and the inequalities of the class system."

These social changes in the role of the state, the impact of globalization on states, and the relationship between dominant and subordinate groups also have major implications for questions of identity. "Is citizenship a useful concept for exploring the problems of belonging, identity and personality in the modern world?" (Shotter 1993; Ong 1999, chapters 1 and 4). Can such a radical change in the conditions for citizenship leave the institution itself unchanged?[1]

Though often talked about as a single concept and experienced as a unitary institution, citizenship actually describes a number of discrete but related aspects in the relation between the individual and the polity. Current developments are bringing to light and accentuating the distinctiveness of these various aspects, from formal rights to practices and psychological dimensions (see Ong 1999; Bosniak 2006; Spiro 2008). They make legible the tension between citizenship as a formal legal status and as a normative project or an aspiration. The formal equality granted to all citizens rarely rests on the need for substantive equality in social and even political terms. In brief, current conditions have strengthened the emphasis on rights and aspirations that go beyond the formal legal definition of rights and obligations.[2] And they have made legible the extent to which some components of citizenship are not inevitably dependent on the national state.

These developments signal the possibility that the new conditions of inequality and difference evident today and the new types of claim-making they produce may well bring about further transformations in the institution. Citizenship has historically grown and expanded through the claim-making and the demands of the excluded. Further, by expanding the formal inclusionary aspect of citizenship, the nation-state itself creates some of the conditions that may eventually facilitate key aspects of EU and possibly even postnational citizenship. At the same time, insofar as the state itself is changing and has reduced its social obligations to citizens under the framework of the need for states to be competitive, today's states are less likely to do the legislative and judiciary work that in the past produced expanded formal inclusions. This may in turn lead to even weaker attachments of citizens to their national states. Claim-making will increasingly be directed at other institutions as well, notably the European Court of Human Rights.[3]

The tension between the formal status and the normative project of citizenship has also grown. For many, citizenship is becoming a normative project whereby social membership becomes increasingly comprehensive and open ended. Globalization and human rights are further enabling this tension and therewith furthering the elements of a new discourse on rights. These developments signal that the analytic terrain within which we need to place the question of rights, authority, and obligations is shifting (Sassen 1996, chapter 2; Sassen 2008, chapter 6). Some of these issues can be illustrated by the actual complexity of immigrant membership in Europe, especially if we review the data through a sufficiently long history.

## Beneath New Nationalisms: A Blurring of Membership Politics

Unlike the "citizen," the "immigrant" or, more formally, "the alien," is constructed in law as a very partial, thin subject. Yet the immigrant and immigration are actually thick realities, charged with content. In this tension between a thin formal subject—the alien—and a rich reality lies the heuristic capacity of immigration to illuminate tensions at the heart of the historically constructed nation-state and national citizenship (Sassen 2008, chapters 2, 3, and 6). These tensions are not new, historically speaking, but as with citizenship, current conditions are producing their own distinct possibilities. Further, the change in the institution of citizenship itself, particularly its emergent debordering of formal definitions and national locations, has implications for the definition of the immigrant. Confronted with postnational and denationalized forms of citizenship, what is it we are trying to discern in the complex processes we group under the term immigration? On the other hand, the renationalizing of citizenship narrows what we might refer to as the customary definition of the citizen and thereby that of the immigrant.

As a subject, then, the immigrant filters a much larger array of political dynamics than its status in law might suggest. Working with the distinctions and transformations discussed thus far, we can discern the possibility of two somewhat stylized subjects that destabilize formal meanings and thereby illuminate the internal tensions of the institution of citizenship, specifically the citizen as a rights-bearing subject. On the one hand, we can identify a formal citizen who is fully authorized yet not fully recognized. Minoritized citizens who are discriminated against in any domain are one key instance. This is a familiar and well-researched condition. On the other hand, we can identify a type of informal citizen who is unauthorized by the law yet recognized by a potential community of membership, as might be the case with undocumented immigrants who are long-term residents in a community and enact membership the way citizens do. Thus, unauthorized immigrants who demonstrate civic involvement, social deservedness, and national loyalty can argue that they merit legal residency, and often get it. But even if they do not gain legal residency, we can posit a condition akin to informal citizenship that binds long-term residents, even if they are undocumented immigrants, to their communities of residence.[4]

These are dimensions of formal and informal citizenship and citizenship practices that do not fit the indicators and categories of mainstream academic frameworks for understanding citizenship and political life. (For a fuller development of these two stylized cases see Sassen 2008, chapter 6.) Some scholars point to the fact of the multiple dimensions of citizenship and how this engenders strategies for legitimizing informal or extrastatal forms of membership (Soysal 1997; Coutin 2000). The practices of these undocumented immigrants are a form of citizenship practices, and their identities as members of a community of residence assume some of the features of citizenship identities (see Sadiq 2007). Supposedly this could hold even in the communitarian model, according to Bosniak (2006), where the community can decide on whom to admit and whom to exclude, but once admitted, proper civic practices earn full membership.[5]

The origins and reasons for entry of migrants of the past differ from those of today. But the fact remains that all of the current major European countries have taken in immigrants for centuries. And historical demography, notwithstanding its limitations, makes clear that most European nation-states have historically incorporated foreigners. Today's populations evince a significant incidence of foreign-born parents and grandparents. How did European nations handle this as societies in the recent and in the remote past? Can we learn something from this integration history?

## Europe and Its Migrations

Europe's immigrant groups of the past are today reasonably well absorbed, though there are important differences. These older immigrant groups, dating three or four generations or even centuries back, have given us many of today's citizens. They are not at issue in today's debates. But in their time, the picture was very different. They *were* the issue.

Anti-immigrant sentiment and attacks happened in each of the major immigration phases in all these countries. No labor-receiving country survives closer investigation with a spotless record—not Switzerland, with its long admirable history of international neutrality and not even France, the country often noted for its generations of immigrants, refugees, and exiles. But there were always, as is the case today, individuals, groups, organizations, and politicians who believed in making our societies more inclusive of immigrants. History suggests that those fighting for incorporation, in the long run won, have had demographic trends to support them. Just to focus on the recent past, one quarter of the French can identify a foreign-born ancestor within the past three generations (Tribalat et al. 1991), and 32 percent of Viennese can similarly claim a foreign-born heritage (Statistik Austria 2007).

Part of the difficulty for Europe is, ironically, the lack of a historical perspective. Europe has a barely recognized history of several centuries of internal labor migrations. This is a history that hovers in the penumbra of official "European History," dominated by the image of Europe as a continent of emigration, never of immigration. Yet, in the 1700s, when Amsterdam built its polders and cleared its bogs, it brought in northern German workers; when the French built up their vineyards, they brought in Spaniards; when

Milan and Turin developed, they brought in workers from the Alps; when London built its infrastructure for water and sewage, it brought in Irish. In the 1800s, when Haussmann remade the boulevards of Paris, he brought in Germans and Belgians; when Sweden decided to become a monarchy and needed to construct royal palaces, it brought in Italian stoneworkers; when Switzerland built the Gothard Tunnel, it brought in Italians; and when Germany built its railroads and steel mills, it brought in Italians and Poles.

At any given time there were multiple significant intra-European migration flows. All the workers involved were seen as outsiders, as undesirables, as threats to the community, as people that could never become part of that community. But significant numbers did become part of the community, even if it took more than two generations; typically, it seems, it took three. Even when they kept their distinctiveness, they functioned as members of the community, and part of the complex, highly heterogeneous social order. But at the time of their first arrival, they were treated as outsiders, radicalized as different in looks, smells, and habits, though they were so often the same phenotype, broad religious group, and broad cultural group. They were all Europeans: but the differences were experienced as overwhelming and insurmountable. Elsewhere (Sassen 1999) I have documented the acts of violence and the hatreds we felt against those who today we experience as one of us.

Today the argument against immigration may be focused on questions of race, religion, and culture, and might seem rational—that cultural and religious distance is the reason for the difficulty of incorporation. But in sifting through the historical and current evidence we find only new contents for an old passion: the radicalizing of the outsider as "other." Today the "other" is stereotyped by difference of race, religion, and culture. Equivalent arguments were made in the past when migrants were broadly of the same religious, racial, and cultural group: they were seen as not fitting in with the receiving society, as having bad habits and the wrong morals. Migration hinges on a move between two worlds, even if within a single region or country—such as East Germans moving to West Germany, who were seen as a different ethnic group and one with undesirable traits.

There is strong evidence of a cyclical character to anti-immigration politics and the clouding of the issues that comes with it. For centuries Europe's major economies have gone through rapid cycles of great demand and then severe expulsion, only to fall back into high demand a few decades later. In the recent past, a country like France had a desperate need for immigrants during the First World War (using Algerian immigrants in its armies) and the reconstruction in the 1920s, only to move into aggressive anti-immigrant politics in the 1930s, to then wind up once again with acute needs for foreign workers in the late 1940s, and so on. In my reading of the features of that history and the current conditions described above, we may well still be following such a cyclical trend. If we consider the growing demand for low-wage workers and sharp population decline in today's EU, it is easy to see that we might actually switch to a phase of sharp demand for more immigrant workers within a decade, if not sooner.

When Italy (1990), Portugal (1991), and Spain (1992) became part of the European Union free movement area (Gelatt 2005), it meant integrating what had been points of origin for large numbers of migrants heading north and who had been barred before 1973 from further entries for work. The policy change generated widespread fears of invasions by masses of poor workers and families. In retrospect we can see how wrong this fear was. In fact, more immigrants returned home to Spain, and Italy, and Greece, and Portugal, and fewer emigrated to the north than had been expected. This was partly because they were free to circulate and partly because their economies were developing in ways that incorporated their people.

The same is likely to hold with the much feared migrations from the new EU members in the East. Indeed the latest figures indicate that up to 50 percent of the Polish migrants who came to the United Kingdom after EU enlargement have recently returned to Poland (Pollard et al. 2008). People with deep grievances in their home countries are far more likely to emigrate permanently than those who might be low income but who are full-fledged members of their communities (MacDonald and MacDonald 1964; Boyd 1989; Stark and Bloom 1985; Massey 1990). We have considerable evidence showing that being low income is not sufficient reason in and of itself to emigrate. We also know that many low-income migrants want to come every year for a few months and then go back to their communities. Thus enlargement will enable far more circular migration and reduce trafficking. Perhaps the best story here is that of the Polish women who teamed up to take care of cleaning and housekeeping in Berlin households. Each wanted to spend a minimum amount of time in Berlin, no matter its comforts, and then go back and live their real life. Teams of four organized for each to spend three months in a given household, and rotate annually (Lutz 2007; Erel 2008). The best strategy for the rich EU countries so worried about receiving masses of low-wage, poorly educated workers from the new EU members is to do whatever can be done to ensure their broad-based development.

There is one set of communities for whom this will be inadequate: the Roma. Europe has failed the Roma for centuries. All those struggles fought in the name of civil society and civic rights fundamentally excluded the Roma. This will have its own backlash effect. The Roma will come. Today we are paying the price for our historic neglect and even persecution of this ethnic community. There are significant numbers of very poor in some of the new EU member countries, and centuries of exclusion have left their marks. Enlargement must be a wake-up call: we need to think of the Roma as part of our future.

At the same time, the Roma also illuminate a key feature of our history of migrations within Europe: most often, particular groups have constituted the core of a country's emigration, rather than massive generalized flows from poverty to prosperity. In the early 1990s, after the fall of the Berlin Wall, Germany received over two million migrants from Eastern Europe and Russia, but the vast majority were ethnic Germans and the rest mostly Roma. There were no high numbers among other nationalities. Similarly, the Turkish emigration to Germany, for instance, has consisted largely of particular groups of Turkish minorities, including Turkish Kurds. In brief, these were not indiscriminate movements from poverty in the East to wealth in the West. These two groups were motivated by very specific and long-term historical conditions.

*Migration as Embedded Process*

Returning to the politics of membership, one critical element is the fact that migrations are embedded in larger systems. That is to say, it is not simply a matter of the poor deciding to come to rich countries.[6] If this were the case, we should plan on well over three billion people engaging in such movements, when in fact today there are only about one hundred million who have migrated to the rich countries (including North America), less than

4 percent of the world's poor. So poverty itself is not enough to explain emigration. Nor is it helpful for politicians to think that all the poor will come: it leads to the wrong policies.[7]

Establishing whether labor migration is an integral part of how an economic and social system operates and evolves is, in my view, critical to develop the politics of membership. The logic of this argument is, put simply, as follows: If immigration is thought of as the result of individuals in search of a better life, immigration is seen by the receiving country as an exogenous process formed and shaped by conditions outside the receiving country. The receiving country is then saddled with the task of accommodating this population. In this model, as poverty and overpopulation grow, there may be a potential parallel growth in immigration. The receiving country becomes a passive bystander to processes outside its domain and control, and hence with few options but to tighten its frontiers if it is to avoid an "invasion."

If, on the other hand, immigration is partly conditioned on the operation of the economic system in receiving countries, the latter can implement domestic policies that can regulate the employment of immigrants. Thus, if a country such as the United States seeks to make manufacturing more competitive by making production cheaper using sweatshops, it is a participant in the formation of a sweated immigrant workforce. As a corollary to the outflow of the manufacturing sector, there is increasing demand domestically for low-wage service workers. In both cases, the receiving country is not a passive bystander to the immigration process. Further, there is something these governments can do beyond controlling borders—they can make those jobs more attractive to resident immigrants and to citizens. Finally, on a global scale, receiving countries need to recognize that when they outsource jobs to low-wage countries they are building bridges for future migrations. Yes, immigration happens in a context of inequality between countries, but inequality by itself is not enough to lead to emigration. Inequality needs to be activated as a migration push factor—through organized recruitment, neocolonial bonds, and so on.

The economic, political, and social conditions in the receiving country contribute in many ways to set the parameters for immigration flows. Immigration flows may adjust more slowly than changes in levels of labor demand or to the saturation of opportunities, but will tend eventually to adjust to the conditions in receiving countries, even if these adjustments are imperfect. Thus there was a decline in the growth rate of Polish immigration to Germany once it was clear that the opportunities were not as plentiful as rumored, and this movement was replaced by circular migration in many East to West flows, including from the former East Germany to West Germany. The size and duration of flows are shaped by these conditions: they are not an exogenous process shaped only by poverty and population growth elsewhere and hence autonomous from the accommodation capacities of receiving countries.

If size and duration of immigration are shaped overall by conditions in receiving countries, then it should also be possible to craft reasonably effective immigration policies. Managing a patterned and conditioned flow of immigrants is a rather different matter from controlling an "invasion." Implementation of an effective policy does not necessarily mean perfect synchronization between conditions in the receiving country and immigrant inflow and settlement. This will never be the case. Immigration is a process constituted by human beings with will and agency, with multiple identities and life trajectories beyond the fact of being seen, defined, and categorized as immigrants for the purposes of the receiving polity, economy, and society. There is no definitive proof in this matter. But there are patterns, and past patterns, that have lived their full life. They can tell us something about the extent to which immigration has consisted of a series of bounded events with beginnings, endings, and specific geographies—all partly shaped by the operation and organization of receiving economies, polities, and societies.

## Cross-Country Regularities

My examination of the past two centuries and the vast scholarly literature on immigration in Europe points to a number of cross-country regularities. The purpose here is to establish whether immigration flows today have geographic, temporal, and institutional boundaries that indicate a definition of the "where," "when," and "who" of immigration. These cross-country regularities contribute to a far more qualified understanding of immigration and hence of policy options:

(1) *Emigration always encompasses a small share of a country's population.* Except for terror-driven refugees, we now know that most people are quite

reluctant to leave their home villages or towns. Most Mexicans have not left their country and moved to the United States, and most people in Poland are not going to try to come to Germany, nor will most Algerians try to come to France. In fact, the evidence shows that even when there is a massive flow, it often is a persecuted people who dominate such flows. Thus most emigrants from the East to Germany in the early 1990s when the wall came down were Roma people from Romania and ethnic Germans, two populations with very specific reasons for migrating. There are individuals and groups who are determined to come (pent-up demand) and will come no matter what. But this is not the typical case. There is a grey area of potential emigrants who may or may not leave, depending on pull factors; but the vast majority of people in a poor country are not likely to consider emigration.

This was already the case in the nineteenth century when borders were not controlled because the state lacked the technical capacities to do so. Even then emigration was confined to a minority of people. This holds even when we consider subnational regions. For instance, some of the historically highest emigration levels were reached in several southern Italian districts. When we specify such districts in very limited geographic terms, we find high rates, but typically for very short periods of time. Thus Choate (2008) finds that in 1906–11, some Sicilian districts saw between 3,000 and 7,000 per 10,000 inhabitants leave. For the country as a whole, from "1905–1907, one in fifty Italians immigrated abroad," which equates to 40 per 1,000 inhabitants at the peak (1907) of emigration. Today, EU nationals can easily move to another EU country, which might be seen as a reasonable option given considerable variation in earnings levels across member states. Yet, EU figures show cross-country migration among EU residents rose minimally, from 5 percent to 5.5 percent in postenlargement EU (European Commission. Eurostat 2006).

(2) *Immigrants are typically a minority of a country's population.* According to the latest available data (European Commission. Eurostat 2006) 25 million nonnationals (residents who are not citizens of the country where they live) lived in the EU25 in 2004, or 5.5 percent of the population. In half of these countries nonnationals were under 5 percent of the population; they were over 10 percent of the population in Luxembourg, and, mostly due to the long-term former Soviet residents, in Latvia, and Estonia. A good share of

nonnationals are from other EU countries. The highest increases in non-nationals from 1990 to 2004 were in Luxembourg, Greece, Spain, Cyprus, Ireland, and Austria. There were declines in Belgium. In the preenlargement period, immigrants were 5 percent (18.8 million) of the EU population. Then and today, third-country immigrants count for a minority of the total European population. For instance, the eight major preenlargement EU countries had a total immigrant population of 2.5 million from the Maghreb, a group that has engendered considerable debate around questions of cultural and religious obstacles to incorporation. This was 13.3 percent of the total immigrant population in the EU, less than 1 percent of the total European population. These levels have not changed much, even if the numbers may have grown, as has the total EU population, from 350 million to about 470 million. Similar concern has been raised about Turks. The vast majority of all Turkish immigrants in the EU are in Germany, where they are 2.4 percent of the German population.

In the old EU member states, the incidence of nonnationals is not particularly high. In the United Kingdom, nonnationals were 4.2 percent of the total population in 1990 and 4.7 percent in 2004, with the Irish the largest single group. And in Ireland, by 2004 nonnationals were 7 percent of the total population, with British the largest single group. In the Netherlands 4.3 percent of the population was made up of EU nonnationals, and in France the same category of immigrants numbered 5.6 percent. Overall, the levels are not quite an invasion as is so often suggested.

(3) *There is considerable return migration.* Except when the military-political situation in countries of origin makes this unfeasible, a great proportion of immigrants eventually return or move in a cyclical trajectory to and from their country of origin. For example, we now know that about 50 percent of Italians who left for the United States around the turn of the century returned to Italy (Choate 2008). The incidence of cross-border residence by EU nationals has declined since 1970, partly as a function of the return of Italian, Spanish, and Portuguese immigrant workers to their home countries. We are seeing generally more and more circular migration in the Mediterranean and, until the U.S. government militarized the border with Mexico, also in the Americas. This all suggests that the fact of return migration may become a different phenomenon—not a definitive return, but a circular movement. It calls for considering the sending and receiving areas

as part of a single economic, social, and political system. It is within this system that immigrants make their own individual decisions and take action.

(4) *One important tendency is towards the formation of permanent settlements. Alongside the circularity of migration, a varying portion of immigrants will seek permanent residency.* This tendency is likely even when there are high return rates and even when a country's policies seek to prevent permanent settlement. We see this happening in all countries receiving immigrants, including extremely closed countries such as Japan (with illegal immigration from the Philippines, Thailand, and other Asian countries, as well as legal immigrations from several Latin American countries) and Saudi Arabia, as well as in the more liberal Western nations.

No matter what political culture and particular migration policies a country adopts, unauthorized immigration has emerged as a generalized fact in all Western economies in the post–Second World War era, including Japan. This has raised a whole set of questions about the need to rethink regulatory enforcement and the sites for such enforcement. Although the fact of such unauthorized immigration suggests that it is possible to enter these countries no matter what policies are in place, the available evidence makes it clear that the majority of unauthorized immigrants are from the same nationality groups as the legal population and they are typically fewer in number than the legal population. Again, this signals a measure of boundedness in the process of unauthorized immigration and the possibility that it is shaped by similar systemic conditions as the legal population, thereby similarly limited in its scope and scale.

(5) *Immigration is a highly differentiated process.* Immigration includes people seeking permanent settlement and those seeking temporary employment who want to circulate back and forth. The two major patterns that are emerging today are circular migration and permanent settlement. Circular migration was a key pattern in the nineteenth century before border controls were instituted in any systematic way. We also know that there was a significant increase in the permanent resident immigrant population after borders were closed in EU countries in 1973–74, suggesting that some of this growth might not have occurred if the option of circular migration had existed (Hugo 2003; Haas 2005; Bieckmann and Muskens 2008). Much migration has to do with supplementing household income in countries of

origin rather than with permanent settlement. Given enormous earnings differentials, a limited stay in a high-wage country is sufficient.

One important question is whether recognizing these differences might facilitate the formulation of improved policy. There is a growing presence of immigrants who are not searching for a new home in a new country; they think of themselves as moving in a cross-border and even global labor market. We know that when illegal immigrants are regularized, they often establish permanent residence in their country of origin and work a few months in the immigration country, an option that becomes available when they can circulate more freely. We know that some of the Polish women who now work as cleaners in Berlin out of financial necessity only want to do this work for three or four months a year and then return to their home towns. This is also the case with some of the African migrants in Italy. The share and numbers of those who seek to become permanent residents seems to be considerably smaller than the numbers of the total resident foreign population suggest.

## Conclusion

Europe's history of anti-immigrant sentiment shows us that it is a recurrent event, one with variable degrees of virulence. We have been here many times before. It also confirms that over the generations of each immigration cycle we have incorporated vast numbers of immigrants so that today we are actually a mix: the *they* have become the *us* over our five centuries of intra-European migrations. But these facts are easily forgotten in the heat of anti-immigrant sentiment.

From the perspective of nation-based citizenship theory, this trajectory of racisms and incorporations seems a parallel history, one exogenous to that of formal political membership. The effort in this essay was to destabilize this binary. First, European history shows us that the excluded also contribute to the expansion of the politics of membership and, further, that they can benefit from a type of informal citizenship often not granted to minoritized citizens. Secondly, that history also shows us that the effort to negotiate the incorporation of the outsider, often in contexts of virulent and deadly anti-immigrant passions, actually contributed to expanding the civic.

In brief, out of such struggles around inclusion of both immigrants and minoritized citizens have emerged some of the institutions we most admire and count on in our Western tradition—institutions enabling the members of our communities, no matter how poor or ill educated to have access to civil and social rights, even if not always political rights. It was not easy, and at the time, when one reads the record, problems and challenges seemed insoluble. They were never perfectly resolved, nor were remedies immaculately executed. But it did leave Europe with strong institutions that can function as tools to ensure reasonable outcomes when it comes to the politics of membership.

At the same time, precisely this highly developed sense of civic and political community has historically made incorporation of outsiders more difficult. Now more than ever it seems we do not like the new and the different. But when has it not been the case in Europe that just about everybody who was not in was an outsider? Incorporating many, albeit never all, immigrants over the generations always took hard work. Reading the record, it often seems an impossible struggle by those sharing this aspiration—typically some insiders and immigrants themselves; and it took generations to achieve.

But we did it, if imperfectly, over and over again across the centuries. These struggles strengthened our civic and political institutions. Racism is still alive and well, but so are the membership rights that can enable inclusion. The public debate today neglects this history of hard work: it assumes that if there is no ready-made fix, there is no solution. Have we become consumers rather than crafters of inclusion?

NOTES

1. The nature of citizenship has also been challenged by a proliferation of old issues that have gained new attention. Among the latter are the question of state membership of aboriginal communities, stateless people, and refugees (Sassen 1999; Knop 2002). All of these have important implications for human rights in relation to citizenship.

2. This is already evident in a variety of instances. One example is the decision by first-nation people to go directly to the UN and claim direct representation in international fora, rather than going through the national state. It is also evident in the increasingly institutionalized framework of the international human rights regime and the emergent possibilities for bypassing unilateral state sovereignty.

3. I distinguish what I would narrowly define as denationalized from postnational

citizenship, the latter term most commonly used and the only one used in the broader debate. In my reading we are dealing with two distinct dynamics rather than only the emergence of locations for citizenship outside the frame of the national state. Their difference is a question of scope and institutional embeddedness. The understanding in the scholarship is that postnational citizenship is located partly outside the confines of the national. In considering denationalization, the focus moves on to the transformation of the national, including the national in its condition as foundational for citizenship. Thus it could be argued that postnationalism and denationalization represent two different trajectories. Both are viable, and they do not exclude each other. The national, then, remains a referent in my work (e.g., Sassen 1996; Sassen 2008). But, clearly, it is a referent of a specific sort: it is, after all, its change that becomes the key theoretical feature through which it enters my specification of changes in the institution of citizenship.

4. Individuals, even when undocumented immigrants, can move between the multiple meanings of citizenship. The daily practices by undocumented immigrants as part of their life in the community where they reside—such as raising a family, schooling children, holding a job—earn them citizenship claims in the United States, even as the formal status and, more narrowly, legalization may continue to evade them. There are dimensions of citizenship, such as strong community ties and participation in civic activities, which are being enacted informally through these practices. These practices produce an at least partial recognition of them as full social beings. In many countries around the world, including those of the EU, long-term undocumented residents often can gain legal residence if they can document the fact of this long-term residence and "good conduct." Liberal democracies recognize such informal participation as grounds for granting legal residency.

5. According to Coutin (2000) and others, movements between membership and exclusion, and between different dimensions of citizenship, legitimacy, and illegitimacy, may be as important as redefinitions of citizenship itself. Given scarce resources the possibility of negotiating the different dimensions of citizenship may well represent an important enabling condition. Undocumented immigrants develop informal, covert, often extrastatal strategies and networks connecting them with communities in sending countries. Hometowns rely on their remittances and their information about jobs in their countries of immigration. Sending remittances illegally by an unauthorized immigrant can be seen as an act of patriotism back home, and working as an undocumented can be seen as contributing to the host economy. Multiple interdependencies are thereby established and grounds for claims on the receiving and the originating country can be established even when the immigrants are undocumented and laws are broken.

6. At some point we are going to have to ask what the term *immigrant* truly means. People in movement are an increasingly strong presence, especially in cities. Further, when citizens begin to develop transnational identities, it alters something in the meaning of immigration. In my research I have sought to situate immigration

in a broader field of actors by asking, who are all the actors involved in producing the outcome that we then call immigration? My answer is that it's many more than just the immigrants, whereas our law and public imagination tend to identify immigrants as the only actors producing this complex process.

7. Immigrants remain under 3 percent of global population. From an estimate of 85 million international immigrants in the world, or 2.1 percent of world population in 1975, the total number of immigrants rose to 175 million or 2.9 percent of world population by 2000, and an estimate of between 185 and 192 million in 2005 (International Organization for Migration 2006). It is important to note the increased concentration of migrants in the developed world, and generally in a limited number of countries. About thirty countries account for over 75 percent of all immigration; eleven of these are developed countries with over 40 percent of all immigrants.

WORKS CITED AND CONSULTED

Basch, Linda, Nina Glick Schiller, and Cristina Blanc-Szanton. 1994. *Nations Unbound: Transnational Projects, Postcolonial Predicaments, and Deterritorialized Nation-States*. Langhorne, PA: Gordon and Breach.

Baubock, Rainer. 2006. *Migration and Citizenship: Legal Status, Rights and Political Participation*. IMISCOE Reports. Amsterdam: Amsterdam University Press.

———, Eva Ersboll, Kees Groenendijk, and Harald Waldrauch, eds. 2007. *Acquisition and Loss of Nationality, Volume 1: Comparative Analyses*. Amsterdam: Amsterdam University Press.

Beck, Ulrich. 2006. *Cosmopolitan Vision*. Cambridge: Polity.

Benhabib, Seyla. 2004. *The Rights of Others: Aliens, Residents, and Citizens*. Cambridge: Cambridge University Press.

Bieckmann, Frans, and Roeland Muskens. 2008. "Creating a Virtuous Circle." *The Broker*. http://www.thebrokeronline.eu/en/articles/creating_a_virtuous_ circle/#f10 (accessed August 5, 2008).

Body-Gendrot, Sophie, and Catherine Wihtol de Wenden. 2007. *Sortir des banlieues: Pour en finir avec la tyrannie des territoires*. Paris: Eds. Autrement.

Bosniak, Linda. 2006. *The Citizen and the Alien: Dilemmas of Contemporary Membership*. Princeton, NJ: Princeton University Press.

Boyd, Monica. 1989. "Family and Personal Networks in International Migration: Recent Developments and New Agendas." *International Migration Review* 23(3): 638–670.

Choate, Mark I. 2008. *Emigrant Nation: The Making of Italy Abroad*. Cambridge, MA: Harvard University Press.

Coutin, Susan B. 2000. "Denationalization, Inclusion, and Exclusion: Negotiating the Boundaries of Belonging." *Indiana Journal of Global Legal Studies* 7(2): 585–594.

Erel, Umut. 2008. "Book Review: Migrant Domestic Workers in Germany a New Perspective on a Global Phenomenon: *Helma Lutz, Vom Weltmarkt in den*

*Privathaushalt: Die neuen Dienstmädchen im Zeitalter der Globalisierung."* European
*Journal of Women's Studies* 15: 47–50.

European Commission. Eurostat. 2006. *European Business Facts and Figures 2006:
Data 1995–2005.* Luxembourg: Office for Official Publications of the European
Communities.

European Monitoring Centre on Racism and Xenophobia (EUMC). 2002. "Racism
and Xenophobia in the EU Member States: Trends, Developments and Good
Practice in 2002." *Annual Report-Part 2.* Vienna: EUMC. http://fra.europa.eu/
fra/material/pub/ar02/AR_trends_2002–EN.pdf

European Union. 2005. "Luxembourg Income Study." Various publications, working papers, and datasets. http://www.lisproject.org (accessed June 5, 2008).

Flores, W. V., and R. Benmayor, eds. 2000. *Latino Cultural Citizenship: Claiming
Identity, Space, and Rights.* Tempe, AZ: Bilingual Review Press.

Gelatt, Julia. 2005. "Schengen and the Free Movement of People across Europe."
Washington DC: Migration Policy Institute. http://www.migrationinforma tion.
org/Feature/display.cfm?id=338 (accessed August 5, 2008).

Giugni, Marco, and Florence Passy, eds. 2006. *Dialogues on Migration Policy.* Lanham, MD: Lexington Books.

Haas, Hein de. 2005. "International Migration, Remittances and Development:
Myths and Facts." *Third World Quarterly* 26(8): 1269–1284.

Hollifield, James. 2000. "Migration and the 'New' International Order: The
Missing Regime." In *Managing Migration: Time for a New International Regime?*,
ed. Bimal Ghosh, 75–109. London: Oxford University Press.

Hugo, Graeme. 2003. "Circular Migration: Keeping Development Rolling?"
*Special Report: Global Population. 2001.* Vienna: International Institute for Applied Systems Analysis (IIASA). http://www.migrationinformation.org/Feature/
display.cfm?id=129 (accessed August 5, 2008).

International Organization for Migration (IOM). n.d. *Trafficking in Migrants: Quarterly Bulletin.* Geneva: IOM.

———. 2006. *World Migration 2005: Costs and Benefits of International Migration.*
Geneva: IOM.

Jacobson, David, and Galya Benarieh Ruffer. 2006. "Social Relations on a Global
Scale: The Implications for Human Rights and Democracy." In *Dialogues on Mi-
gration Policies*, ed. Marco Giugni and Florence Passy. Lanham, MD: Lexington
Books.

Knop, Karen. 2002. *Diversity and Self-Determination in International Law.* Cambridge: Cambridge University Press.

Koh, Harold Hongju. 1997. "How Is International Human Rights Law Enforced?"
*Indiana Law Journal* 74: 1379–1417.

Laguerre, Michel S. 1998. *Diasporic Citizenship: Haitian Americans in Transnational
America.* New York: St. Martin's Press.

Lustiger-Thaler, Henri. 2004. "Social Movements in a Global World." *Current Sociology* 52(4): 657–674.

Lutz, Helma. 2007. *Vom Weltmarkt in den Privathaushalt: Die neuen Dienstmädchen im Zeitalter der Globalisierung*. Opladen: Barbara Budrich.

MacDonald, John S., and Leatrice D. MacDonald. 1964. "Chain Migration Ethnic Neighborhood Formation and Social Networks." *The Milbank Memorial Fund Quarterly* 42(1): 82–97.

Marshall, T. H. 1977. *Class, Citizenship, and Social Development*. Chicago: University of Chicago Press.

Massey, Douglas. 1990. "The Social and Economic Origins of Immigration." *The ANNALS of the American Academy of Political and Social Science* 510(1): 60–72.

Morawska, E. 2001. "Structuring Migration: The Case of Polish Income-Seeking Travelers to the West." *Theory and Society* 3: 47–80.

Munger, Frank, ed. 2002. *Laboring below the Line: The New Ethnography of Poverty, Low-Wage Work, and Survival in the Global Economy*. New York: Russell Sage Foundation.

Naoki, Sakai, Brett de Bary, and Toshio Iyotani, eds. 2005. *Deconstructing Nationality*. Ithaca, NY: Cornell University East Asia Program.

Noiriel, Gerard. 2007. *A quoi sert l'Identite Nationale*. Paris: Agone.

Ong, Aihwa. 1999. *Flexible Citizenship*. Durham, NC: Duke University Press.

Pollard, Naomi, Maria Latorre, and Dhananjayan Sriskandarajah. 2008. "Floodgates or Turnstiles? Post-EU Enlargement Migration Glows to (and from) the UK." London: Institute for Public Policy Research. http://www.ippr.org.uk/publica tionsandreports/publication.asp?id=603 (accessed August 5, 2008).

Ribas-Mateos, Natalia. 2005. *The Mediterranean in the Age of Globalization: Migration, Welfare, and Borders*. Somerset, NJ: Transaction.

Roulleau-Berger, Laurence, and S. L. Radt. 2003. *Youth and Work in the Post-Industrial Cities of North America and Europe*. Boston: Brill Academic Publishers.

Rubenstein, Kim, and Daniel Adler. 2000. "International Citizenship: The Future of Nationality in a Globalized World." *Indiana Journal of Global Legal Studies* 7(2): 519–548.

Sadiq, Kamal. 2007. "Illegal Immigrants as Citizens in Malaysia." In *Deciphering Globalization: Its Scales, Spaces and Subjects*, ed. Saskia Sassen, 301–320. New York and London: Routledge.

Samers, Michael. 2002. "Immigration and the Global City Hypothesis: Towards an Alternative Research Agenda." *International Journal of Urban and Regional Research* 26(2): 389–402.

Sassen, Saskia. 1996. *Losing Control?: Sovereignty in an Age of Globalization*. New York: Columbia University Press.

———. 1999. *Guests and Aliens*. New York: New Press.

———. 2007. "Response to Seyla Benhabib." *European Journal of Political Theory* 6(4): 431–444.

———. 2008. *Territory, Authority, Rights: From Medieval to Global Assemblages*. Updated ed. Princeton, NJ: Princeton University Press.

Saunders. Peter. 1993. *Deregulation and Inequality*. Kensington, N.S.W.: Center for Applied Economic Research, University of New South Wales.

Shotter, John. 1993. "Psychology and Citizenship: Identity and Belonging." In *Citizenship and Social Theory*, ed. Bryan Turner, 115–138. London: Sage.

Soysal, Yasemin Nohuglu. 1997. "Changing Parameters of Citizenship and Claims-Making: Organized Islam in European Public Spheres." *Theory and Society* 26: 509–527.

Spiro, Peter J. 2008. *Beyond Citizenship: American Identity after Globalization*. Oxford: Oxford University Press.

Stark, Oded, and David E. Bloom. 1985. "The New Economics of Labor Migration." Papers and Proceedings of the Ninety-Seventh Annual Meeting of the American Economic Association, May 1985. *American Economic Review* 75(2): 173–178.

Statistik Austria. 2007. 1.353 Mio Menschen in Oesterreich mit Migrationshintergrund. Wien. http://www.statistik.at/web_de/dynamic/statistiken/bevoelkerung/bevoelkerungsstruktur/bevoelkerung_nach_staatsangehoerigkeit_geburtsland/027382 (accessed August 5, 2008).

Tribalat, Michele, et al. 1991. *Cent Ans d'Immigration, Etrangers d'Hier, Francais d'Aujourd'hui: Apport Démographique, Dynamique, Familiale et Economique de l'Imigration Etrangère*. Paris: Presses Universitaires de France.

Tunstall, Kate E., ed. 2006. *Displacement, Asylum, Migration: The 2004 Oxford Amnesty Lectures*. Oxford: Oxford University Press.

Turner, Brian S. 2000. "Cosmopolitan Virtue: Loyalty and the City." In *Democracy, Citizenship and the Global City*, ed. Engin Isin, 129–147. New York: Routledge.

Vertovec, S., and C. Peach. 1997. *Islam in Europe: The Politics of Religion and Community*. London: Macmillan Press.

Weil, Patrick. 1996. "The Transformation of Immigration Policies: Immigration Control and Nationality Laws in Europe: A Comparative Approach." In *The Protection of Human Rights in Europe, 1996, VII/2*, 87–157, *Collected Courses of the Academy of European Law*. Florence: European University Institute.

———. 2008. *Liberte, Egalite, Discriminations*. Paris: Grasset & Fasquelle.

White, Gregory. 1999. "Encouraging Unwanted Immigration: A Political Economy of Europe's Efforts to Discourage North African Immigration." *Third World Quarterly* 20(4): 839–854.

Wihtol de Wenden, Catherine, ed. 1988. *La Citoyenneté*. Paris: Edilic, Fondation Diderot.

———, and Madeleine Benoit-Guyod. 2005. *Atlas des Migrations dans le Monde*. Paris: Ed. Autrement.

Wilpert, Czarina. 1988. *Entering the Working World: Following the Descendants of Europe's Immigrant Labor Force*. Aldershot: Gower.

# CHAPTER THREE

# Ethnicity in Post–Cold War Europe, East and West

ROGERS BRUBAKER

Questions of ethnicity—along with closely related questions of migration and statehood—have been among the most salient and politically charged issues of the last two decades in Europe. They have figured centrally in political, cultural, and social transformations throughout the continent. In Eastern Europe, they have often been understood to be linked in a vicious circle. States founded on ethnicity—and understood as the states *of* and *for* particular ethnocultural nations—have been seen as engendering violent conflict and forced migration. Ethnic cleansing has come to epitomize this dangerous and destabilizing intertwining of ethnicity, migration, and statehood. In Western Europe, by contrast, some observers have seen a more benign intertwining. The postnational erosion of sovereign statehood, on this view, has produced a continent-wide space for free migration, and has allowed previously suppressed ethnoregional cultures to flourish. Darker accounts of Western Europe, to be sure, have stressed migration from outside Europe, seen as generating unwanted ethnocultural and ethnoreligious pluralism, reactively ethnicized understandings of nationhood, and the emergence of a "fortress Europe" whose reinforced external walls keep outsiders at bay. While these accounts are not particularly nuanced, they point to the importance of the intertwined themes of ethnicity, migration, and statehood, and together they suggest that these issues can be configured in quite different ways. In this essay, I seek to specify persisting differences in the way these questions are posed in different parts of Europe. I will draw broad contrasts between Western and Eastern Europe, since such contrasts are indispensable in any attempt to sketch the configuration of ethnicity in Europe as a whole; yet I seek to avoid the often caricaturally oversimplified East-West contrasts that inform many accounts of contemporary Europe.

*Ethnicity*

Almost all European societies, like most societies worldwide, are ethnically heterogeneous, but that heterogeneity takes sharply differing forms. In order to reveal crucial differences in the configuration—the genesis, form, and political consequences—of ethnic heterogeneity in Europe, I begin with a basic, though admittedly oversimplified, distinction between two ways in which ethnic heterogeneity can be socially organized and politically expressed. The first I call "immigrant ethnicity," and the second, "territorial nationality."[1]

On the first model, relevant mainly to Western Europe (and even more characteristic, of course, of North America), ethnic groups arise through migration and are generally territorially dispersed.[2] On the second model, relevant mainly to east central and Eastern Europe, ethnic groups are indigenous (or at least make claims to be so); they are in many cases generated by the movement of borders across people, rather than that of people across borders; and they are generally territorially concentrated. Their members are ordinarily citizens of the country in which they reside, yet they often identify culturally—and sometimes politically—with a neighboring "kin" or "homeland" state, to which they see themselves as "belonging" by shared ethnicity or culture but not by legal citizenship (Brubaker 1996; Brubaker and Kim 2009). Lastly, and crucially, they define themselves in national terms. They see themselves as belonging not simply to a distinct ethnic group but to a distinct nation or nationality that differs from the nation or nationality of their fellow citizens. In this second model, then, ethnicity takes the form of nationality, and ethnic heterogeneity is coded as national heterogeneity.[3] This territorial ethnicity-cum-nationality is very different from immigration-engendered polyethnicity. Using the same term—"ethnicity" or "ethnic minorities"—to designate both can be misleading.

The political claims that can be made in the name of ethnicity differ sharply in the two cases. Immigrant ethnicity evokes a politics of anti-discrimination, civic inclusion, and "soft multiculturalism" (involving claims to recognition, resources, and sometimes immunities and exemptions). Territorial nationality, on the other hand, involves claims for national self-determination; for symbolic recognition as a state-bearing "nation" rather than as a mere "minority"; for rapprochement, in some cases, with a neighboring "kin" or "homeland" state; for extensive language rights; for territorial autonomy; or even for full independence.

Clearly, the claims of territorial nationality can threaten the basic nature of the state in a way that the claims of immigrant ethnicity generally do not. (The main exception is that some claims made for the accommodation of Islam have been seen as threatening to basic principles of the secular state.)[4] When ethnic claims are framed as national claims, based on putative territorial nationhood and nationality, they become more fundamental, and potentially more threatening, precisely because they raise what Linz and Stepan (1996) have called the "stateness" problem—the problem of the integrity and boundaries of the state.

In east central Europe, ethnicity speaks this potentially explosive language of nationality. Nationality or nationhood, in turn, is understood as based on ethnicity (language, culture, a vague sense of shared descent, and so on) rather than—as in the putatively civic model of nationhood—on political citizenship.[5] One might say that ethnicity is nationalized, while nationality and nationhood are ethnicized. In Western Europe, in contrast, after decades of heavy labor migration and subsequent family reunification, public attention has focused on immigrant ethnicity, while ethnic claims have not generally been framed as national claims.

There are, of course, important exceptions to this pattern on both sides. In much of east central Europe, there are fundamental issues associated with the large, socially stigmatized, spatially segregated, and in large part economically marginalized Gypsy or Roma population (Barany 2002). These issues are sui generis and cannot be neatly subsumed under our usual conceptual rubrics. Depending on how Roma are represented by others, and how they represent themselves, they can be conceived as an ethnic group, a national group, a caste, or a social underclass (Vermeersch 2003).[6]

In Western Europe, on the other hand, ethnicity sometimes involves claims to territorial nationality or nationhood, and the politics of ethnicity then becomes a politics of national autonomy and self-determination. This is true above all in Spain, Belgium, and Britain, all of them multinational (and not simply multiethnic) polities. There is also the interestingly ambiguous case of Italy, where the Northern League sometimes claims that northern Italy, or Padania, is a distinct nation. Yet only in the case of Northern Ireland—the Western European case most similar to the classic national conflicts of central and Eastern Europe—is a cross-border "kin" state or ethnic homeland involved in any significant way. As a result—and notwithstanding the political violence associated with Irish, Basque, and Corsican nationalist movements—this type of ethnonationalist politics is less threatening to states than the characteristic Eastern European configuration.

A further crossover, blurring the sharp outlines of the East-West distinction, is that just as ethnicity is nationalized—understood as nationality—in some Western European as well as in most east central European cases, so too nationality and nationhood may be ethnicized in Western as well as in Eastern Europe. And this is true not only for ethnoregional nationalisms. In response to growing Muslim and non-European immigrant populations, national self-understandings have also been ethnicized, to some degree, even in the so-called state-nations of northern and Western Europe, in countries with traditionally state-framed understandings of nationhood.

Ethnicity in east central Europe, I have suggested, often takes a specifically national—and nationalist—form. Yet despite this potentially explosive configuration, and despite the resurgence of nationalism that accompanied the collapse of communist regimes, ethnic violence has been less widespread, ethnic mobilization less strong, and ethnic identity less pervasively significant than is ordinarily assumed. Having made a good part of my professional living recently off ethnicity and nationalism in Eastern Europe, I have no interest in minimizing their significance. In general, however, I think that discussions of the region are overly ethnicized and that an exaggerated focus on ethnicity and nationalism risks crowding out other, often more important theoretical and practical perspectives (Brubaker et al. 2006, chapter 6).

Of the ghastly violence in Yugoslavia and parts of the former Soviet Union since the end of the Cold War we need no reminder. But as Tom Nairn (1995, 91–92) put it, even though one would certainly not want to make light of these terrible conflicts, one should also beware of "making dark" of them. Ethnonationalist violence has been limited to a relatively small part of Eastern Europe and the former Soviet Union—overwhelmingly concentrated in the former Yugoslavia, Transcaucasia, and the North Caucasus. One should remember, moreover, the violence that has not occurred, the dogs that have not barked. In this perspective, what is striking is the relatively peaceful character of the disintegration of the Soviet Union. Consider, for example, the twenty-five million Russians stranded as minorities in nationalizing successor states by the breakup of the Soviet Union. Many analysts—myself included, in the early 1990s—thought that at least some of these Russians would be the flashpoints of ethnonational conflict and violence. Yet outside the self-proclaimed "Dniester Republic" in Moldova, successor state Russians have been neither the objects nor the perpetrators of nationalist violence (Laitin 1998, chapter 12; Melvin 1998; Braun 2000).

What about ethnic and nationalist mobilization? Here too there is a case-selection bias at work. We pay attention to the spectacular moments of high mobilization—the human chain across the Baltic republics in 1989, the great crowds that filled the main squares of Yerevan, Tbilisi, Berlin, Prague, and other cities in 1988–90. But these have been the exception, not the rule. Moments of high mobilization have been few and ephemeral. Even where "nation" was a galvanizing category at one moment, it was not at the next. On the whole, especially since 1990, people have remained in their homes, not taken to the streets. In conspicuous contrast to interwar east central Europe, demobilization and political passivity, rather than fevered mobilization, have prevailed. Much has been written on the strength of nationalist movements in the former Soviet Union, not enough on their comparative weakness.[7]

There is, moreover, a kind of optical illusion involved in the view from afar. From a distance, one risks taking too seriously the claims made by ethnonational entrepreneurs—who have indeed proliferated as ethnic modes of claims-making have become more legitimate—and not asking to what extent they really speak for those in whose name they claim to speak. This is what anthropologist Katherine Verdery (1991, 6) has called the "is-anyone-listening problem." One should not forget that people do not necessarily respond particularly energetically or warmly to the nationalist utterances of politicians who claim to speak in their name.

In the Transylvanian town of Cluj, where I conducted fieldwork for a recent book, a bitterly nationalist local politics set majority Romanian against minority Hungarian claims (Brubaker et al. 2006.) Yet there was very little nationalist mobilization by ordinary people, and there was considerable public indifference to the endless cycles of nationalist talk, and to the Romanian national colors in which the town's public space was saturated during the twelve years in which a radically nationalist mayor occupied city hall. This made palpable for me the striking discrepancy between nationalist politics—which often seems to run in a sphere of its own, unmoored from its putative constituencies—and the cares and concerns of ordinary people in everyday life. And there are many parallels elsewhere in the region. The general political passivity of Russians in Soviet successor states, for example, has been striking, despite various attempts to mobilize them.

Nearly a half century ago, sociologist Dennis Wrong (1961) criticized Parsonian functionalism for its "oversocialized conception of man." Much social analysis today is informed by what might be called an *overethnicized* conception of history, politics, and social interaction. The ethnic categories deployed by political entrepreneurs are often uncritically adopted by social analysts. As a result, the salience of ethnicity tends to be assumed rather than demonstrated; ethnic identities are ascribed to persons who may define themselves in other terms. Ethnicity and nationalism need to be understood as particular ways of talking about and experiencing the social world and as particular ways of framing political claims, not as real boundaries inscribed in the nature of things. Reducing this to a formula, I would say that ethnicity is a perspective on the world, not a thing in the world (Brubaker 2004, chapters 1 and 3). In some contexts, ethnicized ways of talking about the social world and framing political claims have deep resonance, and they powerfully structure how people think and talk and act in everyday life, as well as how they understand and act on their political interests. At other times and places, the language of ethnicity and nationalism deployed by political entrepreneurs falls on deaf or simply indifferent ears.

## Migration

Like ethnicity—and in part, of course, in connection with ethnicity—migration too has become a central issue throughout Europe. But just as patterns of politicized ethnicity differ, so too do patterns of migration. First, and most obviously, the problematics of migration in Western Europe have focused on *immigration*, especially from outside the region,[8] while in Eastern Europe questions of migration have been, in the first instance, about *emigration*—seen both as a problem (insofar as it involves the disproportionate out-migration of highly educated or skilled younger people) and as a solution (a solution for individuals, insofar as temporary work abroad or permanent emigration offers a means of coping with economic dislocation or a way of getting ahead; a solution for the state, in that it generates remittances; or a solution for nationalists, if it removes or weakens "unwanted elements").

As a corollary of this basic difference, migration has been experientially marginal in Western Europe. Migrants and their distinctive cultural practices have of course become conspicuously visible and central to everyday experience in many Western European cities and towns. But migration itself—even in former countries of emigration such as Greece, Italy, Portugal, and Spain—is something that *others* do. In Eastern Europe, by contrast, migration has become experientially central, figuring pervasively in the way ordinary people think and talk about their plans, strategies, dreams, and hopes (Brubaker et al. 2006, chapter 11).

Within Western Europe, migration has of course become more free with the enlargement of the European Union (EU), the (delayed) introduction of free movement for citizens of new EU member states, and the abolition of internal frontiers within the Schengen zone. But in much of Eastern Europe and the former Soviet Union, migration has become less free, in certain respects, as political space has contracted; as borders, visas, and new citizenships have been introduced; and as the initially open door with which Western countries welcomed migrants fleeing collapsing communist regimes quickly closed. In other respects, to be sure, migration possibilities there have expanded. In particular, citizens of most east central European countries no longer require visas to travel to EU countries. This does not, of course, grant them the right to work, and even after the eastward enlargement of the EU in 2004 and 2007, existing member states can limit labor migration from new member states for a transitional period of up to seven years, though not all have done so. But the ability to travel without the hurdles and indignities of having to seek a visa nonetheless marks a significant improvement for citizens of these countries (and also, of course, makes it easier to work without documents).

In Western Europe—to highlight a final stark dimension of difference—migration involves mixing, and generates new forms and degrees of ethnic, racial, linguistic, and religious heterogeneity, together with the new challenges to national self-understandings and the new forms of politicized ethnicity sketched above. In Eastern Europe, much migration—not only in the last decade but over the last century—has involved ethnic *unmixing*, reducing rather than increasing heterogeneity (Brubaker 1995). This is notoriously the case, of course, for the infamous instances of forced migration—starting with the Balkan Wars at the beginning of the twentieth century, via the massive displacements during and after the Second World War, to the Balkan wars at century's close—that have come to be known as "ethnic cleansing" (Naimark 2001; Ther and Siljak 2001). But it is also the case for quieter, less dramatic forms of ethnic unmixing, involving, for example, the migration of Germans from Poland, Russia, and the former Soviet Union to Germany; of Hungarians from Romania, Yugoslavia, Ukraine, and Slovakia to Hungary; of Russians from various Soviet successor states to Russia; and of Jews from the former Soviet Union to Israel (Brubaker 1998; Joppke 2005).[9]

Of course, patterns of migration are a great deal more complicated than this. "Western Europe" and "Eastern Europe" are not single places but differentiated series of places, differently positioned—for economic, political, and geographic reasons—with respect to migration flows. Consider just one example. In the more prosperous east central European countries—especially Poland, the Czech Republic, Hungary, and Slovenia[10]—emigration pressures are weaker, while labor migration from points further east, and requests for political asylum from Asian and African as well as Eastern European countries, have emerged as significant issues. In this respect, these countries may be following in the path of Spain, Portugal, Italy, and Greece, which made the transition from emigration to immigration countries during the last quarter century. Russia, too, has become a key destination for migrants, mainly from other Soviet successor states.

More than a decade and a half after the end of the Cold War, it is worth keeping in mind the migration that has *not* occurred from—and within— Eastern Europe. In 1990, experts warned of an "exodus," a "human deluge,"[11] an "invasion" of "hungry hordes," a "mass migration on a scale unseen since World War II,"[12] a "flood of desperate people," a modern-day *Völkerwanderung* like that in which "the Germanic people[s] moved west and destroyed the Roman Empire" as Peter Jankowitsch, chair of the Foreign Relations Committee of the Austrian parliament, put it. "How many Poles will stay in Poland?" Jankowitsch asked rhetorically. "How many Romanians will stay in Romania?"[13] Plenty, it turned out. Sizeable though westward migration has been in the experience and, even more so, in the social imagination of ordinary citizens of Eastern Europe, its magnitude, for Western countries, has remained modest. In the "frontline" states of Germany and Austria, such migration has been much more significant, but even there its rhythms have been measured, not cataclysmic.

Around the same time, haunted by the Yugoslav refugee crisis, analysts envisioned convulsive episodes of forced or politically induced migration on a much vaster scale, pointing with special concern, in this context too, to the twenty-five million Russians outside Russia. Yet while many Russians have left Central Asia and Kazakhstan, the migration has been comparatively orderly, and the large majority of Kazakhstani Russians have chosen so far to remain in Kazakhstan.

## Statehood

My final cluster of themes concerns the state. The restructuring of the state has been a major issue throughout Europe. But in this domain, too, questions have been posed in very different ways in different parts of Europe.

The most striking difference would seem to be this: while the reorganization of political space in Western Europe has pointed—at least in anticipation—*beyond* the nation-state, the spectacular post–Cold War reconfiguration of Central and Eastern Europe has involved a move *back to* the nation-state. Apart from unified Germany, twenty-one of the twenty-three successor states to the multinational Soviet Union and Yugoslavia and binational Czechoslovakia expressly understand themselves as nation-states, that is, as the states of and for the particular nations whose names they bear (and the two exceptions—the Russian Federation and Bosnia and Herzegovina—are themselves closely linked to particular nations). If Western Europe is entering a postnational age, the political context for much of Eastern Europe is *post-multinational*. Just as the great Habsburg, Romanov, and Ottoman empires crumbled at the beginning of the "short twentieth century" (Hobsbawm 1994), leaving an array of nationally defined successor states, so too, at the close of the century, multinational states have again fragmented into sets of would-be nation-states.

Yet this view requires qualification, and not only because the massive eastward enlargement of the EU in 2004 and 2007 has blurred the West-East distinction. More fundamentally, the EU does not represent a linear or unambiguous move "beyond the nation-state" to a supranational form of political authority. As Milward (1992) argued, the initially limited moves towards supranational authority worked—and were intended—to restore and strengthen the authority of the nation-state. What has been occurring is a complex unbundling and redistribution—upwards, downwards, and in various oblique directions—of previously tightly bundled powers and competencies. The resultant "multi-level" or even "neo-medieval" polity does not look much like a supranational superstate: an oft-quoted remark describes the EU as an "economic giant, a political dwarf, and a military worm."[14] Events of the last decade and a half, notwithstanding the Treaty of Maastricht and the announced formation of a common security and defense policy, have done little to undermine that view.[15]

Although there is no clear move beyond the nation-state, the classical model of unitary, centralized, sovereign statehood, in which all authority derives from a single central point, no longer comes close to describing political reality. Authority has been reconfigured, and competencies unbundled and redistributed—not only to the EU (itself a set of institutions and authorities, not a single entity) but also to other international organizations, and to subnational polities and jurisdictions. This raises fundamental questions about the changing nature of statehood and political authority.

Granted that the EU is not very statelike at present, how might it become more statelike in the future? What attributes historically associated with statehood might it come to acquire? What does its development imply about the statehood—or, following J. P. Nettl (1968), the "stateness"—of existing states? Are they becoming less statelike as they give up conventional sovereign powers, such as control over borders and over monetary and fiscal policy?

Once we revise our understanding of statehood to allow for the unbundling and sharing of powers and competencies previously monopolized by a single sovereign center, then questions of stateness also arise for lower-level polities emerging within federalizing or otherwise decentralizing states. To what extent do more or less autonomous but nonsovereign polities such as Catalonia, Flanders, and Scotland take on attributes of stateness as they gain new and often quite considerable powers and competencies,[16] even while remaining parts of larger, more embracing states? This is a familiar issue in the literature on federalism, but that literature has been quite separate from the historical and political sociological literature on the development of the modern state. The latter has defined the modern state as centralized and sovereign—as monopolizing the means of coercion within a particular territory, in Weber's classic formulation—and has cast the story of its development in teleological form, involving the progressive appropriation of previously dispersed powers by a single center. This perspective has marginalized the experience of federal states. Their very existence is something of an anomaly; they are by definition not very statelike.

The complex unbundling and redistribution of powers and competencies, in short, is forcing a fundamental rethinking of the very notion of "the state." The notion may prove too heavily encumbered by the political theory of sovereignty and its monist, unitarist connotations to be of much analytical use in conceptualizing the complex multilevel polity that is emerging.

The unbundling and redistribution of powers and competencies has important implications for ethnicity. These implications are particularly far-reaching where ethnicity is organized and expressed as territorial nationality.[17] The devolution of power to regions may have no relation to ethnocultural nationality; but where regions with substantial powers of self-government coincide more or less closely with the territories of ethnocultural nations (as they do in the United Kingdom, Spain, Belgium, and to a certain extent in Switzerland), this provides a potential way of satisfying the claims of national self-determination *within* the framework of a wider state, rather than by secession. Ethnoterritorial federalism, however, has been vehemently rejected in east central Europe and (despite—or precisely because of—the legacy of Soviet ethnoterritorial federalism) in Soviet successor states (Kymlicka 2001b).

The deepening and widening of the EU also has important implications for ethnicity. The EU provides various institutional sites for recognizing non-state actors, including ethno-nationally distinct regions and transborder populations such as the Roma. Moreover, the eastward enlargement of the EU to include Hungary, Slovakia, and Romania has in a certain sense—largely but not exclusively symbolic—reunified the state-spanning Hungarian ethnocultural nation, which had been torn apart after the First World War.

In Eastern Europe, questions of statehood and stateness have been posed in quite different terms.[18] There is, in the first place, the sheer proliferation of new states. Almost all of them, as noted above, have defined and constituted themselves as sovereign nation-states, drawing on highly institutionalized— if outdated—rhetorics and models of sovereignty and nationhood (Meyer 1987). These institutionalized "performances" of sovereign nation-statehood do not represent an unambiguous move "back to the nation-state." Almost all the new states are involved, in one way or another, in processes of regional integration, notably as members or candidate members of the North Atlantic Treaty Organization and/or the EU on the one hand, or the Commonwealth of Independent States on the other. Yet the invocations of sovereignty and nationhood are not mere rhetoric. There is a real tension between the model of sovereign nation-statehood and that of supranational integration; the latter does not automatically trump the former. The model of sovereign nation-statehood remains normatively more robust in Eastern than in Western Europe; it has its attractions not only for newly constituted states but also for those newly freed from the Soviet economic and security embrace.

Second, the successor states to the Soviet Union and Yugoslavia are not only nation-states but *nationalizing states* (Brubaker 1996, 2007).[19] They are discursively construed as the states *of* and *for* the "core" ethnocultural nations whose names they bear, and not as the states of and for all of their citizens, regardless of ethnicity. Nationalizing states, moreover, involve not simply a claim to primacy or "ownership," but a call to action. The core nation is represented as being in a weak or unhealthy condition, and action is needed, it is argued, to promote its language, cultural flourishing, demographic robustness, economic welfare, or political hegemony. Such action is understood and justified as remedial or compensatory, needed to redress previous discrimination or oppression suffered by the core nation. To varying degrees, and in varying ways, these states have adopted formal and informal policies and practices informed and justified by these ideas.

Third, there are the special "stateness" problems—in Linz and Stepan's sense, not Nettl's—posed by politicized ethnicity in Eastern Europe. As I indicated earlier, the ethnically framed challenges—or perceived challenges[20]—to the territorial integrity and boundaries of existing states are particularly delicate in Eastern Europe because they often involve cross-border links connecting ethnonational claimants within particular states and a patron state abroad that represents the same ethnocultural nationality.

Finally, while early understandings of postcommunist "transition" posited the need to liberate economy and society from the grip of an overly strong state, more recent analyses have made almost the opposite argument.[21] The post–Cold War moment of triumphant antistatism has long passed. As Stephen Holmes and others argued in the late 1990s with respect to pre-Putin Russia—although the point had broader relevance for the region—it was not the strength of the state but its weakness that threatened the basic rights and well-being of citizens.[22] The "withering away of the state" in Russia and elsewhere in the 1990s destroyed the capacity to provide the most elementary public goods and services. Neoliberals increasingly concede what paleoliberals knew all along: a strong, even powerful state is a precondition for everything that they hold dear, including the orderly workings of markets, the protection of citizens against violence, and the enforcement of human rights. Hence the calls to strengthen and build up the state, to liberate what are in theory the distinctively public powers of the state from the clutches of those who have expropriated and in effect privatized them.

The force of renewed calls for a "strong" or "powerful" state depends of course on how we understand these terms. Here Michael Mann's (1993, 59–60) distinction between "despotic" and "infrastructural" power is helpful, the former denoting arbitrary power *over* civil society, the latter the power of state institutions to coordinate and regulate social life by penetrating and working *through* civil society. Despotically "strong" states may be infrastructurally "weak," and vice versa. What is urgently needed in much of Eastern Europe—and throughout the Third World—is an infrastructurally strong state, one that can keep the peace, punish force and fraud, enforce contracts, collect taxes, provide basic services, protect public health, implement legislation, and prevent wholesale plundering of the land and its people by criminal and quasi-criminal networks.

State-building, then, is still very much on the agenda in Eastern Europe. While Western and parts of east central Europe move towards the unbundling and redistribution of previously concentrated powers, in much of Eastern Europe we see (or at least hear about the need for) moves in the opposite direction, toward the rebundling and reconcentration of previously dispersed—and in considerable part privately appropriated—powers.[23] Whether such changes will succeed—whether an effective, infrastructurally strong state can be built—is by no means certain. Over the long sweep of European history in the last millennium, sustained military competition eventually led to the weeding out of the most blatant forms of patrimonial administration.[24] Today, however, pressures to reform conspicuously corrupt, grossly inefficient state administrations are much weaker. States (and other actors) continue to make war, but war no longer makes states the way it used to.[25] The worldwide club of states includes a large and perhaps increasing number of "quasi-states" (Jackson 1990)—organizations that are officially recognized and certified internationally as "states" yet fail to do the most elementary things that states are supposed to do, such as maintaining order throughout a given territory. Today, thanks to the reification and sacralization of existing state borders in prevailing international discourse and practice,[26] such quasi-states can continue to exist, irrespective of their abysmal performance, with little threat that they will go out of business. Eastern Europe may not harbor the worst specimens of this lamentable genre, and of course there are great differences within the region. In much of the region, however, the making of the modern state, far from being a completed chapter of history, remains a matter of great contemporary urgency.

NOTES

An earlier version of this essay appeared under a slightly different title in Michel Seymour, ed., 2004, *The Fate of the Nation-State*, Montreal and Kingston: McGill-Queen's University Press.

1. As the rich comparative literature on ethnicity makes clear (see, e.g., Akzin 1966; Schermerhorn 1970; Francis 1976; Rothschild 1981; van den Berghe 1981, part two; Horowitz 1985), these are not the only ways in which ethnic heterogeneity can be socially organized and politically expressed. But this distinction does

capture a key dimension of variation in the organization and expression of ethnicity in Europe. A broadly similar distinction has been introduced into political theory—especially into discussions of multiculturalism—by Kymlicka 1995. For an attempt to bring Western political theory to bear on ethnicity in Eastern Europe, see Kymlicka 2001a.

2. Even when immigrants are concentrated in immigrant neighborhoods or enclaves, the nature and consequences of such territorial concentration are quite different than they are in the case of territorial nationality.

3. It is important to emphasize that ethnic heterogeneity is not intrinsically "national" in Eastern Europe; rather, it came to be understood in national terms (Brubaker et al. 2006, 30).

4. This is obviously an important and contested topic in its own right, but it is beyond the scope of this essay.

5. For a critical analysis of the distinction between civic and ethnic nationalism, see Brubaker 2004, chapter 6.

6. Just as Roma straddle conceptual borders, they cross state boundaries as well. Some of the ugliest episodes of immigration control in the 1990s were driven by efforts to control their unwanted movement.

7. A similar point could be made about Western Europe. Substantial literatures address the rise of xenophobic, radical-right, or national-populist parties (for overviews, see Betz 1994; Betz and Immerfall 1998) and of anti-immigrant violence (Björgo and Witte 1993). Again, without minimizing the significance of the new right parties, or still less that of the appalling attacks on asylum seekers and other foreigners in Germany and elsewhere, one should not overestimate the strength of xenophobic nationalism in Western Europe.

8. There has been a good deal of concern with intra-EU migration, but mainly in terms of how it articulates with immigration from outside the region, given the need—since abolition of internal frontiers within the Schengen zone—for EU states to harmonize external admissions policies.

9. Even as it involves a reduction in ethnic heterogeneity in the countries of origin, such migrations of ethnic unmixing generate new forms of ethnic or quasi-ethnic heterogeneity in the putative national homelands: ethnic Hungarians from Romania are treated as "Romanians" in Hungary, while Jews from the former Soviet Union are treated as "Russians" in Israel. On the ambiguous and contested national identity of ethnic Hungarian migrants to Hungary, see Fox 2003.

10. These are the main "buffer" or "transit" countries between Eastern and Western Europe.

11. *Independent*, November 29, 1990.

12. *Los Angeles Times*, December 3, 1990.

13. *Boston Globe*, November 1, 1990.

14. Mark Eyskens, former Belgian foreign minister, quoted in William Drozdiak, "Once Again, Europe Follows American Lead," *Washington Post*, March 26, 1999.

15. Leading European intellectuals critical of the war in Iraq called for a "core Europe" capable of serving as a counterweight to American hegemony (Derrida and Habermas 2003), but as Paul Kennedy (2003) pointed out in reply, there are substantial political and institutional obstacles to this occurring.

16. In certain respects these powers and competencies may be more substantial, and more statelike, than those of the EU.

17. The unbundling and redistribution of powers and competencies has implications for immigrant ethnicity as well. The German *Länder*, for example, have adopted differing policies regarding the wearing of Islamic headscarves by teachers (Joppke forthcoming).

18. In this context, of course, "Eastern Europe" and "Western Europe" increasingly overlap, thanks to the eastern enlargement of the EU.

19. One could also include Slovakia in this category; and while Poland, Romania, Bulgaria, and Hungary are not new states, they too have displayed certain nationalizing tendencies since the change of regime.

20. What constitutes a challenge to the territorial integrity of a state is open to dispute. In Romania, for example, the demands made by the ethnic Hungarian party for autonomy are perceived (or at least publicly represented) by much of the Romanian political elite as a threat to the territorial integrity of the state, even though Hungarian minority politicians insist that while they are challenging the internal structure of the Romanian state (and its constitutional definition as a unitary nation-state), they pose no threat to its territorial integrity.

21. See Stark and Bruszt 1998, chapter 4, for an analysis and critique of this swing in the intellectual pendulum.

22. Holmes 1997 was writing before Putin's accession to the presidency in 2000. Putin has sought to strengthen and recentralize the state, notably by recovering powers previously appropriated by regions (Orttung 2001).

23. Note that powers may be dispersed in two senses: through the formally acknowledged decentralization of power (as in the various agreements that ethno-federal polities within Russia made with Moscow during the 1990s), and through the de facto appropriation by regional or local officials (or even by persons with no official standing, such as some warlords and criminal bosses) of powers formally held by the central state. On the concept of appropriation, Weber's discussion of patrimonial authority remains pertinent and richly suggestive ([1922] 1978, 231ff).

24. For a comprehensive treatment of this theme, see Ertman 1997.

25. Much warfare in the ex-second and Third Worlds is carried out not by states, but by an array of quasi- and non-state forces (Fairbanks 1995; Kaldor 1999). Another, more fundamental reason, as Tilly notes, is that with the gradual "filling-in of the state system," states have increasingly been made—literally created, and allowed to exist, regardless of their infrastructural strength—chiefly by other states (1975a, 46; 1975b, 636; 1990, chapter 7).

26. Much has been made, in the last two decades, about the weakening of this

tendency. But this confuses the weakening of the model of sovereignty, which has indeed occurred, with the desacralization and de-reification of state borders, which has not, at least not to a very substantial degree. Borders are normatively more permeable, but they remain highly reified, despite the important (though contested) exception of Kosovo. Note that (with the exception of Kosovo) the new states that emerged from the Soviet Union, Yugoslavia, and Czechoslovakia already existed as states within formally federal states and already possessed their own borders, territories, and even (in principle) the right to secede from the wider federal state.

WORKS CITED

Akzin, Benjamin. 1966. *States and Nations*. Garden City, NY: Doubleday.

Barany, Zoltan D. 2002. *The East European Gypsies: Regime Change, Marginality, and Ethnopolitics*. Cambridge: Cambridge University Press.

Betz, Hans-Georg. 1994. *Radical Right-Wing Populism in Western Europe*. New York: St. Martin's Press.

———, and Stefan Immerfall, eds. 1998. *The New Politics of the Right: Neo-Populist Parties and Movements in Established Democracies*. New York: St. Martin's Press.

Björgo, Tore, and Rob Witte, eds. 1993. *Racist Violence in Europe*. New York: St. Martin's Press.

Braun, Aurel. 2000. "All Quiet on the Russian Front? Russia, Its Neighbors, and the Russian Diaspora." In *The New European Diasporas: National Minorities and Conflict in Eastern Europe*, ed. Michael Mandelbaum, 81–158. New York: Council on Foreign Relations Press.

Brubaker, Rogers. 1995. "Aftermaths of Empire and the Unmixing of Peoples: Historical and Comparative Perspectives." *Ethnic and Racial Studies* 18(2): 189–218.

———. 1996. *Nationalism Reframed: Nationhood and the National Question in the New Europe*. New York: Cambridge University Press.

———. 1998. "Migrations of Ethnic Unmixing in the 'New Europe'." *International Migration Review* 32(4): 1047–1065.

———. 2004. *Ethnicity Without Groups*. Cambridge, MA: Harvard University Press.

———. 2007. "Nationalizing States Revisited." Keynote address, Annual Meeting of Central Eurasian Studies Society, Seattle, WA.

———, Margit Feischmidt, Jon Fox, and Liana Grancea. 2006. *Nationalist Politics and Everyday Ethnicity in a Transylvanian Town*. Princeton, NJ: Princeton University Press.

———, and Jaeeun Kim. 2009. "Transborder Nationhood and the Politics of Belonging in Germany and Korea." Unpublished paper.

Derrida, Jacques, and Jürgen Habermas. 2003. "Nach dem Krieg: Die Wiedergeburt Europas." *Frankfurter Allgemeine Zeitung*, May 31. http://www.faz.net/s/Rub117C535CDF414415BB243B181B8B60AE/Doc~ECBE3F8FCE2D049AE808A3C8DBD3B2763~ATpl~Ecommon~Scontent.html

Ertman, Thomas. 1997. *Birth of the Leviathan: Building States and Regimes in Medieval and Early Modern Europe*. Cambridge: Cambridge University Press.

Fairbanks, Charles H., Jr. 1995. "The Postcommunist Wars." *Journal of Democracy* 6(4): 18–34.

Fox, Jon E. 2003. "National Identities on the Move: Transylvanian Hungarian Labour Migrants in Hungary." *Journal of Ethnic and Migration Studies* 29(3): 449–466.

Francis, E. K. 1976. *Interethnic Relations*. New York: Elsevier.

Hobsbawm, E. J. 1994. *The Age of Extremes: The Short Twentieth Century, 1914–1991*. London: Michael Joseph.

Holmes, Stephen. 1997. "What Russia Teaches Us Now: How Weak States Threaten Freedom." *American Prospect* (33): 30–39.

Horowitz, Donald L. 1985. *Ethnic Groups in Conflict*. Berkeley: University of California Press.

Jackson, Robert H. 1990. *Quasi-States: Sovereignty, International Relations and the Third World*. New York: Cambridge University Press.

Joppke, Christian. 2005. *Selecting by Origin: Ethnic Migration in the Liberal State*. Cambridge, MA: Harvard University Press.

———. Forthcoming. *Veil: Mirror of Identity*.

Kaldor, Mary. 1999. *New and Old Wars: Organized Violence in a Global Era*. Stanford, CA: Stanford University Press.

Kennedy, Paul. 2003. "Europe's Old Laggards Will Never Balance US Power." *The Guardian*, June 24. http://www.guardian.co.uk/world/2003/jun/24/eu.politics

Kymlicka, Will. 1995. *Multicultural Citizenship: A Liberal Theory of Minority Rights*. Oxford: Oxford University Press.

———. 2001a. "Western Political Theory and Ethnic Relations in Eastern Europe." In *Can Liberal Pluralism Be Exported? Western Political Theory and Ethnic Relations in Eastern Europe*, ed. Will Kymlicka and Magda Opalski, 13–105. Oxford: Oxford University Press.

———. 2001b. "Reply and Conclusions." In *Can Liberal Pluralism Be Exported? Western Political Theory and Ethnic Relations in Eastern Europe*, ed. Will Kymlicka and Magda Opalski, 345–413. Oxford: Oxford University Press.

Laitin, David D. 1998. *Identity in Formation: The Russian-Speaking Populations in the Near Abroad*. Ithaca, NY: Cornell University Press.

Linz, Juan J., and Alfred Stepan. 1996. *Problems of Democratic Transition and Consolidation: Southern Europe, South America, and Post-Communist Europe*. Baltimore: Johns Hopkins University Press.

Mann, Michael. 1993. *The Sources of Social Power: The Rise of Classes and Nation-States, 1760–1914*. Cambridge: Cambridge University Press.

Melvin, Neil J. 1998. "The Russians: Diaspora and the End of Empire." In *Nations Abroad: Diaspora Politics and International Relations in the Former Soviet Union*, ed. Charles King and Neil J. Melvin, 27–57. Boulder, CO: Westview Press.

Meyer, John W. 1987. "The World Polity and the Authority of the Nation-State." In *Institutional Structure: Constituting State, Society, and the Individual*, ed. George M. Thomas, John W. Meyer, and Francisco O. Ramirez, 41–70. Newbury Park, CA: Sage.

Milward, Alan S. 1992. *The European Rescue of the Nation-State*. Berkeley and Los Angeles: University of California Press.

Naimark, Norman M. 2001. *Fires of Hatred: Ethnic Cleansing in Twentieth-Century Europe*. Cambridge, MA: Harvard University Press.

Nairn, Tom. 1995. "Breakwaters of 2000: From Ethnic to Civic Nationalism." *New Left Review* (214): 91–103.

Nettl, J. P. 1968. "The State As a Conceptual Variable." *World Politics* 20(4): 559–592.

Orttung, Robert. 2001. "Putin's Federal Reform Package: A Recipe for Unchecked Kremlin Power." *Demokratizatsiya* 9(3): 341–349.

Rothschild, Joseph. 1981. *Ethnopolitics: A Conceptual Framework*. New York: Columbia University Press.

Schermerhorn, R. A. 1970. *Comparative Ethnic Relations: A Framework for Theory and Research*. New York: Random House.

Stark, David, and László Bruszt. 1998. *Postsocialist Pathways: Transforming Politics and Property in East Central Europe*. Cambridge: Cambridge University Press.

Ther, Philipp, and Ana Siljak, eds. 2001. *Redrawing Nations: Ethnic Cleansing in East-Central Europe, 1944–1948*. Lanham, MD: Rowman & Littlefield.

Tilly, Charles. 1975a. "Reflections on the History of European State-Making." In *The Formation of National States in Western Europe*, ed. Charles Tilly, 3–83. Princeton, NJ: Princeton University Press.

———. 1975b. "Western State-Making and Theories of Political Transformation." In *The Formation of National States in Western Europe*, ed. Charles Tilly, 601–638. Princeton, NJ: Princeton University Press.

———. 1990. *Coercion, Capital, and European States: AD 990–1992*. Cambridge: Blackwell.

van den Berghe, Pierre L. 1981. *The Ethnic Phenomenon*. New York: Elsevier.

Verdery, Katherine. 1991. *National Ideology under Socialism: Identity and Cultural Politics in Ceausescu's Romania*. Berkeley: University of California Press.

Vermeersch, Peter. 2003. "Ethnic Identity and Movement Politics: The Case of the Roma in the Czech Republic and Slovakia." *Ethnic and Racial Studies* 26(5): 879–901.

Weber, Max. [1922] 1978. *Economy and Society: An Outline of Interpretive Sociology*, ed. Guenther Roth and Claus Wittich. Berkeley: University of California Press.

Wrong, Dennis. 1961. "The Oversocialized Conception of Man in Modern Society." *American Sociological Review* 23(2): 183–193.

# CHAPTER FOUR

# New Ways of Thinking About Identity in Europe

SALVADOR CARDÚS

## On "Ethnicity"

I begin with the Aristotelian maxim to "dare to think," and moreover, in the context of this collection, we must question common assumptions of the saliency of European ethnicity. That is to say, we need to call into question the presumptions of the social world and the evidence that we use to describe it. Such basic questions always entail risk, and one runs even greater risk to test not simply that which is implicit in ordinary commonsense knowledge [sens commun savant], but especially—in the words of Pierre Bourdieu[1]—that which lies in commonsense wisdom. In other words, we must question what constitutes the presumed world and that which is labeled evidence by social scientists. The theoretical basis for sociology, as with any other scientific discipline, should not be understood as a solid starting point, or a stable reference that avoids all risks, but as a provocation. Responding to the provocation will help develop the arguments for or against its worth or the need to revise it.[2]

In this context, I feel an intellectual discomfort using the term "ethnicity" to interpret sociological phenomena. At the root of my misgivings is the question of whether "ethnicity" and "identity" are "social" phenomena or "sociological" descriptors, that is to say, empirical or theoretical artifacts. In this essay I focus on the latter, to interpret social phenomena. My own intuition is to take a page from critical anthropologists and to suspect that using the term "ethnic" has unintentionally rejuvenated the outdated concept of "race." In place of the focus on genetics, the notion of ethnicity would emphasize supposed original cultural traits, and yet it thereby posits a concept that is no less closed or deterministic.[3] I do not go so far as some in anthropology who accuse ethnographers of racist bias. But I do believe that this is a term that cannot be analyzed without closely considering its ideological and political weight, because such instrumental usage dilutes its analytical leverage when it comes to revealing the current processes for negotiating diversity especially in today's globalized Europe.

My reservation regarding the concepts of "ethnic" and "ethnicity" is likely inflected by a European perspective, one that may seem overly critical of American scholarship. My European theoretical and practical viewpoint is not based on a concern that these categories are originating in Europe; in fact quite the opposite is the case. By my reading, notions of ethnicity and related terms are used in Europe as a result of the dominant influence of American academic social science. Such models cross the Atlantic with attractive internal logic, but are applied in Europe without considering the differences between societies and their internal functioning of individual and group identification.

My reflections on this occasion are a first step in criticizing the notion of ethnicity and its uses, more than a fully worked-through argument. I find strong evidence that in Europe the term "ethnicity" has only worked adequately for studying—and in effect to reify—the models of multicultural coexistence of postcolonial countries. European policies toward immigration—including guest-worker programs and related practices of maintaining distinct alien status—make the term convenient and even instrumental to defend models of multicultural society. Such models have depended upon the assumption that cultural differences are essential and irreducible. In these countries, multicultural models are being defended based on a postcolonial "guilt" most clearly manifest in politically correct discourse: such language of ethnic difference, paradoxically, while putatively an attempt to defend cultural diversity, ultimately promotes the idea that national cultures must be protected from melding.

We have recently seen criticism of such consequences of ethnicizing European communities, even in administrations heretofore invested in multiculturalism. The head of the British Commission for Racial Equality, Trevor Phillips,[4] as well as the Commission on Integration and Cohesion (final report, June 2007) have scrutinized the impact of qualifying communities as distinctly ethnic.[5] On the continent, Ayan Hirsi Ali is only the most noted of critics of privileging ascribed authentic ethnic culture in the name of multicultural Europe.[6] Although her fate, including death threats from Islamic fundamentalists, and abandonment by her own party, resulted from a complex mix of circumstances, her story raises questions among supporters and detractors about the effects of ratifying claims to ethnic difference.

Currently, even in progressive quarters, an increasing number of critics—from those who oppose and those who encourage immigration—are voicing their own concerns about the meaning of ethnicity.[7] Such critical reflections on multicultural, multiethnic Europe are spurring reconsideration of theoretical models as well as political and social failures. One important aim of this essay is to consider the role of traditional protection for claims to ethnic difference in the recent constellation of troubling developments in Europe, including the London terrorist attacks in July 2005, the high-profile murders of outspoken critics of multiculturalism such as Pym Fortuyn and Theo van Gogh, the exile of Hirsi Ali, and the rise of racist and xenophobic political parties in liberal Holland and in neighboring democracies hosting immigrants across the expanding European Union.

Multiethnic Europe has been and still is a polity that in the name of respect for diversity obstructs immigrant assimilation. Far from the self-description of the United States as a melting pot for all immigrants, Europe has effectively erected barriers to the integration of newcomers and, one can argue, turned cultural origin into a closed community in which residents obtain the protection of the welfare state, but only on condition of maintaining their characteristic community in isolation. Moreover, according to some authors, the multicultural priority not only locks immigrants in something like a cultural prison, but also accentuates, creates, and multiplies differences, putting social cohesion itself in danger.

One most perceptive analysis on the functioning of multicultural Europe is the study by Giovanni Sartori on pluralism and multiculturalism in multi-ethnic Italy.[8] Sartori considers that the priority for multicultural society, more than "respecting" diversity, is an unreflective and self-perpetuating "diversity machine." At the same time that the priority enforces diversity, it also denies voluntary pluralism. Sartori asserts that "pluralism works on created cleavages that neutralize and minimize among themselves, while multiculturalism is centered on the (cumulative) cleavages that, when joined together, reinforce one another."[9] Multiculturalism would create "reinforced identities," for example, by superimposing language, religion, ethnicity, and ideology. Sartori concludes, "Pluralism manifests itself as an open society that is highly enriched by multiple conditions of belonging, while multiculturalism means the dismemberment of pluralist society into subgroups of closed and homogeneous communities."[10]

Such an argument about self-perpetuating alienation in ethnic Europe has been recently mapped onto related social analysis. At the Universitat Autònoma de Barcelona, Peter L. Berger has perceived a secondary factor contributing to immigrant community isolation: Western Europe's highly secularized society eschews the central role of religious institutions in producing community solidarity.[11] In large part, this secularization could be explained by the role of European states in the organization of community solidarity networks, with such a high level of cultural intervention and social protection that it has left traditional churches with almost no practical function to perform. The crisis of the traditional local churches contrasts with the growth, in Europe, of powerful religious organizations around new immigrant groups, which as long as they are not beneficiaries of the welfare state, develop religious links that have more to do with the transitory need for incorporation in the host society than with their "strictly" spiritual needs, as suggested in the exhaustive study on the establishment of "other religions" in Catalonia carried out by a team at the Universitat Autònoma de Barcelona directed by Joan Estruch.[12]

## Ethnicity and Immigrant Culture

The concept of ethnicity, rather than clarifying, in fact obscures such processes of social change in Europe. In my view, the idea of a strong ethnic factor that socially structures an "essential" and irreducible difference relies on the hypothesis that the home culture can be transported. This assumption has been used to support claims for rights that may be contrary to local and national laws. Moreover, it presupposes that the home culture can be preserved outside the historical, political, economic, and social contexts that shaped it. Such a static view implies an erroneous idea of culture as a closed and stable structure, as opposed to an open process of communication by which groups establish their hierarchical networks of loyalty and belonging in a given social space. When, through the process of immigration, that space changes, as long as no artificial situations of social and cultural isolation are created, the networks and hierarchies also change, and the process of cultural communication adapts to the new circumstances. Culture is not a transportable rigid vehicle of traditions, but rather a piece of software of meanings that is constantly updated to facilitate the functioning of social operating hardware that is also in constant evolution.

Outside the historical and social context that gives it meaning, a cultural tradition is easily reduced to a repertory of beliefs and customs, but thereby becomes folklore communicated via community culture. It is often true that individuals, who in their own countries have never shown any special interest in the products of this communication—in forms such as music, literature, and dress—strongly defend such manifestations once outside their home culture, as if such defense were necessary to preserve respect for their most basic rights and dignity. The need to be recognized as one of the beneficiaries of the privileges that the welfare state has reserved for immigrants might explain this radical rediscovery of an "identity of one's own" outside its original space. One of the most telling facts in Catalonia, where the arrival of Muslims in large numbers is a relatively recent event, is that while the first waves of Muslim immigrants adapted easily to local uses and customs, later, with the arrival of the Imams, who act as intermediaries between the Muslim population and the government, there has been an accelerated deadaptation, with a radicalized and homogenizing reconstruction of the (supposed) original identity. On several occasions, the threat of exacerbating the original identity and the conflict that this could generate has been used by these intermediaries in the negotiation of certain advantages.[13] Far from criticizing such rediscovery among many immigrants, we must see that it is the immigration policies in Europe that have perhaps unintentionally enforced this process of folklorization and segregation.[14] In this way live culture is contained, translated, and "ethnified" as a representation of remote origins.[15]

We may clarify this process by means of comparison. In the United States, unlike in Western Europe, statements of ethnic belonging do not tend to endanger the basic cohesion of the nation, because ethnic identity is conceived in political as opposed to cultural terms.[16] In the United States one might claim to be, for instance, "Polish-American"; or one might say that one is "Polish," despite having been born in the United States. This fluid ethnic identification exemplifies what Michael Billig has called "banal nationalism."[17] Some Americans claim their European origins by maintaining traditions that are unknown or relatively ignored in their places of origin. A representative anecdote serves to illustrate the disjuncture between ethnicity reclaimed and place of origin: in the United States I was assured by a man that he was Italian, although he had never been to Italy, did not speak Italian, and did not know anything about the culture of Italy (either north or south) that he claimed as his own. The fact that he was partly and remotely of Italian descent gave him the necessary pride to claim his part in the founding myth of the nation built by immigrants and to have participated in the "dream of freedom" as is represented in the history of transatlantic westward emigration.

In Europe, claims to ethnicity or identity by outsiders who remain linked to a cultural tradition of their own are still experienced as—and in this sense still are—a threat to national cohesion. Europeans see this kind of ethnicity as founding a "resistance identity." In America, the opposite is true: the American model of a strong political nation and a hyphenated ethnic nationalism effectively enables the individual to claim inclusion by accepting the national culture imposed on him or her—even on oneself—to recreate ethnicity. Ethnicity, in this weak mode, becomes a pliable constituent element of the constructed national heritage. Both ethnic origin and the new national culture are adopted and ascribed, creating what Manuel Castells has referred to as "project identity."[18]

When we discuss "ethnic groups," "ethnicity," and the manifest forms by which they are expressed, we need to define the contested terrain and the public identity at stake. One can probe all the different ways of understanding the cultural significance of the use of the Shador or the Hiyab depending on whether we are talking about the United States, Britain, or France. We can do so not just in terms of the respective degree of religious pluralism, multiculturalism, or laicism in the host country, but also particularly from the point of view of those who use the veil to express different things. The meanings may range from publicly demonstrating religiously prescribed submission to their husbands, to defiantly claiming self-expression in the face of a host nation that imposes cultural norms against free choice of association.[19]

## Toward an Instrumental Identity

In Europe we are experiencing a crisis in multicultural and multiethnic models that have proved politically unviable, or at least insufficient, and in my view cannot be interpreted using the same parameters as in the United States. I refer here to Central Europe and Great Britain, where there is public criticism of the consequences of multiculturalism. But one could also consider the immigration policies of southern Europe, Italy, and more broadly throughout Western Europe. I do not think that northern Europe has yet fully experienced the contradictions of cultural diversity, because the phenomenon there is more recent. In France, the immigration debate and the obstacles to integration have been intense since 2005, following the confrontations in the *banlieues*, but the phenomenon is taking its course according to France's own model of political belonging.[20]

Testing the concept of ethnicity in Europe—and the notion linking ethnicity to the political claims for a right to difference—obliges us to revise the notion of identity itself. In schematic terms, the concept of identity that is implicit in ethnicity would best suit stable and homogeneous societies with little population movement. But in the West this kind of society no longer exists: under the pressures of immigration, especially from increasingly distant origins not characterized by even postcolonial associations, it is increasingly difficult to list the qualities that define the cultural specificity of an ethnic or national identity. In contemporary Europe, we would find it an almost impossible task to answer the questions, "What is British?" or "What is Spanish?" The internal differentiation of every society, its fragmentation into widely diverse social groups, the appropriation and reappropriation of external elements and the incoherence and variability of its components, is so vast that it would be difficult for us to define *anything* specific and characteristic of such putative national identities. When British prime minister Gordon Brown was tested to define Britishness (as Tony Blair had previously attempted), he merely offered some vague ideas that, in trying to transcend stereotypes, were interchangeable with what could equally be said of any other national character in Europe.[21]

There are, however, theories of identity that are intended to gain better traction. The sociologist Zygmunt Bauman suggests an interesting proposal, with his formulation of a "liquid modern life," which also suggests "liquid identity."[22] But in my view this proposal does not get to the root of the problem, in that it continues to concentrate on the content of identity, which is more variable and changing than in previous societies. It may be that identity, using Bauman's metaphor, has become fluid in the sense that the content of a modern identity is inherently unstable. But it is precisely this instability that makes it useless, analytically speaking, to emphasize what constitutes that identity. Quite the opposite, in modern liquid societies, identity cannot be anything other than the container, the recipient that holds the liquid and shapes it to satisfy the need for recognition of any individual or community.

A better metaphor for an identity that emphasizes not content but the container is that of the skin.[23] Identity is the "skin" that gives external shape to certain content and keeps it opaque. It is interesting that in this metaphor of the skin, the external appearance that identifies and distinguishes is as important as the opacity of that which paradoxically makes us most alike: the internal content. It is also worth highlighting the idea that the skin is the limit, or the frontier, as well as the point of contact without which there is no possible relationship. We are not far from the notion of "person" or "persona" derived etymologically from the Greek word for "mask." My suspicion is that what social scientists call identity has always functioned as a skin, even if under certain circumstances what the skin contained was considered the important subject of regard.[24] In the condition of globalized European communities, we should recognize that the impossibility of determining the content of identity has restored to preeminence the level of the metaphorical skin of identity.

The idea of "skin" carries the risk of suggesting superficiality, or thinking of identity as an "epidermal" or surface reality.[25] But in the modern cultural emphasis on image and representation, what could be more relevant for the individual—and for national communities—than their "exterior" image? The focus on container and exteriority may strike social scientists as overly constraining. But our goal should not be to measure the relative value of the bones or the skin, but rather whether the skin most importantly shapes identity, regardless of internal character content.

I suggest, then, that we shift emphasis from a "content identity" to a "surface identity," in which socially meaningful difference is understood to be overdetermined, and mainly shaped by externalities. It must be noted that this change is a consequence of globalization, which means that the cultural "ingredients" can be found in any cultural diet in the world, even if the specific appropriation gives them different meanings and functions.

I expand this with two examples. In the first example, at the end of 2007, the fast-food chain McDonalds carried out an advertising campaign in Spain in which, simply by eating "genuine American" hamburgers, the main characters of a television commercial start to speak English without even realizing it (a kind of multinational corporate Pentecostal toward which one might easily imagine some dispute from the Holy Ghost!). In this commercial, clearly, to speak English indicates a cosmopolitan ability, not a sign of American identity that could be read negatively as an imperialistic hegemony over Spanish identity. The characters and the urban space depicted in the advertisement are in fact very Spanish! In U.S. advertising, the same fast-food chain can, by using the same product—a Big Mac—implicitly affirm an American national branded product as a local identity, while elsewhere it deploys the same representation to symbolize a global, cosmopolitan identity. So it is not a specific ingredient that determines a sense of identity, but the container, and the interpretative context that shapes it.

In a second example, in an international context such as an academic conference, I have said that I am Spanish, and when I do so the other participants automatically recognize my identity without any further questions about the specific content of what or who I am. They attribute to me the knowledge of a language—Spanish—and may shudder at the thought of my probable love for bullfighting. They may even assume that I like to dance flamenco in my free time. These are clichés which do not apply in my case. But my Spanish identity saves me from having to provide any explanation about what I am assumed to be. Recognition, in fact, does not follow from what we know for certain about the other, but from what we do not verify. In other words, it is based on something implicit, or taken for granted, which does not need to be confirmed.

If instead of telling them that I am Spanish I say that despite my nationality, I am not Spanish but Catalan, and if I then add that Catalan is my customary language in my personal life and my academic work, then questions about the content of being Catalan can be endless. What makes me different from the Spanish? Is it really a difference that justifies recognition? Is my affirmation that I am different a throwback to medieval loyalty and typical of a feudal society? And this difference in identity—might it not signal imminent danger of conflict, comparable to that which caused the Balkans crisis? One wonders, then, by what process this new particularity of my Catalan identity may provoke concern where Spanish citizenship likely would not.

I could respond with a few well-worn phrases to satisfy curiosity about the Catalans, representing them as a homogeneous community. But if my interlocutors desired a list of fundamental rather than accidental and folkloric components, I would find myself in the same position as Gordon Brown when he wanted to define Britishness: there would be nothing that could not also be found in any list of qualities of any European community. In short, one tends to question the content of identity as a reflexive response when faced with a new difference, which demands recognition. If Catalonia were an independent state with international recognition, such as Holland or Denmark, questions about Catalan identity would not be asked as well, no matter that its content remained as opaque as that of the Danish case, and like this one wrapped in myriad stereotypes.

The point I wish to stress with these examples is that identity is a question of social interest only when it is in crisis, and when the problem of recognition is at stake. Societies with stable cultural and political hierarchies—for all that one may question their internal homogeneity—do not divide over identity. Instead, societies with leadership crises approach identity as a problem. This is the case not because of the content of those identities, but because in an open society identity is a negotiating tool for the positions that individuals and social groups occupy. That is why, in a global society, claims to identity are multiplied, based on differences of generation, sexual orientation, gender, profession, religion, and indigenous or immigrant status. These are not the so-called liquid or fluid identities of Bauman's model. Instead, these could best be described as instrumental identities—exaggerated and dramatized to be used for negotiating their own recognition. In contemporary Europe, we live in times of tattoos and piercings, the marks (stigmas), literally "skin identities," which provide identity without the need for large investment, and which can be reascribed as the surface sign of cultural *habitus*.

## Conclusion

If I have emphatically critiqued the relevance of ethnicity, it is because I see ethnicity deployed not so much to defend pluralist society, but rather as a nervous response to the spectre of social fracture. Those who read contemporary European society in terms of competing ethnicities perceive a double peril: on the one hand, emphasizing ethnic difference can be an almost desperate effort to defend nearly disappearing minority communities. On the other hand, perceiving Europe as a terrain of contested ethnicity provokes a fear of the disintegration of European communities under stress from newcomers and their apparently incompatible traditions.

In the spring of 2006 I lived for a few months in the East End of London in a mainly Bangladeshi and Muslim neighborhood, taking advantage of an invitation to Queen's College London as a visiting researcher. Every day I asked myself the same question, to which nobody ever managed to give me a conclusive answer: are the large numbers of students who hide their faces behind their black *niqabs*[26]—that disquieting dress that only allows you to see their eyes—affirming membership in a traditionalist religion? Or are they seeking recognition of their existence in British society through a postmodern strategy of negotiating their social position? Should the *niqab*, in fact, be interpreted as the expression of their adherence to traditional religious content and an ethnic identity that resists adaptation to their new society? Or is it, in Europe, merely a container, a skin, or a mask, for retaining a modern identity that is as fluid as that of the native British, but strategically formulated in a way that is culturally and politically threatening?

I believe that the social sciences have to make a constant effort to adapt their analytical concepts to a changing reality. If we fail to test our models, we may unwittingly obscure, and also encourage processes that are much more dynamic than the old concepts allow us to see. We should remember the evangelical admonition against putting new wine into old wineskins. If we do not, we may reify ideological artifacts that invent artificial difference.

NOTES

1. "En fait, c'est toute la tradition savante de la sociologie qu'il faut constamment mettre en doute, dont il faut sans cesse se méfier" [In fact, it is the entire learned tradition of sociology that must be constantly placed in doubt, of which one must constantly mistrust]. And "[le sociologue] risque de substituer simplement à la doxa naïve du sens commun la doxa du sens commun savant, qui donne sous le nom de science une simple transcription du discours du sens commun" [(the sociologist) puts one in danger of simply substituting for the naive doxa of lay common sense the no less naive doxa of scholarly common sense, which parrots, in technical jargon and under the official trappings of scientific discourse, the discourse of common sense]. Pierre Bourdieu, 1992, *An Invitation to Reflexive Sociology*, 217. [Editor's note: the English translation in this note is from Pierre Bourdieu and Loic J.D. Wacquant, 1992, University of Chicago Press edition, *An Invitation to Reflexive Sociology*, 248. English translations of other notes are by the editor.]

2. "Theorize means to make explicit social certainties to [in this way] lay the foundations for doubt in order to localize the doubt correctly." Joan Estruch and Salvador Cardús, 1986, "Teoria i provocació. Reflexions per a una epistemologia paradoxal" [Theory and provocation: Reflections for a paradoxical epistemology], *Papers. Revista de Sociologia* 26:82.

3. "The cultural racism takes for granted that there are some innate characteristics for every collective identity, that works as a genetic programme, which members are hereditary bearers" (155), and "I have to say that the neoracism usually appears as a defender of people's right to keep up their cultural identity." Manuel Delgado, 1998, *Diversitat i integració* [Diversity and integration], 157.

4. The Commission for Racial Equality found research about Britishness with some aims as this: "The attacks [London, July 2005] have been interpreted by many people, regardless of their ethnic or religious backgrounds, as evidence that (at least some sections of) the British Muslim population have loyalties that lie beyond the British nation state and are linked to a worldwide Islamic network whose interests may be at odds with those of Britain. There is a danger that such perceptions could undermine the hard-won achievements of British society with respect to multiculturalism and integration." Commission for Racial Equality, UK, 2005, *Citizenship and Belonging: What Is Britishness?*, 11.

5. In the launch of the British Commission on Integration and Cohesion (August 24, 2006), the secretary of state for communities and local government and minister

of women, Ruth Kelly, said, "I believe it is time to engage in a new and honest debate about integration and cohesion in the UK. . . . Patterns of immigration to Britain are becoming more complex. . . . And one of the outcomes of that complexity is that the global tensions are being reflected on the streets of local communities. New migrants protect the fierce loyalties developed in war-torn parts of Europe." And she adds, "I believe this is why we have moved from a period of uniform consensus on the value of multiculturalism, to one where we can encourage the debate by questioning whether it is encouraging separateness. Trevor Philips and others have put forward these points of view. . . . In our attempt to avoid imposing a single British identity and culture, have we ended up with some communities living in isolation of each other, with no common bonds between them?" Commission on Integration and Cohesion, UK, 2006, www.communities.gov.uk. See also: Commission on Integration and Cohesion, UK, 2007, *Final Report: Our Shared Values*, www.integrationand cohesion.org.uk.

6. Ayan Hirsi Ali, 2006, *Mijn Vrijheid.*

7. Among many works in the past several years on multicultural United Kingdom, see: David Goodhart, 2006, *Progressive Nationalism*; Patrick West, 2006, *The Poverty of Multiculturalism*; Ashley Mote, 2003, *Overcrowded Britain*; and George Alagiah, 2006, *A Home from Home.*

8. Giovanni Sartori, 2000, *Pluralismo, multiculturalismo e estranei: Saggio sulla società multietnica* [Pluralism, multiculturalism and strangers: An essay on multiethnic society]. Here I cite the Spanish edition: 2001, *La sociedad multiétnica* [Multiethnic society].

9. Sartori, 2001, 123.

10. Sartori, 2001, 127.

11. Peter L. Berger, 2007, *Seminar on Religion and Culture.*

12. Joan Estruch et al., 2004, *Les altres religions: Minories religioses a Catalunya* [Other religions: Religious minorities in Catalonia].

13. On the dilution of the immigrant's status in Catalonia, see Salvador Cardús, 2005, "The Memory of Immigration in Catalan Nationalism," *International Journal of Iberian Studies* 18(1): 37–44.

14. Two articles published in the press on the assassination of Theo van Gogh clearly indicate this concern: Henk Spaan, 2004, "I Fear for my Country," *The Guardian*, November 11; and Tahaj Ben Jelloun, 2004, "El trauma holandés" [The Dutch trauma], *La Vanguardia*, November 22.

15. A vivid literary representation may be found in Zadie Smith, 2000, *White Teeth*. It is the story of two brothers born of Indian parents who live in London. The son who is sent away to university in India comes back westernized at the end of his studies. The son who stays in London finds social recognition in a multicultural society through his support for an Islamic fundamentalism that not even his parents had known.

16. This is most clearly exemplified in the American celebration of Saint Patrick's

Day by Irish and non-Irish communities. The date is relatively minor in Ireland, whereas in the United States the large-scale parades in New York and other cities demonstrate little of Irish tradition and more of how the Irish-American immigrant communities participate in creating American hybrid identities based on putative original ethnic culture. This phenomenon was discussed at the International Conference on National Days, 2007, "National Days: Summoning the Nation?" in Glasgow, November 29–30, the papers from which are in the process of being published, at http://www.gcal.ac.uk/nationaldays/.

17. Michael Billig, 1995, *Banal Nationalism*.

18. Manuel Castells, sociology professor at the University of California, Berkeley, and director of the Internet Interdisciplinary Institute of the Universitat Oberta de Catalunya, defines three types of identities: "legitimizing identity," "resistance identity"—both focused on the past and with a closed outlook—and "project identity," an open-minded process oriented toward the future. The latter is the identity that Castells sees as characteristic of the new information society. "Project identity [is manifest] when social actors . . . build a new identity that redefines their position in society and, by so doing, seek the transformation of overall social structure." Manuel Castells, 1997, *The Power of Identity, The Information Age: Economy, Society and Culture*, vol. 2, 8.

19. I remind the reader of the divergent perspectives of the United States and Europe, that each gives the expression "second generation immigrant" radically different connotations. In the United States, the descriptor could be understood as the desire to demonstrate belonging to a country that is made up of immigrants. In Europe, the same descriptor represents the difficulty of throwing off the transitory condition of the outsider. Even when children of immigrants are European born, the political community continues to cast doubt on their loyalty to the nation.

20. One of the most controversial books on multicultural politics and its unexpected consequences is Geoff Dench, Kate Gavron, and Michael Young, 2006, *The New East End: Kinship, Race and Conflict*. The debate about the riots in France in 2005 is discussed in Laurent Mucchielli et al., 2007, *Quand les banlieues brûlent*; and in Chakri Belaïd et al., 2006, *Banlieue, lendemains de révolte*.

21. Gordon Brown, 2006, "The Future of Britishness." See also the Select Committee on the Constitution, House of Lords, UK, 2007, *The Governance of Britain*; and also the discussion of David Beetham's article, 2008, "What Is Britishness? Citizenship, Values and Identity," in Joseph Rowntree's *Seminar on Governance*, http://www.ukwatch.net/article/what_is_britishness.

22. Zygmunt Bauman, 2004, *Identity*.

23. The first time I used this metaphor was in the prologue of the book written by two eminent dermatologists, Francesc Grimalt and Ramon Grimalt, 2006, *Salvem la pell* [To save the skin].

24. In *L'hystérie identitaire*, Éric Dupin, 2004, states that identity "en dépit de sa nature largement chimérique, remplit des fonctions vitales" [in spite of its largely

chimerical nature, fulfills vital functions, 11. Dupin cites Claude Dubar, 2000, *La crise des identités*, to describe the crisis of identities, in the meaning I stated, as "le glissement d'anciennes identités 'communautaires,' où l'individu était fortement enchâssé dans les groupes, à de nouvelles identités 'sociétaires,' collectifs multiples, variables, éphémères auxquelles les individus adhèrent pour des périodes limitées et qui leur fournissent des ressources d'identification qu'ils gérent de manière diverse et provisoire" [the slippage of old 'communitarian' identities, where the individual was strongly inserted in groups, into new 'memberships,' and into collectives, multiple, variable and ephemeral, to which individuals adhere for limited periods and which furnish them with resources of identification which they utilize in varied and provisional manner], 12. These new identities rest on imagery, brands such as Nike or Apple/Mac, and on iconic artists and actors. This is not to speak of "virtual identities" as in the recent phenomenon of "Second Life."

25. This theoretical inversion ascribing content to surface can suggest an effective answer to the question raised by François Laplantine, 1999, in *Je, nous et les autres*: "L'identité est devenue aujourd'hui un slogan brandi comme un totem ou répété de manière compulsive comme une évidence paraissant avoir résolu ce qui précisément pose problème: son contenu, ses contours, sa possibilité même" [Identity has become today a slogan, brandished like a totem or repeated in a compulsive manner as if it were evidence of having resolved that which precisely poses the problem: its content, its contour, its own possibility]. Cited in Éric Dupin, *L'hystérie identitaire*, 10.

26. In October 2006, former UK foreign secretary Jack Straw made some controversial remarks when he suggested that "women who wear veils over their face can make community relations harder." Straw asked, "Would those people who do wear the veil think about the implications for community relations?" The Muslim community reacted with irritation. *BBC News*, http://news.bbc.co.uk/1/hi/uk_politics/5410472.stm.

WORKS CITED

Alagiah, George. 2006. *A Home from Home*. London: Little, Brown.

Bauman, Zygmunt. 2004. *Identity*. Cambridge: Polity.

Beetham, David. 2008. "What Is Britishness? Citizenship, Values and Identity." http://www.opendemocracy.net/ourkingdom/2008/04/25/what-is-britishness -citizenship-values-and-identity/

———. 2008. "Discussion of 'What Is Britishness? Citizenship, Values and Identity.'" In Joseph Rowntree's *Seminar on Governance*. http://www.ukwatch.net/ article/what_is_britishness

Belaïd, Chakri, et al. 2006. *Banlieue, lendemains de révolte*. Paris: La Dispute.

Ben Jelloun, Tahaj. 2004. "El trauma holandés" [The Dutch trauma]. *La Vanguardia*, November 22.

Berger, Peter L. 2007. *Seminar on Religion and Culture*. Department of Sociology, Universitat Autònoma de Barcelona.

Billig, Michael. 1995. *Banal Nationalism*. London: Sage.

Bourdieu, Pierre. 1992. *An Invitation to Reflexive Sociology*. Chicago: University of Chicago Press. [Cited edition: *Réponses*. Paris: Seuil]

Brown, Gordon. 2006. "The Future of Britishness." Keynote address at the Future of Britishness Conference, January 14. London: Fabian Society. www.fabian -society .org.uk

Cardús, Salvador. 2005. "The Memory of Immigration in Catalan Nationalism." *International Journal of Iberian Studies* 18(1): 37–44.

Castells, Manuel. 1997. *The Power of Identity, The Information Age: Economy, Society and Culture*. Vol. 2. Cambridge, MA: Blackwell.

Commission on Integration and Cohesion, UK. 2006. www.communities.gov.uk.

———. 2007. *Final Report: Our Shared Values*. www.integrationandcohesion.org.uk

Commission for Racial Equality, UK. 2005. *Citizenship and Belonging: What Is Britishness?* London: Ethnos Research Consultancy.

Delgado, Manuel. 1998. *Diversitat i integració* [Diversity and integration]. Barcelona: Empúries.

Dench, Geoff, Kate Gavron, and Michael Young. 2006. *The New East End: Kinship, Race and Conflict*. London: New Profile Books.

Dubar, Claude. 2000. *La crise des identities*. Paris: PUF.

Dupin, Éric. 2004. *L'hystérie identitaire*. Paris: Le cherche midi.

Estruch, Joan, et al. 2004. *Les altres religions: Minories religioses a Catalunya* [Other religions: Religious minorities in Catalonia]. Barcelona: Editorial Mediterrània.

———, and Salvador Cardús. 1986. "Teoria i provocació: Reflexions per a una epistemologia paradoxal" [Theory and provocation: Reflections for a paradoxical epistemology]. *Papers. Revista de Sociologia* 26:82.

Goodhart, David. 2006. *Progressive Nationalism*. London: Demos.

Grimalt, Francesc, and Ramon Grimalt. 2006. *Salvem la pell* [To save the skin]. Barcelona: La Campana.

Hirsi Ali, Ayan. 2006. *Mijn Vrijheid*. Amsterdam and Antwerp: Augustus. [English edition: 2007. *Infidels*. New York: Free Press]

International Conference on National Days. 2007. "National Days: Summoning the Nation?" Glasgow: Caledonian University. http://www.gcal.ac.uk/nationaldays/

Laplantine, François. 1999. *Je, nous et les autres*. Paris: Éditions Le Pommier. [Cited in Éric Dupin, *L'hystérie identitaire*.]

Mote, Ashley. 2003. *Overcrowded Britain*. Petersfield: Tanner Publishing.

Mucchielli, Laurent, et al. 2007. *Quand les banlieues brûlent*. Paris: Éd. La Découverte.

Sartori, Giovanni. 2000. *Pluralismo, multiculturalismo e estranei. Saggio sulla società multietnica* [Pluralism, multiculturalism and strangers. An essay on multiethnic society]. Milan: Rizzoli.

———. 2001. *La sociedad multiétnica* [Multiethnic society]. Spanish ed. Madrid: Taurus.

Select Committee on the Constitution, House of Lords, UK. 2007. *The Governance of Britain*. London: The Stationery Office. http://www.publications.parliament.uk/pa/ld200607/ldselect/ldconst/158/158.pdf

Smith, Zadie. 2000. *White Teeth*. Bristol: Hamish Hamilton.

Spaan, Henk. 2004. "I Fear for My Country." *The Guardian*, November 11.

Straw, Jack. 2006. "Straw's Veil Comments Spark Anger." *BBC News*, October 5. http://news.bbc.co.uk/2/hi/uk_news/politics/5410472.stm

West, Patrick. 2006. *The Poverty of Multiculturalism*. London: Civitas.

PART TWO **Dividing Lines**

# CHAPTER FIVE

## Veiled Truths

*Discourses of Ethnicity in Contemporary France*

ALEC G. HARGREAVES

During the last quarter century, discourses of ethnicity in France have been characterized by a major paradox. At one level, with the exception of the extreme right, politicians of almost all shades of opinion and a very large part of the academic and research community have until recently been united in the view that ethnicity has no rightful place in public discourse. Yet, at another level, those same politicians, together with the mass media, have been deeply involved in the ethnicization of French politics, which in turn is just part of a much wider dynamic in which ethnic differences have come to play a central role in many aspects of French society. In recent years, the gap between official discourse and the day-to-day praxis of social relations has become increasingly difficult to conceal, and it has indeed narrowed. Politicians and researchers have become increasingly inclined to acknowledge that, like it or not, ethnicity is a significant factor in many aspects of French society. Moreover, after hanging precariously in the balance, attempts to document the salience of ethnicity through new forms of data gathering now appear to have overcome the main obstacles placed in their way.

My analysis of these developments falls into four main parts. The first of these looks at the new forms of ethnicity which have come to the fore in France in recent years. The second examines the reasons for resistance to the acknowledgment of ethnic differences, with particular reference to the role of the state in the construction of knowledge. The third section discusses the gradual erosion of that resistance, and the fourth looks at recent moves which have now opened the doors to ethnic data gathering.

*New Forms of Ethnicity*

In varying degrees and in different ways, ethnicity has always been a factor in French politics, but in recent decades this has taken new forms, thrown up new debates, and generated new policy responses. During the first half of the twentieth century, Jews were the main minority at issue in public debates, most obviously during the Dreyfus affair at the beginning of the century and later during the Nazi Occupation in the 1940s, when the Vichy regime collaborated in rounding up Jews, who were to perish in the death camps. Since the Second World War, the focus has shifted to postcolonial immigrant minorities, originating principally in North Africa and other parts of France's former colonial empire. Until the 1960s, the overwhelming majority of immigrants in France had come from Europe. Since then, the balance has tilted toward immigrants from outside Europe, above all from former French colonies in predominantly Islamic countries (Hargreaves 2007).

This demographic shift has coincided with major social and economic changes. Since the oil shocks of the 1970s, France has experienced over a sustained period higher unemployment levels than any other West European country, inducing high levels of insecurity amongst the population. Prior to the mid-1970s, most non-Europeans came to France as economic migrants in response to labor shortages during a period of high economic growth. Since the mid-1970s, temporary labor migration has given way to permanent family settlement. The new generations of postcolonial minorities, born in France to immigrant parents or grandparents, have come of age during a period of high unemployment and economic insecurity. Although these minorities have been the principal victims of unemployment, with jobless rates far higher than those of the national population as a whole, they have frequently been scapegoated not only as the causes of that unemployment but also as threats to the integrity of French society and the very foundations of French national identity (Gastaut 2000).

These demographic and social changes have in turn been accompanied by changes in the categorization of immigrant minorities from former colonies. Until the late 1970s, they were most commonly categorized primarily in economic and/or national terms as "*travailleurs immigrés*" [immigrant workers] or as "*Algérians*" [Algerians] or "*Maghrébins*" (Maghrebis, that is, people originating in the three former French North African colonies of Algeria, Tunisia, and Morocco). Since the early 1980s, the word "*travailleur*" [worker] has disappeared almost completely from this lexicon; "*travailleurs immigrés*" has been replaced by "*immigrés*" [immigrants], then by "*jeunes issus de l'immigration*" [youths of immigrant origin] and, increasingly, by "*Musulmans*" [Muslims] (Bonnafous 1997). None of those expressions contains the word "ethnic," which still remains largely taboo in French political discourse, but they are all de facto markers of ethnic consciousness and have frequently served to stigmatize immigrant minorities originating outside France as alien groups that can never really fit into French society.

The growing preoccupation among the majority ethnic population with minorities now more frequently seen as Muslims rather than as immigrant workers has been seen, in its most hysterical forms, in the Islamic headscarf affairs of 1989, 1994, and 2003–4. In media and political discourses, as well as in majority ethnic public opinion, those affairs have been widely misrepresented and misunderstood as signs of a fundamental unwillingness on the part of Muslim minorities to adapt to French social and cultural norms (Tévanian 2005). In reality, there is a massive body of research data showing that minorities of Muslim heritage have overwhelmingly acculturated to French norms, including the code of *laïcité*, that is, the formal separation of organized religions and the Republic, and limitations on religious expression in public spaces (Laurence and Vaisse 2006).

When the settlement of immigrant minorities from predominantly Muslim countries began to become visible to the majority ethnic population, it did so at a time when, following the Khomeini revolution in Iran in 1979, anti-Western variants of Islam were becoming more assertive forces in the international arena. Although few Muslims in France originated in the Middle Eastern countries where the most radical forms of Islam were at work, this was often lost sight of in French media representations of the nation's new immigrant minorities, who were viewed with growing antipathy by a significant part of the majority ethnic population amid worries about unemployment at home and religious fanaticism abroad. It was on the back of those fears that the extreme-right Front National (FN) made its first electoral breakthrough in 1983, trading on a radically anti-immigrant platform. Since then, the Front National has enjoyed the longest sustained electoral successes of any extreme-right party in Western Europe, scoring between 10 and 18 percent of the vote at every parliamentary and presidential election until 2007, when it slipped to below 5 percent in the parliamentary elections which followed the election of Nicolas Sarkozy as president.

Far from betokening a reduction in the political salience of issues relating to ethnicity, Sarkozy's triumph is just the latest in a long series of events reflecting the contaminating effects of the Front National on French politics as whole. For in the face of the FN's electoral threat, politicians in most of the major established parties, not only on the center-right—very obviously Sarkozy—but also on the left, have for the last twenty-five years trimmed and tweaked their discourses and policies in ways designed to woo ethnically prejudiced voters. A notable example of this was the reform of French nationality laws with the aim of excluding second- and third-generation members of minority groups from automatic access to citizenship. First proposed by the FN in the early 1980s, the idea was taken up by the center-right, then led by Jacques Chirac, who attempted unsuccessfully to push it through parliament while serving as prime minister from 1986 to 1988. The measure passed into law in 1993 under the center-right government of Edouard Balladur and was rescinded when the left returned to office in 1997. After regaining power in 2002, the center-right implemented a slew of measures which had initially been proposed by the FN to combat *"insécurité"* (anxieties about law and order associated at a popular level with immigrant minorities) (Nobili 2005). Much of this was the work of the then interior minister, Nicolas Sarkozy, who in his presidential election campaign openly courted FN voters, most notoriously in a February 2007 television appearance, in the course of which he vowed to ensure that Muslims would not be allowed to slaughter sheep in their bathtubs, recycling a crudely Islamophobic urban myth that bears no reality to the everyday lives of Muslims (Ridet 2007). The success of Sarkozy in taking votes from Le Pen through tactics such as this was manifest in exit polls conducted after the first round of voting in April 2007, which showed that many former supporters of Le Pen had switched to Sarkozy (Fourquet 2007).

## Resistance to Ethnically Based Statistics

If the ethnicization of French politics has been plain to see, politicians have nevertheless spent a lot of time denying the salience of ethnicity as a factor in social behavior. Until quite recently, most politicians denied that ethnic discrimination was a sufficiently serious problem to merit their attention. As racial and ethnic discrimination were formally prohibited by the French constitution and by a law passed in 1972, it was frequently contended that the matter had been dealt with (Bleich 2003). The tiny number of court convictions secured on the grounds of discrimination was seen not as a sign of lax enforcement but as proof that racism was a minor problem. When, in the second half of the 1990s, the evidence of discrimination collected by sociologists and pressure groups became so overwhelming that the existence of widespread discrimination could no longer be denied (Hargreaves 2000), the barricades of denial were re-erected around the question of ethnically based data collection.

Before proceeding further in our discussion, it is important to clarify the meaning of certain terms in the debate surrounding what have come to be known in France as "ethnic statistics." Contrary to the impression that might often be gained from this debate, the French Republic has never operated a blanket prohibition on the collection of ethnically based statistics. To the extent that such a ban has existed, it has concerned only certain types of ethnically based data, and it has applied less stringently in the private sector than in public institutions. While rigorously eschewing categories formally labeled as "ethnic," the Republic collects census data on the nationality of all persons living in France. If nationality, an undeniable ethnic marker in the eyes of most social scientists, is not labeled as such by the Republic, this is because French nationality is not officially regarded as an ethnic condition. In this optic, ethnicity is a marker of other groups, based, for example, on culture, color, or other nonstate-bounded categories. In line with this, there are no census questions on religion, "race," or other nonstate-bounded ethnic markers. Data protection laws have also made it difficult, if not impossible, for private corporations as well as public institutions to collect and store information on individuals based on ethnic categories other than nationality, though it should be noted that this has not prevented private polling organizations and publicly funded research institutions from conducting anonymized opinion surveys using ethnic categories based on color and culture ("Blacks," "Muslims," and so on).

In the discussion that follows, "ethnic data gathering" and "ethnic statistics" are to be understood in a generic sense as encompassing all forms of public and privately generated data based on ethnic and racial categories, in contrast with the more narrowly circumscribed (nationality-based) forms of ethnic data gathering which have generally operated in France. Nationality, until quite recently the only ethnic marker in most publicly available census data, distinguishes foreigners from French nationals. As about a third of all immigrants and virtually all the descendants of immigrants are French citizens, they are by the same token invisible in most official statistics. And as ethnic discrimination operates on the basis of color or culture rather than on the basis of formal citizenship, its effects are also statistically invisible. In refusing to collect data based on racial or ethnocultural categories, the Republic has allowed discrimination to remain beyond the reach of the standards of evidence required for successful prosecutions. Convictions generally require evidence of direct discrimination, that is, a statement showing that the defendant treated an individual unfairly for explicitly racial or ethnic reasons. Knowing this, racists have become adept at camouflaging their motives, thereby escaping prosecution. Indirect discrimination, in which individuals or institutions engage in behavior which, intentionally or not, has the effect of treating members of certain groups unfairly, has recently become an offense in French law, in line with a European Union directive implementing the 1997 Amsterdam Treaty. But as indirect discrimination cannot be proved without institutional data gathering, this new legal tool remains largely a dead letter in the absence of data based on ethnic categories other than nationality.

Despite this statistical and juridical occultation, the effects of discrimination are all too apparent. In the early 1990s, when the unemployment rate was around 10 percent for the nation as a whole, with youth unemployment at about 20 percent, a trailblazing, ethnically based survey found that unemployment among youths of Algerian origin was running at about 40 percent (Tribalat 1995, 175). A further survey conducted at the end of the 1990s found similar disparities, with second-generation non-Europeans experiencing much higher unemployment levels than young people of French origin with the same level of qualifications (Meurs, Pailhé, and Simon 2005). There was not (and still is not) a single *député* [member] of North African origin or of Muslim heritage in the 577–seat National Assembly. Minorities are also very visibly underrepresented in the French media. This was clearly documented in 1999 when Hervé Bourges, head of the Conseil Supérieur de l'Audiovisuel (CSA), the regulatory agency responsible for overseeing French television and radio, was persuaded to commission a study entitled "The Presence and Representation of Visible Minorities on French Television," which computed the proportional presence of "Blacks," "Arabs/North Africans," and "Asians" in relation to the "other," that is, white or European faces seen on French television. When preliminary results were published in June 2000 (Conseil Supérieur de l'Audiovisuel 2000), the outcry by politicians and journalists against the use of racial and ethnic categories (though not against the underrepresentation which they revealed) was such that the CSA cancelled publication of the full report.

Most of the arguments against ethnic data gathering are couched in a discourse of "republican" principles, which are held to be incompatible with the public acknowledgment of ethnic differences (see, for example, Blum, Guérin-Pace, and Le Bras 2007). The two main lines of argument advanced in this way point on the one hand to the sinister purposes to which ethnic data were put during the Vichy period and on the other hand to the alleged dangers of weakening national cohesion inherent in using categories that might fuel "*communautarisme,*" that is, divisive forms of ethnic consciousness. The authoritarian Vichy regime, which broke radically with the Third Republic, remains a deeply troubling episode in French history, not simply because the French government presided over by Marshall Pétain collaborated with Nazi Germany but, more specifically, because it pursued a policy of anti-Semitism which resulted in tens of thousands of Jews being rounded up and deported to death camps. These deportations were facilitated by the compilation of registers of Jews by officials in the Vichy government.

Opponents of ethnic data gathering frequently confuse or deliberately misrepresent modern, anonymized databases as if these were synonymous with ethnically categorized records of individual persons, and claim that the compilation of such data is motivated by or at the very least open to misuse against vulnerable groups and must therefore be eschewed. On this logic, ethnic data gathering is incompatible with republican governance, for it threatens to lead to a police state and to the persecution of minorities.

The second main argument made against ethnic data gathering claims that the Republic recognizes only individuals, not groups, and would be betraying a fundamental principle if it were to recognize differences between ethnic groups. In reality, the Republic recognizes and dialogues with numerous groups, from trades unions and employers' organizations to churches and other religious bodies. Those who, in opposing ethnic data gathering, present themselves as the guardians of self-evident republican principles are in reality arguing for a particular version of republicanism constructed in the context of postcolonial migration from mainly Muslim countries, which many believe cannot be assimilated into mainstream French society. Within this optic, Muslims are fundamentally at odds with a further key principle of the Republic, *laicité*, and inclined toward *communautarisme*, which if given the apparent backing of ethnically based data collection, would lead to French society splintering between rival ethnic communities.

Proponents of both of these arguments prioritize theoretical dangers which would allegedly flow from ethnic data collection, relegating concerns over actual discrimination to a secondary level. Not uncommonly, they claim—without, of course, any empirical evidence to back this claim, since their near-stranglehold on the institutions of the Republic has made the collection of such evidence impossible—that the purity of the nation's republican principles has saved France from the levels of discrimination seen in other countries. In its most extreme forms, this kind of argument suggests that inquiries supposedly designed to measure racism actually generate it. A fierce battle has raged, for example, over an annual opinion survey commissioned by the Commission Nationale Consultative des Droits de l'Homme (CNCDH), which since 1990 has been charged by the government with publishing an annual report on racism in France and measures designed to combat it. Every year, most respondents questioned in the survey have declared themselves to be in some degree racist. In response to these findings, some members of the CNCDH's governing body have claimed that the survey is itself generating racism by asking such questions and should therefore be discontinued (Morice 2002). Where the existence of discrimination is acknowledged, existing tools are said to be sufficient to deal with it. It is also frequently asserted—again, without any empirical evidence—that ethnic data gathering would be a Trojan horse leading inevitably to policies of "positive discrimination" (French nomenclature for U.S.-style affirmative action) and ethnic quotas that would instill ethnic strife in place of social harmony. This kind of argument is often advanced by an appeal to anti-Americanism. During the postwar period, there has been a long tradition of French statesmen trying to offset the global domination of the United States by insisting on specifically "French" ways of doing things. In French debates over immigration and "integration" policy during the last twenty-five years, the United States has frequently been cited as an antimodel, an example of the dreadful consequences which could follow if France were to follow so-called Anglo-Saxon approaches to ethnic relations. Policies such as affirmative action and ethnic monitoring, introduced in the United States to combat discrimination, are in France often blamed for producing the problems they were designed to remedy: racial discrimination, ethnic segregation, urban ghettoes, and so on. Through this back-to-front logic, it has frequently been asserted that France can avoid the development of comparable problems only by refusing to follow the policies which allegedly produced them.

The trouble with this seemingly noble vision of French republican principles is that, in failing to address the realities of everyday discrimination in many parts of French society, it allows that discrimination to go unchecked, breeding precisely the kinds of social divisions against which opponents of ethnic data gathering warn. In other words, the refusal to collect ethnic data deprives the Republic of an important tool with which to enforce—as distinct from merely incanting—the principle of equality for all before the law.

## Toward Ethnic Data Gathering

Until only a few years ago, the question of ethnic data gathering was almost completely taboo in French public debate. To even raise the matter was to invite immediate condemnation on the grounds of alleged antirepublicanism and/or the promotion of alien, Anglo-Saxon ideas. Gradually, however, doors toward ethnic data gathering have been opening as part of a wider recognition of the need for more forceful action against discrimination. At least three main factors have contributed to this shift.

First, by the late 1990s, a growing body of evidence collected in studies by sociologists such as Michèle Tribalat (1995) and Philippe Bataille (1997) together with tests conducted by pressure groups such as SOS Racisme made it increasingly difficult to deny the existence of widespread discrimination. The evidence collected in this way used existing legal provisions which, while falling well short of full-scale U.S.-style ethnic monitoring, nevertheless produced findings which were difficult to ignore. Under the terms of the 1978 Data Protection Act, it is in general unlawful to collect data on the "racial or ethnic origins" of individuals. The Commission Nationale de l'Informatique et des Libertés (CNIL), the state agency responsible for overseeing compliance with the law, can authorize exceptions for research purposes. In addition, private or public organizations which gain the written consent of respondents can ask ethnically based questions and compile anonymized findings without needing to request authorization from the CNIL. Since the early 1990s the almost exclusive reliance on nationality as an index of ethnicity in data gathering by public agencies has been gradually eroded by exploiting previously underutilized criteria permitted by the CNIL, notably place of birth, and by securing approval for a number of ethnically based surveys. The Institut National de la Statistique et des Etudes Economiques (INSEE) began complementing nationality-based data with the publication of census data referencing place of birth, which it had long collected but seldom published. Factoring in place of birth gave a much more accurate picture of France's immigrant population than had previously been afforded by data referencing only nationality, but it still left largely out of account second- and third-generation members of minority ethnic groups, who were neither foreigners nor immigrants. A team of researchers at the Institut National d'Etudes Démographiques (INED) and INSEE led by Michèle Tribalat scored a major advance when they secured approval to conduct a survey in the early 1990s which, by factoring in the place of birth of respondents' parents, allowed them to study a large sample of second-generation minority ethnic members of the national population (Tribalat 1995, 1996). While the place of birth of parents remained off-limits in full-scale nationwide censuses, that criterion was again included in a survey of a substantial population sample carried out in parallel with the 1999 census (Meurs, Pailhé, and Simon 2005). This, like Tribalat's survey, yielded evidence on unemployment rates which pointed incontrovertibly to the effects of discrimination in labor markets. At the same time, pressure groups such as SOS-Racisme produced more direct evidence of discrimination by adopting a testing procedure which had already been widely used in the United States and the United Kingdom. Individuals from different racial or ethnic groups, who in all other significant respects were identical, were shown to receive differential treatment in job applications and at the entrances to nightclubs and other social facilities, where non-whites were frequently rejected out of hand.

In parallel with the accumulation of such evidence, the victims of discrimination were becoming increasingly restive. Postcolonial immigrant minorities are concentrated mainly in disadvantaged urban areas known as the *banlieues*, which have been the scene of a steady stream of confrontations between minority ethnic youths and the police. The most widespread of these confrontations were of course the riots of 2005, which forced the government to declare a state of emergency. But at a lower level of intensity, similar disturbances—typically involving attacks on the police and the burning of cars and public buildings in response to police methods seen as emblematic of a discriminatory social order—have been flaring up periodically in the *banlieues* since the late 1970s, to the point where, by the mid-1990s, there were serious concerns that threats to public order might spin out of control if nothing were done to pacify young victims of discrimination (Beaud and Pialoux 2003).

A third factor favoring a change in public policy lay in new political opportunities opened up by the elections of 1997, in which the left—typically more sympathetic than the right to the plight of minorities—returned to power just as unemployment levels began to fall after more than twenty years of almost uninterrupted rises. In 1998, Martine Aubry, minister for employment and solidarity, announced that for the first time, the fight against racial discrimination was to be made a priority area of "integration" policy. In practice, progress toward more effective action against discrimination remained painfully slow. Aubry received reports favoring the establishment of an independent antiracism authority modeled on the UK's Commission for Racial Equality (CRE) and a system of ethnic monitoring similar to that used in Britain (Haut Conseil à l'Intégration 1998; Belorgey 1999). She balked at both proposals, preferring initiatives aimed at consciousness-raising and mediation rather than new institutions armed with fresh powers to detect and prosecute individuals and institutions engaging in discrimination. By the time the left lost office in 2002, virtually nothing of substance had been done to make a reality of Aubry's promise to curb discrimination. It was not until June 2005 that center-right president Jacques Chirac inaugurated the Haute Autorité de Lutte Contre les Discriminations et pour l'Egalité (HALDE) to bring France into compliance with the 1997 Amsterdam Treaty, which required every member state of the European Union to establish an independent antiracism authority to assist victims of discrimination. The move came too late to avert the eruption of the *banlieues* in November 2005. Moreover, Chirac remained implacably opposed to the collection of ethnically based statistics, as did Prime Minister Dominique de Villepin and the head of the HALDE, Louis Schweitzer. In the absence of such data, institutional and indirect discrimination would continue to go largely unchecked. There thus remained an unresolved tension between changes in public discourse and the policies which would be necessary to close the gap between that discourse and the daily realities experienced by minority ethnic groups.

Changes in public discourse did at least signal acknowledgment of discrimination as an issue that needed to be addressed. As noted earlier, a publicly financed report on "The Presence and Representation of Visible Minorities on French Television" was withdrawn from publication in 2000 because of the outcry against its use of racial and ethnic categories. Yet almost simultaneously, Catherine Tasca, minister of culture and communications, announced that television channels would in the future be required to "pay due attention to the richness and diversity of the origins and cultures which make up contemporary society," an unmistakable reference in all but name to respect for ethnic differences (Chirot 2000). By 2004, when the CSA teamed up with the High Council for Integration and other public agencies to sponsor a conference entitled "Ecrans pâles?" [Pale screens?], terms such as "diversity" and "visible minorities," previously considered as taboo, had become part of the common currency of public debate (*Ecrans pâles?* . . . 2004). The Equal Opportunities Law of 2006, drawn up in response to the riots of 2005, made it a statutory requirement that television channels reflect the "diversity" of French society and report annually on their efforts to achieve this. Yet in the absence of a legally sanctioned method of measuring ethnic diversity (of which nationality is patently an inadequate indicator), it was difficult to see how compliance with this requirement can be determined. French public policy had thus painted itself into an uncomfortable corner. On the one hand, there was now almost universal support for the slogan of "diversity," a lightly camouflaged way of acknowledging ethnic and cultural differences and the need to ensure equal treatment irrespective of such differences, while on the other hand politicians and public officials generally remained reluctant to embrace the statistical apparatus necessary to measure compliance with that slogan.

## Cutting the Gordian Knot

The political impetus that now appears to have unlocked the door to ethnic data gathering has come from what in many ways may seem an unlikely quarter: Nicolas Sarkozy. In pursuit of his presidential ambitions, which came to fruition when he beat the Socialist candidate, Ségolène Royal, in the second round of voting in May 2007, Sarkozy proved himself a master of promising something to virtually every part of the electorate, no matter how at odds with each other those segments might be nor how seemingly contradictory his promises might appear. While serving as interior minister in the run-up to the presidential elections, he courted with great success voters on the extreme right by trading on Islamophobic stereotypes and dismissing disruptive youths in the *banlieues* as *"racaille"* [scum]. This was the same Nicolas Sarkozy who, in 2003, had become the first senior politician in France to call for the seemingly unspeakable by advocating "positive discrimination," who prided himself (and scandalized others) in announcing the appointment of a "Muslim" prefect, thereby helping to rectify the underrepresentation of minorities in the senior echelons of the French civil service, and who opposed Jacques Chirac's 2004 law banning the Islamic headscarf in French public schools.

This delectation in political opportunism continued after Sarkozy's election as president. In his election campaign, he promised to set up a new Ministry for Immigration and National Identity, brazenly pandering to those, especially on the right of the political spectrum, who saw immigration as a threat to national identity. In legislation introduced after the elections by the man appointed to head the new ministry, Sarkozy's right-hand man, Brice Hortefeux, a whole raft of new measures designed to curb immigration including language tests and highly controversial DNA tests stood cheek by jowl with an amendment to the 1978 data protection law designed to authorize the collection of data for the purpose of "measuring diversity of origins, discrimination and integration." This amendment, which its proponents had openly stated was aimed at legalizing data gathering based on racial and ethnic categories, was immediately challenged by old-style guardians of republican rhetoric, who asked the Constitutional Council to declare it void. While their efforts appeared initially to prevail, it has now become clear that they have lost the battle to block the collection of ethnically based data. This defeat, sealed in 2008, constitutes a major step in a process of change that began incrementally more than a decade earlier.

Since the early 1990s, the criteria used in French census and other official data-gathering exercises have widened beyond nationality to include the birthplace of respondents and of their parents. Yet discrimination is frequently triggered by factors—skin color, cultural markers such as names or items of clothing, and so on—with no empirical correlation to nationality or place of birth. A growing number of researchers and minority ethnic activists therefore began pressing for data collection using racial or ethnic categories that are tied to neither nationality nor birthplace. The survey of television program content conducted for the CSA in 1999 was an early result of such pressures. Following the riots of 2005, which were driven to a large extent by resentment and despair among the victims of discrimination, researchers at INED and INSEE began planning a major survey entitled "Trajectoires et origines" [Trajectories and origins, or TeO] in which respondents would be asked about perceptions of their skin color, their religious beliefs, and other ethnic markers, which would then be cross-referenced to empirical indicators of social status such as educational qualifications, employment, and so on, which would in turn assist in detecting the effects of discrimination. Simultaneously, the CNIL began to discuss for the first time the possibility of approving data collection employing subjectively perceived ethnic and racial criteria alongside the objective factors (nationality and place of birth) to which CNIL-approved research had hitherto been limited. In the fall of 2006, the CNIL announced that it was conducting hearings with a view to making recommendations on ethnic data gathering, which would then be submitted to candidates campaigning in the 2007 presidential elections. This was a remarkable move, explicitly placing the question of ethnic data gathering—hitherto regarded as politically taboo—squarely on the electoral agenda. No less remarkable was the fact that Sarkozy, front-runner in the race for the Elysée, indicated his support for better data collection on "diversity" while his Socialist opponent, Ségolène Royal, demurred (Gabizon 2006). Sensing the danger of a major political shift, opponents of wider forms of ethnic data gathering launched a petition in which they once again cast themselves as the guardians of republican orthodoxy (Amadieu et al. 2007). The controversy stirred up by the petition was sufficiently intimidating to persuade the CNIL to delay the release of its report until after the elections.

Amid the wave of media coverage surrounding Sarkozy's victory against Royal on May 6, little attention was paid to an announcement by the CNIL a few days later in which it recommended widening the criteria permissible for ethnic data gathering and indicated its support for the TeO project (Debet 2007). Four months later, two members of the CNIL, Michèle Tabarot and Sébastien Huyghe, who were also members of Sarkozy's center-right UMP party and *députés* (members of the National Assembly), inserted into the bill on immigration then making its way through parliament under the aegis of Hortefeux an amendment permitting the collection of data designed to measure "diversity of origins, discrimination and integration" (Leclerc 2007). When the bill was adopted by parliament, SOS-Racisme immediately launched a widely publicized petition against it, denouncing the CNIL-inspired amendment on ethnic data gathering as an affront to republican principles (SOS-Racisme 2007). Simultaneously, the Socialist group in the National Assembly asked the Constitutional Council to rule that the amendment (article 63 in the finalized text) was unconstitutional.

It was neither surprising nor particularly damaging that, in ruling on the matter on November 15, 2007, the Constitutional Council invalidated article 63 on the procedural grounds that it did not belong in a parliamentary bill dealing with immigration. Members of the CNIL and of the TeO research team were, however, stunned when the Constitutional Council ruled not only that article 63 of the new law was procedurally invalid but also that data collection based on racial or ethnic origins was prohibited because it was substantively at odds with article 1 of the constitution, guaranteeing "equality before the law for all citizens, irrespective of origin, race or religion."

Supporters of the proposal tabled by Tabarot and Huyghe were baffled by the finding that measuring the diversity of racial or ethnic origins meant treating people differently before law (Türk 2007). As there was seemingly no judicial recourse beyond the Constitutional Council, they were also at a loss to chart a new way forward. Legal counsel suggested that there was little or no prospect of overturning the ruling by appealing beyond the national level to either the European Union or the European Court of Human Rights. The only flicker of hope appeared to reside in case-by-case court actions designed to test the precise meaning of the Constitutional Court's ruling and the extent to which this might still allow certain kinds of ethnically related data gathering. The Gordian knot might in theory be cut by a revision of the constitution, which almost no one expected. But in yet another unanticipated twist in the road, that is precisely what suddenly came into prospect when, in January 2008, Sarkozy announced that he wanted to inscribe the principle of "diversity" in the preamble to the constitution and was setting up a commission headed by former centrist minister Simone Veil to advise on how this and other constitutional changes might be made (Sarkozy 2008a; Chemin 2008). Although Sarkozy did not explicitly say that he wanted to use such a revision to facilitate ethnic data gathering or "positive discrimination" in favor of minority groups, it was widely assumed that the proposed constitutional amendment foreshadowed steps of this nature (Fourest 2008).

It was not until December 2008 that the Veil Commission delivered its report, initially promised for the summer of that year. The report recommended firmly against the constitutional revision for which Sarkozy had called and the ethnically based policies of "positive discrimination" for which such a revision might have paved the way. While these negative recommendations grabbed the headlines, the small print of the report noted with approval that on a separate but closely related matter the path had in fact been recently cleared for the collection of ethnically based data without the need for a constitutional revision. In February 2008, the Constitutional Council had made a surreptitious but significant addition to the section of its website in which it explains and comments on its formal rulings. In its original commentary on the ruling of November 15, 2007, the council had stated that while evidence of diversity could be collected based on "objective data" such as the name, geographical origin, or former nationality of respondents, the constitution did not permit the collection of data based on "racial or ethnic origins" (Conseil Constitutionnel 2007). In the absence of any explicit indication permitting the use of subjectively constructed categories, the council's statement was generally interpreted to mean that the constitution permitted only the use of "objective" criteria recognized as such in French law, and by the same token prohibited not only the collection of data based on skin color ("black," "white," "colored," and so on) but also the gathering of data based on other, more obviously subjective, markers of ethnic identity. However, a new sentence was added to the council's website in February 2008 which now stated that data gathering was not limited solely to "objective" criteria and that it was permissible under the constitution to collect "subjective data, such as those based on *'ressenti d'appartenance'* [literally, feelings of belonging]" (Conseil Constitutionnel 2008). It was surely no coincidence that *ressenti d'appartenance* was precisely the designation used by INSEE and INED in their "Trajectoires et Origines" research project to denote perceptions of skin color, religious beliefs, and other ethnic markers, which after seemingly being prohibited under the terms of the council's initial commentary on its November 2007 ruling were now apparently permitted categories, provided they were understood as being subjective rather than objective in nature. Neither was it perhaps entirely coincidental that the additional, more permissive, commentary issued by the council in February 2008 was concordant with the direction in which President Sarkozy had pointed a month earlier in calling for the constitutional recognition of "diversity."

In noting the Constitutional Council's commentary of February 2008, the Veil Commission said that existing constitutional provisions made it possible to collect data "that can be read in a fashion comparable to that of an ethno-racial system of categories" (Comité de Réflexion sur le Préambule de la Constitution 2008, 77). Far from opposing this, the commission unequivocally supported the collection of ethnic statistics, which it said were essential in the fight against discrimination. Its recommendation against a constitutional revision enshrining the principle of "diversity" was thus grounded, not in opposition to ethnic statistics but in the observation that as the collection of such data was already permitted by the constitution, such a revision was unnecessary.

These subtleties attracted far less media attention than the commission's recommendations against a constitutional commitment to "diversity" and the prospect of ethnically based policies of "positive discrimination." In an attempt to conceal the loss of face resulting from these recommendations, Sarkozy delivered a high-profile speech in which he accepted that instead of policies of "positive discrimination" grounded in ethnically based categories the Republic should strengthen and expand measures aimed at assisting socially disadvantaged groups, a significant proportion of which were of minority ethnic origin, while at the same time collecting statistics on "diversity" so as to measure progress in the field (Sarkozy 2008b). Although the president stated that data collection of this nature "must not present an ethnic reading of our society," his insistence on the need for "statistics designed to measure inequality and discrimination linked to people's origins" amounted in practice to support for ethnically based statistics in all but name, a bridge that had already been quietly crossed by the Veil Commission and before it by the Constitutional Council. Sarkozy announced that he was appointing Yazid Sabeg, a French businessman of Algerian origin, as commissioner for diversity and equal opportunities, with responsibility for proposing a program of action in this field. In March 2009, Sabeg set up a committee of experts charged with hammering out the details of a system of data collection for the measurement of "diversity" in which ethnicity was patently pivotal, though the committee chair, François Héran, sought to disarm opponents of this initiative by formally eschewing the label "ethnic statistics" (Héran 2009). While lightly camouflaged by circumlocutions of this nature, the collection of ethnically based data now appears set to expand substantially. That said, in the absence of additional policy initiatives based directly on ethnic criteria concerning resource allocation and/or anti-discrimination, it remains to be seen how more broadly based policies addressing socially disadvantaged groups—defined, for example, in terms of personal income or residential concentrations of poverty—will rectify the specific forms of inequality resulting from racial and ethnic discrimination. Whatever the outcome of these "color-blind" policies, there is now a much better prospect of measuring ethnically based inequality and discrimination together with such progress as may or may not be made in curbing them.

Among the many ironies which have punctuated the bumpy road toward the public recognition of ethnicity in France is the fact that the left, generally more sympathetic than the right in relation to minority groups, has been dominated by a Socialist Party leadership hostile to data gathering designed to help combat discrimination, while the right, frequently inclined to scapegoat immigrants for electoral purposes, has under Sarkozy appeared far more willing than the left to embrace not only ethnic data gathering but also "positive discrimination" in favor of minority groups. Of course, much depends on what is meant by "positive discrimination," and the modus operandi of data gathering on "diversity" may remain lightly camouflaged compared with that seen in the United Kingdom or the United States, where openly racial and ethnic categories are a routine part of nationwide censuses. But after a roller-coaster ride in which those pressing for ethnic data gathering seemed to have reached a constitutional impasse, the road toward a clearer understanding of the role of ethnicity in French society now appears open.

WORKS CITED

Amadieu, Jean-François, et al. 2007. "Engagement républicain contre les discriminations." *Libération*, February 23.

Bataille, Philippe. 1997. *Le Racisme au travail*. Paris: La Découverte.

Beaud, Stéphane, and Michel Pialoux. 2003. *Violences urbaines, violence sociale: Genèse des nouvelles classes dangereuses*. Paris: Fayard.

Belorgey, Jean-Michel. 1999. *Rapport sur la lutte contre les discriminations*. Paris: Ministère de l'emploi et de la solidarité.

Bleich, Erik. 2003. *Race Politics in Britain and France: Ideas and Policymaking since the 1960s*. Cambridge: Cambridge University Press.

Blum, Alain, France Guérin-Pace, and Hervé Le Bras. 2007. "La statistique, piège ethnique." *Le Monde*, November 10.

Bonnafous, Simone. 1997. "Où sont passés les 'immigrés'?" *Cahiers de la Méditerranée* 54: 97–107.

Chemin, Anne. 2008. "La Discrimination positive bientôt dans la Constitution?" *Le Monde*, January 10.

Chirot, Françoise. 2000. "La télévision publique devra mieux refléter la diversité de la population." *Le Monde*, May 21.

Comité de Réflexion sur le Préambule de la Constitution. 2008. *Rapport au Président de la République*. Paris: La Documentation Française. http://lesrapports.ladocu mentationfrancaise.fr/BRP/084000758/0000.pdf (accessed January 22, 2009).

Conseil Constitutionnel. 2007. "Cahier de commentaires" on ruling number 2007–557 DC of November 15, 2007. www.conseil-constitutionnel.fr (accessed November 24, 2007).

———. 2008. "Cahiers du Conseil Constitutionnel," no. 23, commentary on ruling number 2007–557 DC of November 15, 2007. www.conseil-constitutionnel.fr (accessed March 19, 2008).

Conseil Supérieur de l'Audiovisuel. 2000. "Présence et représentation des minorités visibles à la télévision française." *La Lettre du CSA* 129 (June): 12–14.

Debet, Anne. 2007. *Mesure de la diversité et protection des données personnelles*. Paris: Commission Nationale de l'Informatique et des Libertés.

*Ecrans pâles? Diversité culturelle et culture commune dans l'audiovisuel*. 2004. Paris: La Documentation française.

Fourest, Caroline. 2008. "La Diversité contre l'égalité." *Le Monde*, January 18.

Fourquet, Jérôme. 2007. "La Capitation réussie de l'électorat du Front National." *Le Monde*, June 7.

Gabizon, Cécilia. 2006. "Statistiques: Nicolas Sarkozy est pour, Ségolène Royal est réservée." *Le Figaro*, October 17.

Gastaut, Yvan. 2000. *L'Immigration et l'opinion en France sous la Ve République*. Paris: Seuil.

Hargreaves, Alec G. 2000. "Half-Measures: Anti-Discrimination Policy in France." *French Politics, Culture and Society* 18(3): 83–101.

———. 2007. *Multi-Ethnic France: Immigration, Politics, Culture and Society*. London and New York: Routledge.

Haut Conseil à l'Intégration. 1998. *La Lutte contre les discriminations: Faire respecter le principe d'égalité*. Paris: La Documentation française.

Héran, François. 2009. "Statistiques ethniques, non! Mesure de la diversité, oui." *Le Monde*, March 25.

Laurence, Jonathan, and Justin Vaisse. 2006. *Integrating Islam: Political and Religious Challenges in Contemporary France*. Washington, DC: Brookings Institution.

Leclerc, Aline. 2007. "Un amendement au projet de loi sur l'immigration autorise la statistique ethnique." *Le Monde*, September 13.

Meurs, Dominique, Ariane Pailhé, and Patrick Simon. 2005. "Mobilité intergénérationnelle et persistance des inégalités: L'accès à l'emploi des immigrés et de leurs descendants en France." *INED Documents de travail* 130: 1–35.

Morice, Alain. 2002. "Le Sondage annuel sur le racisme: Suite (et fin?)." *Hommes et migrations* 1236 (March–April): 94–99.

Nobili, Christophe. 2005. "Plus de la moitié du plan sécuritaire de Le Pen déjà cannibalisé par la droite." *Le Canard enchaîné*, December 14.

Ridet, Philippe. 2007. "Sur TF1, Nicolas Sarkozy se rêve en 'président de l'ouverture'." *Le Monde*, February 7.

Sarkozy, Nicolas. 2008a. "Déclaration et conférence de presse de M. Nicolas Sarkozy, Président de la République, [ . . . ] à Paris, le 8 janvier 2008." http://discours.vie-publique.fr/notices/087000082.html (accessed April 25, 2008).

———. 2008b. "Discours de M. le Président de la République à l'Ecole Polytechnique de Palaiseau," December 17. http://www.elysee.fr/documents/index.php?mode=cview&press_id=2142&cat_id=7&lang=fr (accessed January 22, 2009).

SOS-Racisme. 2007. "Fiche pas mon pote. Appel contre la statistique ethnique." http://www.fichepasmonpote.com/index.php (accessed February 27, 2008).

Tévanian, Pierre. 2005. *Le Voile médiatique. Un faux débat: "L'affaire du foulard islamique."* Paris: Raisons d'agir.

Tribalat, Michèle. 1995. *Faire France. Une enquête sur les immigrés et leurs enfants.* Paris: La Découverte.

———. 1996. *De l'immigration à l'assimilation. Enquête sur les populations d'origine étrangère en France.* Paris: La Découverte.

Türk, Alex. 2007. "Sur les statistiques ethniques, 'nous n'avons pas été compris'." *Libération*, November 23.

# CHAPTER SIX

## Europe's Internal Exiles

*Sound, Image, and Performance of Identity in Želimir Žilnik's Films*

PAVLE LEVI AND ŽELIMIR ŽILNIK

Ever since he began making films, in the mid-1960s, in what was then the Socialist Federative Republic of Yugoslavia, Želimir Žilnik has been at the forefront of the socially and politically engaged European cinema. In fact, there is probably no filmmaker who has explored the dynamics of postwar European politics, economy, and culture with more persistence and rigor than he has. Over the period of some four decades, Žilnik has produced around eighty films—short and feature-length, documentary and fiction, on topics as diverse as modalities of socialist and liberal-democratic state governance (*Early Works*, 1969; *Fortress Europe*, 2000); political oppression and terrorism (*Pretty Women Passing Through the Town*, 1985; *Offentliche Hinrichtung*, 1974); immigrant communities in Western Europe (*Inventory*, 1975); links between economic crime and homophobia in the postcommu-

---

In this essay, text in boldface is by Želimir Žilnik. Translations, where necessary, are by Pavle Levi.

nist "transitional" societies (*Marble Ass*, 1994). He has explored the Marxist revisionist movements of the 1960s, documented the 1968 student demonstrations (*June Turmoil*, 1968), analyzed the contemporary rampage of European ethnic intolerance (*Old Timer*, 1988; *Wanderlust*, 1998), and dissected ways in which the notions of nationhood and citizenship have been transformed by the establishment of the European Union (*Kenedi Comes Home*, 2003).

Žilnik's oeuvre constitutes a piercing cinematic chronicle of contemporary Europe—an extensive audiovisual analysis that reaches eastward and westward alike, but feels most at home while drifting *along* the borders and camping in the margins. A major recent project, *Fortress Europe*, shot primarily in the border regions of Slovenia, Italy, and Hungary, most literally instantiated this inclination to ground one's sociopolitical as well as aesthetic views in the "no-man's-land." Žilnik is a persuaded transnationalist, an advocate of the political force—the community—composed of the oppressed, the marginalized, and the excluded. His is the cinema of society's inherent self-alterity: a cinema about the people whose lives embody a variety of European ideological contradictions, sociopolitical exclusions, and paradoxes of identity formation. It is a cinema of Europe's internal exiles.

Žilnik's investment in politicizing the underprivileged and the ostracized represents the lasting legacy of his Marxist intellectual heritage. Today, in the postcommunist times, the continuing relevance of this Marxism manifests itself most forcefully in the filmmaker's manner of understanding the processes of globalization, more specifically in his assessment of the changing role of the nation-state from a perspective resistant to the normativized opposition between liberal democracy and ethnic essentialism. A merciless critic of ethnonationalism, Žilnik is also a foremost denaturalizer of the supposedly spontaneous and nonideological rampage of liberal politics and market economy. Desire of a truly equitable distribution of wealth—material and cultural alike—is the driving force behind his ongoing pursuit of a cinematically constituted *demos*.

What follows is a textual montage, a series of analytical quips that seek to situate Želimir Žilnik's cinema in relation to a variety of European ideological and political currents. It "intercuts" fragments of an analysis of Žilnik's film practice with the author's own reflections on the political history of his medium.

## Document, Fiction, Identity

In 1967, *Newsreel about the Village Youth in Winter* inaugurated a number of thematic, technical, and stylistic features, which subsequently became the common traits of Žilnik's cinema. Particularly notable among these are a tendency to blur all distinctions between documentary and fiction, and an interest in *heterological* subjects—social outcasts, marginalized individuals and groups.

Filmed in the manner in which the state-sponsored newsreel journals were being made at the time, this short work documents the leisurely activities of the rural socialist youth, ways in which the "free time" is spent by the teenagers living in the villages of the multiethnic Vojvodina region of Serbia. Their cultural life—announced in the film's opening title as the author's primary point of interest—is revealed as a series of rituals revolving around an insatiable desire to suspend all kinds of social norms. The village youths, mostly men, are filmed in a multitude of situations involving drunken stupor, orgiastic singing and dancing, ecstatic self-mutilation with broken glasses and bottles, and even a private, amateur production of a historical play! *Newsreel* is a cinematic sketch composed by stringing together a number of loosely related acts, confessions, and performances, all expressive of the marginalized socialist youths' lacking sense of purpose, their sexual obsessions, and their uncontrolled outbursts of surplus energy.

On the formal level, *Newsreel* is distinguished by a dual tendency. On the one hand, it seeks to present its content in the manner of a "style-less," direct cinema-type of reportage. On the other hand, however, it repeatedly and directly intervenes into the reality it depicts by employing a number of fictionalizing tropes, such as (re)enactments and preplanned staging of action.

**I never hide the camera. I do not hide the sound recorder either. I do not conceal from the people I am shooting the fact that I am making a film about them. To the contrary! I seek to help them recognize the situations they are in and to express their views of these situations. They, in turn, help me to make a film about them that will be as solid as possible. While working on a film, I am aware of the fact that I am in a way betraying the found reality. My manner of treating individuals who populate these films is, at the bottom, a way of giving them an opportunity to act. The people act themselves. They know that they have been recognized as interesting**

**characters, and they tend to perform precisely those among their own features that are particularly photogenic.**

Identities are, then, always performed. As such, they are also ideological constructs. Articulated through the narratives, which we tell ourselves about ourselves, identities exist within the frameworks of coherence and sets of values, which we impose upon ourselves (in order, subsequently, to entertain the illusion that we are, in fact, freely choosing these). Reality is an enactment in the first degree. "Ideology is," as Roland Barthes claimed, "the Cinema of a society."[1]

The performative and constructed foundation of identity is thoroughly explicated in Žilnik's short documentary *Inventory*, made in West Germany in 1975. The film's thematic ambition seems deceivingly simple: to be a record, a collective biographical sketch, of a group of *Gastarbeiter* [guest workers] living in the same building in Munich. Toward this goal the film engages an effective, straightforward structure: all tenants in the building are lined up along its central staircase; one by one they step into the stationary camera's field of vision and briefly introduce themselves. Some tenants speak in German, others in their native languages—Greek, Serbo-Croatian, Turkish, and so on. Žilnik's structurally predetermined documentary, realized in a single uninterrupted long take, gives visible form to the social dynamic which Louis Althusser termed "ideological interpellation." One's identity (political, cultural, ethnic) is here revealed as something other than a natural "essence"—it is a social artifact, assumed at the same time as it is being produced. Ideological interpellation has its "place" within the structure of the society, and Žilnik's camera renders that place almost palpable.

Interpellation takes place when the individual is called upon ("hailed," is the term Althusser uses) to assume "his/her" identity within an existing structure. In *Inventory*, the site of interpellation is literally the space in front of the camera, while "hailing" takes the form of the act of filming itself. Through the processes of "primary" and "secondary" cinematic identification (that is, the spectator's identification with the look of the camera and the on-screen protagonists, respectively), the film apparatus produces a set of relations formally analogous to those which the apparatus of the State commonly entertains with its subjects.[2] In this particular case, the State is the 1970s German state, while its subjects are those who pass in front of the camera, assuming and expressing—acting and acting out, one might say—

the dualities inherent in their status as *gastarbeiter*. These guest workers are at the same time the legal, if temporary, citizens of the German state (legitimate subjects of its laws, political norms of conduct, as well as dominant sociocultural customs) *and* the normative German subject's ethnic others (within the German nation they embody the "non-German" identities—Turkish, Greek, Yugoslav). Their performances in front of the camera thus make apparent the role they play in the German state: their equivocal, half-assimilated status as lodgers in another's national house. Significantly, the extent to which the guest workers tend to foreground their "authentic" ethnic and cultural backgrounds is not simply a measure of the distance, of the difference, they seek to *retain* in relation to the German *Hausordnung* [house ordinance].[3] The variety of ethnic "types" that may be glimpsed from the tenants' brief acting stints also bespeak a wish to *assume* that distance, to *produce* a difference, which would give them a sense of agency and freedom vis à vis the laws and the norms of their host nation.

·   ·   ·

Questions of identity, in particular of ethnicity and interethnic relations, are at the core of the conflicts that brought about the socialist federative Yugoslavia's disintegration. It is, however, imperative to recognize that the contemporary outbursts of ethnic nationalism in the region are by no means symptomatic of some "intrinsic," centuries-old regional tribalism. Rather, the widely and successfully disseminated nationalist hatred among the South Slavs originated as an ideological, discursive instrument utilized by the participants in the political battles that were being waged in the late, rapidly collapsing state-socialist context. The death of the multiethnic Yugoslavia directly resulted from a certain deadlock of politics, from an inability on the part of the regional authorities in the country's six constitutive republics—Slovenia, Serbia, Croatia, Bosnia and Herzegovina, Montenegro, and Macedonia—to uphold the identity of the federation (of the Yugoslav nation and the state) at the time when its economic and political reform had become unavoidable. This failure to reform the existing socialist system went hand in hand with the activation of the ideological tropes of reactionary identity politics: ethnic essentialism, exclusivism, and collectivism. Ever since the 1980s, the intellectual and cultural elites in the region have openly and systematically worked on nurturing these nationalist mythomanias. They were the principal instigators, promoters, and rationalizers of ethnic animosity—

theirs is, therefore, the lion's share of responsibility for the manufacture of hatred that brought about the demise of the multinational Yugoslavia.

During the 1970s the bureaucracy of the Yugoslav Communist Party became increasingly afraid of the various manifestations of the rapidly spreading, reformist sociopolitical tendencies. It was at this time, out of this fear, that it began to dig the grave for the federal state. In order to prevent further growth of the reformist social consciousness and of solidarity among the workers and the intellectuals, the bureaucracy *invented a return to tradition* and encouraged the ethnic divide to set across the country. For the first time since the end of the Second World War, there was ideological pressure to identify with a particular ethnic group. At the age of twenty-five or thirty, people were suddenly learning that they were Slovenian or Serb, and that their friends were Croat, Muslim, and so on. Until the 1970s, ethnic differences had played no role whatsoever in the political life of the country.

This invitation to tribalization began to induce artificial conflicts, to encourage social tensions, and to rechannel the energy which had previously been displayed in the protests against the reified bureaucracy. Social and economic issues were increasingly interpreted in the ethnic key (who is more privileged—Serbs, Croats, or Slovenes?). Nationalist manipulations also took hold in certain intellectual circles. In 1980, the death of Josip Broz Tito, Yugoslavia's president for life, further reinforced a medieval-like squabbling inside the federal political apparatus about the country's existence in the post-Tito era. At the time, Slovenia was the strongest advocate of a version of Eurocommunism—it first promoted a loose federal, then a confederal model of the state. Serbia, on the other hand, assumed a hardline state-socialist position, and was arguing in favor of a strongly centralized Yugoslavia. Most simply put, after hundreds of hours spent in the central committee and party meetings, when the regional political elites realized that no single perspective was prevailing, they decided to turn to nationalism in order to mobilize local populations in support of their diverging causes.

In 1988, Žilnik made *Old Timer*, a rare example of a film which openly sought to expose and discredit—to audiovisually deconstruct—the so-called antibureaucratic revolution: the skillfully orchestrated ethnonationalist campaign also known as "the happening of the people," which served as the populist backbone of Slobodan Milošević's total usurpation of political power in Serbia. *Old Timer* is a road movie. Its central protagonist is a free-spirited Slovenian rock critic who travels along the arteries of Yugoslavia's "brotherhood and unity"—roads and highways that used to connect various parts of the country, bringing together its diverse ethnic communities. But the longhaired rebel's motorcycle journey unfolds intermittently. His voyage across Yugoslavia is presented with regular structural interruptions in the form of inserted documentary footage depicting the "happenings of the people" and meetings organized in support of Milošević's political campaign. Ironically, while filming *Old Timer* in Serbia, Žilnik and his crew repeatedly crossed paths with the "cast and crew" of these political spectacles. Much of the footage incorporated into the film was therefore shot by Žilnik's own cinematographer, and some of it even features *Old Timer*'s libertarian protagonist directly mingling with the ecstatic nationalist masses. This serendipitously earned structural device enabled the filmmaker to rely on his character's diegetic status as an outside observer, in order to offer some subtle pedagogical advice on how to analyze political imagery—more specifically, how to read through the simulated spontaneity of Milošević's antibureaucratic revolution.

In the summer of 1988, when I was shooting the film, Yugoslavia was still in existence. The bloodiest tools from the arsenal of European political history—national-socialism and fascism—had not yet been fully activated. But they would have to be used if the country was to be definitively divided; a war was needed, violence and bloodletting—soon enough they would, indeed, take place. . . . Today, things are often interpreted simplistically, as if the political tensions were only manifesting themselves in Serbia and not in other Yugoslav republics as well. It is true that the concentration of a Stalinist-type of dogmatism and of destructive energy was highest in Serbia, but political leaderships in other republics had also consolidated their power on openly ethnocentric platforms. Milošević was the one who decisively pushed Yugoslavia into the final phase of its physical disintegration, by aggressively instrumentalizing the question of Serbia's southern province, Kosovo.

Six or seven centuries ago Kosovo used to be—as the Serb nationalist mythology never fails to remind us—the "cradle" of Serbian statehood.

Subsequently, however, during the times of the Ottoman Empire, the majority of Serbs migrated northwards and settled in the southern parts of Austria, around the Danube River. They served in the military and protected the borders of their new homeland, which in turn gave them land to work and granted them educational and religious autonomies. With the arrival and the settling of the Albanians, Kosovo, too, changed its demographic structure over the course of time. Historical dynamics of this sort are not at all uncommon in Europe—huge migrations of peoples caused by occupations, wars, and economic depressions affected other territories as well. But in the late 1980s, in the heat of the debate about Yugoslavia's course in the post-Tito era, Milošević's political apparatus misinterpreted the history of Kosovo in order to align it with the events of the "anti-bureaucratic revolution." Marches of "dissatisfied and threatened Serbs and Montenegrins from Kosovo" began to be organized; protests were held in front of federal institutions in the capital of Belgrade; police and state intervention in Kosovo were called for. Soon the demonstrations spread all over Serbia. In the autonomous province of Vojvodina the objective was to overthrow the "bureaucratic authorities insensitive to the plight of the people." The first mass rally of this sort that I directly encountered took place in my hometown of Novi Sad. It took ten minutes of conversation with some of the participants to figure out the true nature of their protest: everything was well-coordinated with the secret police and fully funded—mass transportation had been provided; banners and speeches had been prepared and dictated in advance.

I made *Old Timer* out of a desire to document some of this masquerade. In the process, I also directly witnessed the paramount role the modern media technologies were playing in promoting these rallies. Around this time, Belgrade Television had just acquired beta video cameras, which drastically improved production schedules: events could now be taped in the course of an afternoon and broadcast the same evening. Thanks to this technology, the entire ethnonationalist "revolution," the "awakening" of the Serb people, actually began to resemble a tightly directed film. Groups of people were being driven by buses from one town to another; they would change their costumes on the go, and within a single day one group of protesters could appear in up to four "performances." They were the real movie extras! As a filmmaker, I was extremely interested in the language of images and the repertory of nationalist slogans that were being used at the rallies—everything revolved around the topics of Serb resentment, territorial expansion, the "reclaiming" of Kosovo, and the personality cult of Slobodan Milošević.

During the 1990s, ethnic performances and nationalist spectacles, staged with the intent of promoting and feeding the wars, prominently figured in the cinema of the formerly Yugoslav lands. The manufacture and naturalization of hatred—the two key political and ideological mechanisms of the project that was the murder of the federation's interethnic "brotherhood and unity"—were explored in films such as Srdjan Vuletić's *I Burnt Legs* (1993), Žilnik's *Marble Ass* (1993), Danis Tanović's *No Man's Land* (2001), and more recently, Miloš Radivojević's *Awakening from the Dead* (2005) and Rajko Grlić's *Border Post* (2006). But the vast majority of the mainstream cinema in the region demonstrated a serious lack of interest in conducting sobering, rationally grounded analyses of the political and the socioeconomic foundations of the nationalist menace. Generally speaking, over the course of the 1990s, the post-Yugoslav cinema was marked by a tendency to either actively promote ethnocentric collectivisms, rampant irrational stereotyping, patriarchal machismo, and the culture of violence (the cinema of Emir Kusturica is a case in point), or to ignore these issues altogether. On the aesthetic front, this situation led to an inflation of stylization, artifice, and not infrequently grotesque formalism. Realism, naturalism, verism, and other cinematic styles traditionally associated with critical portrayals of contemporary reality were for the most part pushed aside.

In 1994, Žilnik made a film that remains to this day his most direct attack on homophobia. *Marble Ass* is the first properly speaking queer film produced in the ex-Yugoslav lands, and a work distinguished by a "trash" aesthetic that seems to have been partially inspired by such Warhol-Morrissey productions as *Flesh* (1968), *Trash* (1970), and *Women in Revolt* (1971). Thoroughly staged, yet shot in the manner of *direct cinema*, *Marble Ass* is set in Belgrade in the mid-1990s, the time when Serbia seemed to have reached an economic, social, and cultural bottom. It confronts and discards many of the carefully nurtured nationalist myths about ethnic masculinity, potency, and bravery, by juxtaposing the story of a macho sociopath—a young man who returns to Belgrade from the war zone, where he was freely killing and pillaging—with the tale of two friendly and easygoing transvestite prostitutes.

In the summer of 1994 there was no end in sight to the carnage in the former Yugoslavia. State propaganda machineries were "lubricating" the war by producing outrageous stereotypes. An "authentic" Serb adorns himself with ammunition and knives. He is also a macho, a heavy drinker, who surrounds himself with brass music. He violates girls behind counters. Such were the most popular screen heroes at the time, those in whom the culture industries invested millions of dollars. For their part, Western coproducers were also ever ready to participate in such projects. The television news developed in the atmosphere of a cabaret, dominated by the paramilitary and "weekend" warriors. What was happening at the time in the spheres of media and culture was a spectacle designed to conceal the truth of killing, pillaging, and trafficking in arms and human lives. A new, post-Yugoslav ruling class was being produced. These were the circumstances under which *Marble Ass* also went into production, on an extremely low budget and within an environment highly restrictive of free individual expression.

The moral of the film was clear: Belgrade's transvestite prostitutes—who prefer free and rampant sexual activity to violence and bloodletting—are the only true guardians of humanity and sanity in 1990s Serbia. The patriarchal heteronormativity of the Serb ethnonational collective thus received its first ever, overt on-screen negation.

## Cinema Is Praxis

What is quite specific to filmmaking is that those involved in it are commonly aware of the extent to which an entire social atmosphere or a cultural climate can be affected through their practice. I began to make films in the mid-1960s—the time when the socialist Yugoslavia and President Josip Broz Tito's system of self-management were at their prime. My generation, the post–Second World War generation of cineastes, was a group of people whose goal was to radically change the structure of filmmaking in the country, to engage in an open polemic with the state's authoritarian ideological dogma and its propaganda machinery. In a broader perspective, we recognized and sought to join the powerful reformist tide that was, at the time, impacting systems and ideologies worldwide.

Cinema does not depend on reality pure and simple. It depends on the filmmaker's transformation of that reality. This is true of documentary and fiction films alike. To me, the only inexhaustible theme in the cinema has to do with the relationship between individual destinies and the society at large. Documentaristic impulse in particular can be strongly expressive of a general concern for human destinies. The duty of the cinema ought to lie beyond a naked registration of actuality, in searching, analyzing, asking questions, and exciting the audience.

What is cinema? Andre Bazin famously asked. Different ontologies of the medium can and have been proposed, but a Marxist answer to this question necessarily grounds itself in an understanding of the cinema as (a mode of) *praxis*. Being a realm—an instrument as well as a creative expression—of humankind's general power to transform itself and the world around it, filmmaking brings together consciousness and material action, exercises in critical thinking and practical labor. As such, the cinema has played a steady role in the history of the revolutionary processes that have in no small measure defined the twentieth century: from Sergei Eisenstein and Dziga Vertov, to Luis Bunuel and Jean Vigo, then Jean-Luc Godard (and The Dziga Vertov Group) and Chris Marker (and the Groupe Medvedkin); from Miklos Jancso, Dušan Makavejev, and Jan Nemec, to Glauber Rocha, Pier Paolo Pasolini, Marco Belocchio, Jean-Marie Straub, and others.

However, in today's post–Cold War, "postideological" world, Marxist filmmakers are few and far between. Amidst a historical reality distinguished by an all but total discrediting of the "utopia" of communist internationalism and a forceful onset of the supposedly much more "natural," particularist forms of identity politics—the most rampant among which are various ethnic essentialisms—one of the few remaining bearers of the torch of Marxist cinema is Želimir Žilnik. This is not so because his work has maintained the unaltered course of a radical aesthetico-political program, outlined back in the 1960s. Didactic cine-Marxism (of the kind once made famous by the Dziga Vertov Group) was, to begin with, never a trait of Žilnik's filmmaking. His cinema today still successfully functions as a form of praxis simply because it remains committed, as passionately as it was four decades ago, to a total demystification of the processes of production in all their manifestations: film production and sociopolitical activity alike. When the dynamics of production are made explicit, ideological delusions—be they Stalinist, liberal-democratic, or ethnonationalist—are more easily debunked. The notions of identity and community are thereby also, inevitably, submitted to critical reevaluation.

Žilnik has steadily operated on very low budgets and has developed a distinct method and style of "guerilla" filmmaking, highly suitable to the almost permanent state of cinematic production in which he seems to exist. He came of age as a filmmaker in the context of the 1960s Yugoslav New Film movement. In an atmosphere of widespread sociopolitical progress and substantial relaxation of the state and Communist Party control, filmmakers sought to discard the inherited armor of ideological rigidity by demanding that "one collective mythology be replaced with endless individual mythologies."[4] Many among the most engaged film authors working at the time aligned their artistic endeavors with the ideational currents of Marxist revisionism, felt not only in Yugoslavia and the East European socialist block (and epitomized in the events of the Prague Spring in the late 1960s Czechoslovakia) but also in the leftist political circles in the West (Maoism, Althusserian structuralism, and so on). In Yugoslavia, the most influential trajectory of Marxist revisionism was paved by the so-called Praxis School— a group of humanist thinkers particularly influenced by Karl Marx's early writings. Praxis demanded "a merciless critique of everything existing," advocated individual freedom as "a precondition of collective freedom," and promoted "man [as] essentially a being of *praxis*, i.e., a being capable of free creative activity by which he transforms the world, realizes his specific potential faculties and satisfies the needs of other human individuals."[5]

To understand cinema as a mode of human praxis is to situate it at the creative crossroads of critical theory, sociopolitical engagement, and the practice of everyday living. Referencing both Marx and the contemporary revisions of his thought, Želimir Žilnik titled his first feature film *Early Works*.

**The film was made in the aftermath of the 1968 student demonstrations in Belgrade. Directed against the ruling state-socialist bureaucracy, the demonstrations called for a return to the true principles of Marxism and communism. This was an early movement of solidarity. The younger generation was asking about its place in a society which, like other Stalinist societies, had become gerontocratic, despite its earlier declarations of commitment to building a "democratic socialism with a human face." The demos took place in Belgrade in June, but soon afterwards,**

in August, came the Russian invasion of Czechoslovakia. At the time, Yugoslavia was one of the most open of the Stalinist systems, and the bureaucratized state structure was genuinely being put under pressure by the student demonstrators. There were no brutal police or army interventions against the protesters. A discussion about these events even took place inside the apparatus of the Communist Party, and in June and July it seemed that the Belgrade demos would be victorious and that they would effect a positive change.

On the other hand, however, the occupation of Czechoslovakia gave rise to a widespread fear—encouraged by the bureaucracy and the apparatchiks—that Yugoslavia, despite being outside the Soviet bloc, might be next in line for an intervention by the Soviet Army. The events in 1968 thus raised a lot of questions concerning the future of socialism, the meaning of the revolution, and how it is to be practically implemented. In August and September, these questions crystallized themselves into a concept for a film, *Early Works*.

The film came out in early 1969, and was initially very successful because it addressed many of the issues that had been in the air for some time. But after two months, its distribution was suddenly interrupted because President Josip Broz Tito had apparently seen the film and was very displeased with it. The police confiscated all prints of *Early Works*. I took the issue to court; the outcome was an interesting reflection of the still relatively open political situation in the country: the court decided to free the film and to allow its distribution to continue. Shortly afterwards, the film won the Grand Jury Prize at the Berlin Festival. However, by the time I returned to Yugoslavia from Germany, a damaging propaganda campaign had been launched against me by the state bureaucracy. My work was declared to be "anarcho-liberal" with additional "Maoist deviations." I was thrown out of the party and denied further opportunities to make films in the country. Other young, progressive filmmakers—Dušan Makavejev, Aleksandar Petrović, Živojin Pavlović, Lazar Stojanović—also suffered a similar fate.

*Early Works* follows a group of student radicals who, in the wake of 1968, set out to enact a "return to Marx" and to spread their revisionist gospel across rural Serbia. The film thematizes exactly those conceptual and structural dynamics which form the core of Žilnik's authorial method: a direct immersion of the filmmaking apparatus into the sphere of social production. In the spirit of Marx's thesis 11 on Feuerbach ("Philosophers have hitherto only interpreted the world in various ways; the point is to change it"), one could say that Žilnik's cinema reaches beyond or, more properly, beneath the realm of audiovisual representation: its immediate significance resides in the arena of production itself. More specifically, it resides in the process, the series of relations, which constitute the making of a film and which are here conceived as already a direct and worthy intervention into the social sphere. In this type of cinema, the act of filming is at least as important as the (finished) film. Deprived of the aura of a privileged creative activity, art/film practice thus becomes a situation of common labor. In a sense, Žilnik's films may be thought of as chronicles left by a group of workers—the director, the cast, the crew—of their attempted exercises in grassroots social and cultural productivity. They are films-as-documents of their own production, which is conceived as first and foremost an end unto itself: a dereified collective engagement in "sensuous human activity."[6]

In Žilnik's case (even more so than in the case of other New Film authors, Makavejev included), "cinema-as-praxis" decidedly casts filmmaking as a mode of play. Each new project functions as yet another installment of an experimental social game. An issue is introduced, a situation is established, and the process of filming is set in motion. The making of a film functions simultaneously as (1) an incentive to resolve the issues at hand; (2) an exercise in giving birth to a new subcultural cell/formation; and (3) a reflection on what, if anything, will have been accomplished in or through the production process. Thus, even if by the time the filming has come to an end the issues that are being dealt with have not yet been successfully settled, the making of the film will still have constituted a worthy exercise in social activism.

*Black Film*, realized in 1971, already fully demonstrated this type of approach. In this short piece of cinema verité, the director explored the problem of homelessness in the socialist Yugoslavia. The film opens with Žilnik standing in a street, surrounded by a randomly gathered group of homeless men. He declares into the camera that the film he is about to make will document a series of attempts to find homes for the people he has gathered. A temporary community has thus been formed, and a set of objectives— a "mission"—has been clearly stated. The rest of the production finds the director, his homeless protagonists, and his crew playing as a team—acting together toward a common goal. The resulting film is, in turn, more than anything else an audiovisual trace of this collective action aimed at improving the housing conditions of the most underprivileged socialist subjects.

## In Pursuit of the Heterological

Protagonists of Žilnik's cinema are the marginalized subjects, those excluded from, at times even entirely inassimilable into, the existing social frameworks—the "accursed share" of the society, the human waste. Žilnik's is a tireless pursuit of the *heterological* (Bataille).[7] In the early days, he found it among the socialist practitioners of sloth (*Newsreel*), the homeless urban types (*Black Film*), and the systematically abused (sexually and otherwise) Roma children (*Little Pioneers*, 1968). More recently, the "unavowable" modes of existence depicted in Žilnik's films have included transvestites living amidst a macho war culture (*Marble Ass*); economic migrants/illegal immigrants caught and detained while crossing the borders of the European Union (*Fortress Europe*); and ethnic subjects moving in the opposite direction—those who have been deported from the EU to their countries of origin (*Kenedi Comes Home*).[8]

In all these cases the function of the *heterological* is to render the existing categories of identity as questionable as possible. By definition, the notion of identity connotes a certain, if minimal, measure of stability. Žilnik's films are, on the other hand, interested in subjectivizing—that is, in attributing political agency—to the most unstable forms of social existence. The heterological is here to be understood as a dynamic category, a process whereby the existing social, political, cultural, and economic institutions—in short, reality as discursively constituted—are forced to recognize their own limits, to accept their exteriority, and to thus open themselves up to various possible forms of criticism. Sometimes, as in *Black Film*, *Fortress Europe*, and the beginning of the *Kenedi* saga, Žilnik's protagonists are the true *homo sacer*: their existence is reduced to the possession of nothing but bare life.[9] But even when they belong to an already articulated (if radically marginalized and stigmatized) subculture—as is the case with the transvestite prostitutes of *Marble Ass*—the role these characters play "within" the society at large is still mainly that of the "nonexistent."[10] Žilnik's protagonists have, at most, *clandestine identities*. They serve as liminal cases between the real, existing societies (within which they do not really have a proper place) and the possible, alternative, transformed societies (within which, if these were to come to existence, they could have more stable and defined identities). They are the material, so to speak, for the process described by Etienne Balibar as "the constitution of a 'people' (or *demos*) that begins as nonexistent on account of the exclusion of those who are considered unworthy of the status of citizen (depending on the epoch and the circumstances: slaves or servants, workers or paupers, women, foreigners, and so on)."[11]

In an almost ritualistic fashion, *Early Works* already sought to strip all traces of recognizable identity off of the human subject. Film critic Goran Gocić perceptively noted that the "entire film is like a carnal performance, a synaesthetic version of body-art, in which everything revolves around . . . the body: the body is subjected to the scrutiny of the gaze, beaten, rolled in leaves and mud, tortured by fire, squeezed, dragged by a car; it is fed and cleansed, buried, caressed, pleasured, shaved, imprisoned, carried around, poisoned and re-animated, raped, soiled, carefully washed, exposed to the cold, killed and burnt." *Early Works*, concludes Gocić, "is a truly 'proletarian' film, in unexpectedly literal ways: the protagonists' investment in their adventure takes place solely on the level of the body."[12]

More recently, the bodies of Žilnik's protagonists have been exhibiting the marks left upon them by the contradictory dynamics of Europe's post–Cold War democratic "realignment." Today's subjects without identity, "men without [symbolic] content" (Agamben), are Kenedi (the title character in *Kenedi Comes Home*)—a Roma youth forced to leave the European Union and to return to his "native" Serbia despite the fact that he was born, raised, and schooled in Italy; and the protagonists of *Fortress Europe*—the countless men and women who seek to live in the EU, but are forbidden entry into the same. In their very existence, they all negate the ideological foundation upon which rest all normative oppositions structuring the field of contemporary liberal-democratic politics: the foundation of *particularist identity politics*. In this regard, the success of the ideological fiction about the "insurmountable ethnic differences," which ensured Yugoslavia's disintegration, represented an early sign of the more general onset of this ideological paradigm.

**The multiethnic Yugoslavia did not disappear due to the will of its peoples, but because of the power struggles waged among its political elites. The country is now history, but what of the current social and political de-**

sires of the young generation from the formerly Yugoslav lands? They do not dare declare openly that they would like to have continued to live together (and this would anyway no longer be possible given how much killing and destruction took place in the 1990s in the name of ethnonational interests), so they say it in a roundabout manner: the young wish to leave the region, to "go to Europe." The country has been violently torn apart, new national borders have been drawn, we swore never to live together again, and now . . . here are the ex-Yugoslavs knocking at the door of the European Union. The EU is still deciding whether to let us "in," but we are hopeful.

But the new Europe itself rests upon a major contradiction. Its governing political-economic force, big international capital, knows no limits—this is the only way it can survive. However, while there is much talk about an open Europe, a Europe without borders, in reality a new wall has been erected to keep certain groups of people outside Europe. This immaterial wall is even thicker and higher than the Berlin Wall was at its time. For the entire region of Eastern Europe, currently undergoing tremendous economic distress, travel to Western Europe has become more restrictive than ever before. Many people undertook a journey to the West nurturing illusions about its democratic openness and egalitarianism. In fact, the terms of border-crossing established by the Schengen Agreement facilitate travel mainly for the criminal elements and the new political apparatchiks from the East—former dictators, Stalinists, and even murderers. On the other hand, thousands of ordinary people, many of them hardworking and incredibly talented, end up trapped in the no-man's-land between the states.

The contemporary project of European "unification" depends on the exclusionary violence directed against certain nation-states and ethnic communities, those considered insufficiently democratic, tolerant, and prosperous to be granted entry into the European political "club." Of course, our intention here is by no means to negate the fact that at any given point in time, some states and societies are indeed more democratic and tolerant than others. The irony, however, is that the (liberal) democratic imagination behind the project of European unification does not seem capable, or willing, to truly reach beyond the ethnic and national categories of identity politics—those categories which enable the process of unification to remain underwritten, first and foremost, by the interests and the imperatives of global capital. In other words, the idea of Europe without borders, open and inclusive, rings true primarily in the "sacred" sphere of economic currents—the notion of "free flow" applies more than anything to merchandise (legal and trafficked); borders are far less porous where migrations of the population are concerned. Contrary to its legitimizing ideological discourses, the project of European unification is not simply resulting in erasure of borders. In order to make some borders disappear, the EU is in fact making other lines of separation more prominent than before. Ever less-restricted advancement of multinational capital, and a carefully regulated movement of the people—such is the antinomic foundation of the New Europe. National and ethnic identities—these fundamental symbolic, ideological differences—are themselves carefully maintained precisely so that a lack of balance can be preserved in the economic base. Thus, on the one hand, the national and ethnic forms of political imagination seem to be growing increasingly irrelevant, obsolete, and backwards; on the other hand, however, they are not being entirely eliminated, because this might give rise to the idea of a continent unified on the truly universal(ized) grounds of human solidarity, not of economic inequality.[13]

In light of the above, both Kenedi and the innumerable protagonists of *Fortress Europe*—those who wish to live in Europe but are not permitted to do so—may be said to embody the highest ideal of the European Union itself: the ideal, in Balibar's words, of "a 'European right to citizenship' understood as a 'right to citizenship in Europe'—that is, an [unlimited] expansion of democracy by means of European unification."[14] Such is the ideal which the EU wishes to claim, but does not dare implement. From this perspective, Kenedi and others with a similar fate are not so much illegal immigrants as they are, in fact, political refugees from the New Europe.

## Coda: Community

"Communism, like cinema, is the promise of a counter-society."[15] Serge Daney's words certainly ring true where Želimir Žilnik's praxis of sounds and images is concerned. His filmmaking incessantly articulates possible future communities: it urges for a political solidarity—for a cinematically constituted collectivity—among the disenfranchised, the marginalized, and the socially inassimilable individuals and groups. As Žilnik himself recently put it, "For millions of people from out-of-the-way corners of the globe, the only chance to surface, to become visible and to show their intelligence and creativity, resides in the establishment of a unified world on an LCD screen."[16]

"[O]ne cannot make the world with simple atoms," asserts Jean-Luc Nancy. "There has to be a *clinamen*. There has to be an inclination or an inclining from one toward the other, of one by the other, or from one to the other. Community is at least the *clinamen* of the 'individual'."[17]

Each film made by Želimir Žilnik is an exercise in creating a new and authentic human collective; an attempt at inserting this collective as deeply as possible into the existing social fabric. This is, ultimately, why these films are at the same time fictional and documentary, and why they can hardly be otherwise: their protagonists are always playacting, regardless of whether they are portraying themselves (through documentary reenactments) or someone else (as characters defined within the framework of acted fiction). Žilnik's cinematographic subjects are the laborers and the operatives of a (permanently) approaching film commune.

Cinema, clinamen!

NOTES

1. Roland Barthes, "Upon Leaving the Movie Theater," in *Apparatus*, ed. Theresa Hak Kyung Cha, 3.

2. For a canonical elaboration of the notions of primary and secondary cinematic identification, see Christian Metz, *The Imaginary Signifier*. For a strongly related discussion of the primary and secondary forms of political/ideological identification, through which ethnic, national, and civic identities are negotiated, see Etienne Balibar, *We, the People of Europe?*, 25–30.

3. *House Ordinance* is the title of another short documentary, which Žilnik made in 1975 on the topic of guest workers in Germany.

4. Dušan Stojanović, *Velika avantura filma*, 84.

5. Mihailo Marković, "Introduction," in *Praxis: Yugoslav Essays in the Philosophy and Methodology of the Social Sciences*, ed. Marković and Gajo Petrović, xii.

6. See Giorgio Agamben, *The Man Without Content*, 72–73, 79–85. See also Etienne Balibar, *The Philosophy of Marx*, 40–41.

7. See Georges Bataille, "The Use Value of D.A.F. de Sade," in *Visions of Excess: Selected Writings, 1927–1939*, ed. Allan Stoekl, 91–104.

8. I borrow the term "unavowable" from Maurice Blanchot. See his reflections on Bataille and Marguerite Duras in *The Unavowable Community*.

On account of Žilnik's pursuit of the heterological, a useful analogy may be drawn between him and the Italian filmmaker Pier Paolo Pasolini. Pasolini locates radical otherness first in the Roman *borgata* (the city suburbs which disappeared in the 1960s, with the sweeping industrial modernization of Italy, are the central location of Pasolini's first feature, *Accatone*), then among the Italian peasantry (*Teorema*), and ultimately, when all other spaces of radical alterity have been eradicated from the country's socioeconomic reality, in the realm of myth (*Porcile*).

9. See Giorgio Agamben, *Homo Sacer*, esp. 85–100.

10. As Jacques Ranciere put it, "Politics exists through the fact of a magnitude that escapes ordinary measurement, this part of those who have no part that is nothing and everything. . . . Politics exists simply because no social order is based on nature, no divine law regulates human society." See Jacques Ranciere, *Disagreement: Politics and Philosophy*, 15–16.

11. Balibar, *We, the People of Europe?*, 72.

12. Goran Gocić, "Prerani i prekasni radovi," in *Želimir Žilnik: Above the Red Dust*, 21.

13. I draw here on Rastko Močnik's perspicacious analysis of the multiple roles the institution of the nation plays in the era of globalized capitalism. See Rastko Močnik, *Koliko fašizma?*, 9–23.

14. Balibar, *We, the People of Europe?*, 9.

15. Serge Daney, *Postcards from the Cinema*, 120.

16. Želimir Žilnik, "Instead of Esperanto—Video," in *Divided God and Intercultural Dialogue*, ed. Tomislav Žigmanov, 26.

17. Jean-Luc Nancy, *The Inoperative Community*, 3–4.

WORKS CITED

Agamben, Giorgio. *Homo Sacer*. Stanford, CA: Stanford University Press, 1998.

———. *The Man Without Content*. Stanford, CA: Stanford University Press, 1999.

Balibar, Etienne. *The Philosophy of Marx*. London: Verso, 2007.

———. *We, the People of Europe?* Princeton, NJ: Princeton University Press, 2003.

Barthes, Roland. "Upon Leaving the Movie Theater." In *Apparatus*, ed. Theresa Hak Kyung Cha. New York: Tanam Press, 1980.

Bataille, Georges. "The Use Value of D.A.F. de Sade." In *Visions of Excess: Selected Writings, 1927–1939*, ed. Allan Stoekl. Minneapolis: University of Minnesota Press, 1985.

Blanchot, Maurice. *The Unavowable Community*. Barrytown, NY: Station Hill Press, 1988.

Daney, Serge. *Postcards from the Cinema*. Oxford: Berg, 2007.

Gocić, Goran. "Prerani i prekasni radovi." In *Želimir Žilnik: Above the Red Dust*. Belgrade: Institut za film, 2003.

Marković, Mihailo. "Introduction." In *Praxis: Yugoslav Essays in the Philosophy and Methodology of the Social Sciences*, ed. Marković and Gajo Petrović. Dordrecht: D. Reidel Publishing, 1979.

Metz, Christian. *The Imaginary Signifier*. Bloomington: Indiana University Press, 1986.

Močnik, Rastko. *Koliko fašizma?* Zagreb: Arkzin, 1998–99.

Nancy, Jean-Luc. *The Inoperative Community*. Minneapolis: University of Minnesota Press, 1991.

Ranciere, Jacques. *Disagreement: Politics and Philosophy*. Minneapolis: University of Minnesota Press, 1999.

Stojanović, Dušan. *Velika avantura filma*. Belgrade: Institut za film, 1998.

Žilnik, Želimir. "Instead of Esperanto—Video." In *Divided God and Intercultural Dialogue*, ed. Tomislav Žigmanov. Ljubljana: Dijaški Dom Ivana Cankarja, KUD Pozitiv, 2008.

PART THREE  **Promising Ties**

# CHAPTER SEVEN

# The Return of Ethnicity to Europe via Islamic Migration?

*The Ethnicization of the Islamic Diaspora*

BASSAM TIBI

It is beyond dispute that contemporary Europe attracts millions of immigrants but has a poor record of integrating them. Today, approximately twenty million Muslim immigrants have transferred their residence to Europe, and for the foreseeable future immigration is expected to reach record numbers.[1] For reasons explored here, today's immigrants increasingly resist social integration and in turn are cast as aliens by choice. This essay offers an explanation and possible solution using a concept of ethnicity.[2] We begin with the puzzle: Islam is founded on tenets of a humanity beyond ethnic distinction, and proponents of Europe in the era of the European Union make a similar claim. Islam, according to its foundational *umma* community, is a universal and inclusive civilization, and Europe, based on a concept of civic society, promotes itself as well to offer transparent principles for inclusion. What, then, provokes Muslims and Europeans to identify with ethnic difference? Do these identifications principally inflame conflict? Why is the Islamic Diaspora, apparently beyond other immigrations, challenging the project of creating a cohesive Europe?

I begin with the observation made in the United Kingdom by a prominent liberal Muslim. Hanif Kureishi, who resides in Britain and writes of his South Asian perspective, has observed what he sees as an alarming phenomenon in mosques across the United Kingdom. He writes:

> In all the mosques I visited I listened to ardent Imams. One preaching demagogue followed the other in a never subsiding torrent. Their inflammatory and demagogic incitements were directed at the West, and against the Jews. It was possible to find out that this is not only taking place in mosques, but also in a similar manner throughout and across the religious communities, including their faith schools where these anti-Western and anti-Jewish ideas are propagated.[3]

The combination of anti-Westernism and anti-Semitism which Kureishi observes in Britain is most frightening. Within his testimony one finds twin points of concern: an ethnicization of the Islamic Diaspora in Europe, and the Islamization of European anti-Semitism.[4] To be sure, ethnicity is not consistent with a universal Islam, nor does Islam contain anti-Semitism in itself. Anti-Semitism is originally a European ideology alien to Islam.[5] This Islamist variant of anti-Semitism is a relatively recent phenomenon whose origins and prospects must be deliberately laid bare. Only then may we derive a viable response.

## Terms and Concepts

Although it is possible to make a case for an organic origin for ethnicity, today's ethnic Islamic and ethnic European identities, as expressed by immigrants, native-born Europeans, political leaders, and popular culture, are the result of social disruption and instrumentalization. The Muslim Diaspora in Europe can be deconstructed in numerous sectarian, ethnic, and subethnic communities often inimical to one another (for example, Kurds versus Turks, and Sunnis versus Alawis.) However, the alienated status of the majority of Muslim immigrants in Europe contributes to uniting these diverse communities in a fantasy *umma* community. The social imaginary is provoked by the essential condition of shared exclusion—itself hardly resembling the origin of Islamic faith. It is most perplexing that European politicians, in particular in Germany, take public stances that in effect support this imagined community of separation. Public policy is based on a principle of identifying and recognizing official representatives of one Muslim community. This politics enforces the deepening ethnicization of those who share only adherence to an instrumentalized version of an Islamic identity. Accordingly, such political representation may be motivated by an effort to overcome ethnicity within the framework of modernity, but in effect it engages Muslim immigrants in a framework of ethnic-communitarian politics.

To look deeper into this phenomenon, we must define essential terms and concepts. The term "ethnicity" refers by definition to an exclusive identity, since it is based on a perception of the self in a group distinct from an ethnically defined other. Ascribing ethnicity, therefore, creates borders not to be crossed and thereby creates conditions for conflict.[6] Though Islamic immigrants in Europe today are considered part of organic ethnic communities, their self-awareness is defined by a notion of a universal civilization. The Islamic *umma* community, in this way, should be understood as "an imagined community." In its history Islam's claims were never based on ethnicity but rather on a religious doctrine of universal inclusion. Anyone could join through a simple act of conversion to Islam. Similarly, European citizenship is in its self-image a kind of club that anyone can join through naturalization. The European nation, and the *umma* community, in principle deny the politicization of ethnicity and replace this with alternative principles of inclusion. However, the realities on the ground belie the claims of both concepts. Muslims in Europe are not integrated, and the obstacles come from both sides.

What, then, does it mean to belong to Europe? European civic inclusion, beyond or besides legal citizenship, is not, as Islamists insist, based on Christian belief. In its first stage as an *"Abendland"* Europe was defined by Christianity. Today, it is secular. Historically, the identity of Europe changed with the Renaissance, and even more since the French Revolution. In principle, modern Europe is today no longer defined by Christianity but rather by Western and secular values. The historian and sociologist Leslie Lipson defines the issue aptly in this manner, that with the emergence of the Renaissance,

> The main source of Europe's inspiration shifted from Christianity back to Greece, from Jerusalem to Athens. Socrates, not Jesus, has been the mentor of the civilization that in modern times has influenced or dominated most of the planet.[7]

It is important to note that during the Middle Ages Muslims adopted Hellenism, and they were the ones who passed it later on to Europe. Therefore we must ask why Europe and Islam at present are not able to establish commonalities, as they did before. In light of the fact of global migration, the world of Islam and Europe are being brought together. In fact, Islamic migration is changing the identity of Europe and of Islam as well, but both parties suppress a debate on this change.

To be sure, I do not view all ethnicities as constructed. However, in the present case of two strange bedfellows in Europe, ethnicity matters as one constructed identity posed against another equally constructed identity. The possibilities available to both "actors" are ignored. In the present study, the concept of ethnicity discussed in the context of Europe of the twenty-first century is set opposite the concept of the nation viewed in civic terms. There are subnational local ethnic groups within the European nations, as is the case with the Basques in Spain. In the present age of global migration further ethnic identities are added. The focus of this study, however, is on the two strange bedfellows, Europeans and Muslim immigrants, and addresses the question of whether they could be accommodated in the non-ethnic French model of a nation based on *citoyenneté*. It is a fact that all European modern nations are based on citizenship or *citoyenneté* in the Anglo-Saxon or French meaning. The German and Spanish concepts are ethnic but not religious; all are secular.

Europe's Muslim immigrants also for their part believe that they have overcome the constraints of ethnicity, but their community is based on the religious *umma*, the world community of Islam, that is, not on the secular, as in the European model of nation. In this understanding, the encounter of Muslims and Europeans is not related to the nation-state but rather to a simultaneity of the unsimultaneous. Neither the European Union nor the European Muslim Diaspora is a nation-state. The encounter takes place under conditions of global migration that brings both parties together on a continent of civil societies attempting to formulate a postnational union. Both parties are compelled to engage in a search for solutions.

The third concept to be introduced, next to ethnicity and the nation, is the concept of pluralism of religions and cultures. Such a notion of pluralism helps to facilitate combining diversity with an idea of a consensus of shared civic rules and values. European and Muslim immigrants need to engage in such a venture to overcome the exclusivism of "ethnicity," which is its meaning as employed by the involved communities themselves. They construct fault lines between "we" and "they" resulting in the ethnic conflict taking place at present in Europe. This essay proposes pluralism of religions and cultures as the solution for the pending ethnic conflict.

It has been stated that ethnicity is alien to the universalist and inclusive religious doctrine of Islam. That is, however, the model. In reality, ethnicity exists not only today, but also it existed in medieval Islam. The relation between ethnicity, conflict, and war[8] within the Islamic *umma* and in its relations with the outside world is an essential part of Islamic history. The historical records indicate that ethnicity was a well-known phenomenon in Islam, and it contradicted the religious doctrine in Islam. The scripture of Islam reflects an ideal which is firmly opposed to creating exclusive ethnicities, and it shares in this the same foundational principle at the core of the modern idea of a civic nation in Europe.

### Ethnicization in Europe: A Working Hypothesis

Today, the ethnic divides within Islam are being introduced into Europe. In its history the Islamic world has never achieved its ideal of one *umma* community; it has suffered from ethnic subdivisions. Europeans, however, have no reason to be self-congratulatory; they too are supporting the creation of ethnic communities and states. Thus in both the host and immigrant societies, realities indicate a corruption of inclusive ideals. In particular, the ideology of Islamist internationalism represented by political Islam denies its own inner tensions. The Islamist opposition to integration contributes to European fears and in turn promotes the construction of a "European ethnicity." From this we arrive at a working hypothesis for this essay: in today's Europe there are two constructed ethnicities reinforcing one another; one is Islamic, the other is European.

For the purposes of this argument we should highlight the civic premise of the nation-state as the clear and modern alternative to ethnic community. Scholars acknowledge the ethnic origins of their nations, which are supposed to have been overcome in a civic nation in Europe.[9] This narrative of nationhood, however, is belied by today's reality. There is also in today's ethnicized Europe a parallel ethnicization of the Islamic *umma*. Of course, there are European nations like those of Germany and Spain, where ethnicity is still avowed, not renounced as in the French and British model. Nevertheless, in official pronouncements, Europe accepts more or less the French model. In reality, however, ethnicity prevails. In my life in Europe as a Muslim from West Asia, who spent forty-five years in Germany, I experienced that even professed civic Europeans behave towards the new immigrants in an ethnic-exclusivist manner. Blame games are not a promising avenue, and this has never been my style. It is better to engage in an inquiry that squarely addresses the issue and aims to illuminate the underlying constraints. Only on these grounds could one propose a solution. It has to be based on a combination of the civic idea of Europe with an enlightened and reformed Islam. The concept of Euro-Islam claims to deliver this solution, but it cannot be discussed in this essay due to a lack of space. The focus here is the ethnicization process.

One must begin by understanding the self-ethnicization of Muslims in Europe. This cannot be explained merely by a reference to the belief in Islamic doctrine. At issue is also a Muslim-ethnic response to the equally ethnicizing host societies. The response is, in this sense, a process of cultural self-defense. In the two cases, ethnic identity is constructed, and this leads to conflict. One is persistently reminded of the need for the study of ethnicity in this context. From this perspective, immigrants constitute in Europe newly created ethnic communities with their own culture in parallel societies. If their alienated condition continues and intensifies, then conflict could lead potentially to disunite the project of the new Europe.

The hypothesis of ethnicizing Muslims in Europe is combined with a reference to the already addressed parallel process in which Europeans are betraying their own civic ideals. These ideals are rooted in European history in a model identified by the late Reinhard Bendix as a process of transformation "from kings to people." This is also the transformation from an "ethnic community" to a modern "nation" as a model on which the common European understanding of the civic nation rests.[10] The ethnic self-perception of the German nation of being a distinct "*Kulturgemeinschaft*," or the even worse "*Volksgemeinschaft*," stands in contrast to the French notion of a nation based on *citoyenneté*. It is also racist and exclusivist, because it supposes that the others have no "*Kultur*." There is also the implied contrast between collectivity and individualism. The German notion is utterly exclusive, and its *"Gemeinschaft"* resembles a big ethnic tribe based on a collective identity, in contrast to the "nation" that consists of *"citoyens"* as individuals. The exclusive design and the supremacist attitudes of a collectivity named *"Gemeinschaft"* or *"Volk"* could never integrate the Muslim newcomers. The ethnic German and Spanish cases are not consonant with a civic nation based on *citoyenneté* or citizenship.

To be sure, even though the French model is more positive, it is not fully reflected in reality. Despite all odds, the British and French models are more promising than the ethnic German notion of a *"Staatsvolk"* that fails to include immigrants as *citoyens* or citizens. However, French and British claims are belied by the realities on the ground. Underlying this statement is the empirical fact that even French- or British-born Muslims are not yet accepted as members of society and polity.[11] The turmoils in the United Kingdom and upheavals in France's *banlieues* herald a counter-ethnicity directed at the existing ethnicity.

The assumption of mutually reinforced ethnicities in a perilous process of an overall ethnicization of Islam and Europe acknowledges that this emerging reality runs counter to the idea of civic "nations" and also to the concept of a universal *umma*. We must beware of the trap of an essentializing ethnicity, and therefore I am inclined to follow Davydd Greenwood in his challenge to the traditional "wisdoms." In his case study on "ethnic persistence or resurgence of Spain," Greenwood does not essentialize ethnicity, but he instead relates ethnic identity politics to political economy. Greenwood is aware of the fact that the "reformulation of the traditional demands of the poor" are translated "into an ethno-regional idiom."[12] In the case of the unfolding of "Basque ethnicity as a historical process," "cultural identities" are constructed and associated with economic demands. One has to add that this happens by conviction in an ethnic primordiality, and it is not instrumentally done. The conclusion Greenwood draws is that "the complexity of multi-layered and dynamic cultural identities"[13] underpins the ethnicization fully incorporated into social and economic issues, and then leads to an "ethnic conflict."[14]

The argument that Basque ethnicity clashes with Spanish ethnicity points not merely to economic conflict. Parallel processes are taking place in the Islamic Diaspora in Western Europe,[15] and similarly they cannot be convincingly explained merely by a reference to social exclusion. Of course, there is a difference: Muslims in Europe are newcomers, not ethnic locals. They are becoming ethnicized not only due to their social exclusion and marginalization but also in this context due to an identity politics[16] based on a religious-ethnic indoctrination. I do not dispute the fact that third-generation Muslims are becoming more locally integrated, but they continue to constitute an Islamic diaspora with the related ethnic-religious identity politics. In some parts of Berlin—as in other German cities—Turks form a kind of rural Anatolia, even though they physically live in Western Europe. Intellectually and emotionally, they think and behave as if they were in Anatolia (for example, "honor murder"). Europe's Muslim communities even persist in imposing such alienated thinking on their youngest generation.

For analyzing these issues while employing the concept of ethnicity I refer to the work of a cross-cultural group of scholars who engaged in the study of the Muslim Diaspora and the emergence of a related radicalization in the West. In this cross-cultural project chaired by two Muslim immigrant scholars teaching in Australia, the Iranian-born Shahram Akbarzadeh[17] and the Tunisian-born Fethi Mansouri, a research project was conducted that is summarized in their introductory chapter to the edited volume in this manner: "The emergence of the Muslim question in the West has added a worrying dimension: . . . The changing nature of Islamism . . . [and its] far-reaching implications . . . for the Muslim diaspora."[18] Akbarzadeh and Mansouri add,

> Muslim migration to Europe . . . diluted the binary divide between Islam and the West. The classical division of the world between the land of Islam (*dar al-Islam*) and the land of the disbelief (*dar al-harb*) has become irrelevant as Muslims have made the West their home. By the same token, social discontent among Muslim youth in the diaspora due to racial, socio-economic and/or religious discrimination has made them vulnerable to neo-Islamist propositions.[19]

Muslims living in Europe act in this context and, as Akbarzadeh and Mansouri argue, "navigate between connections and emotional attachment to the country of residence . . . such navigation may prove hazardous . . . Neo-Islamism, therefore may find a receptive audience among alienated Muslims who feel marginalized and excluded from society."[20]

These findings support my hypothesis of an identity politics taking place within the Islamic Diaspora, reacting to a parallel and mutually reinforcing process in Europe. To be sure, and to avoid any misunderstanding, the argument for deethnicization is not an argument against the nation-state. I continue to take the civic foundations of the nation at face value. The scenario described here of an "ethnicity of fear" is based on an analysis of the escalating process of ethnicization. It is not related to questioning the value or efficacy of the nation but rather to the fact that Europe is currently not delivering on the promise of its model of a civic community.

### Islam, Tribes, Ethnicity, and the Nation

The reader is reminded of the major concept in Islam of a universal *umma*, which runs in principle counter to any ethnic community. Therefore, Islam was since its birth in conflict and at war with the then existing tribes, and it preached against their local identity[21] in favor of an Islamic universal identity pattern. The respected British scholar of Islam, W. M. Watt, contends, however, that Islam never reached its goal of fully overcoming ethnicity and overcoming the existing tribal divisions. In short, Watt believes Islam did not deliver what its doctrine had promised. Watt therefore describes in his work the *umma* either as a "federation of tribes" or even as "super-tribes."[22] This contention applies only to the inner tribal structure of the Islamic *umma*, which was in its origin an Arabic one. In the course of the Islamic expansion this *umma* was enhanced and encompassed non-Arabs, who were not integrated. In its worldview the *umma* was and still is designed to map the entire globe and include the whole of humanity. The Prophet provisioned, "*La farqa bain Arabi wa ajami illa bi al-taqwa*" [There is no difference between an Arab and a non-Arab except in piety]. However, the realities of early Islam do not reflect a corresponding pattern, which would be in line with this laudable mind-set. The divides have always characterized the *umma* (see note 8). It is a fact that these persisted throughout Islamic history. I remind the reader that in the doctrine of Islam *umma* resembles the civic nation of Europe, in that it is a model and not a reflection of reality.

In the history of Islam one encounters first the tensions between Arab tribes. Then it is followed by the conflict with non-ethnic Arabs who were Muslims, like Persians, but were despised as *mawalis* [non-Arab Muslims].

The term "*shu'ubiyya*" [ethnicity] was coined to qualify non-Arab Muslims always as "the other," even though they were supposed to be part and parcel of the imagined inclusive *umma*. Even among Arabs, the tribes prevailed. The "connect" between Arab tribes and the *umma* was always a weak one in comparison to the loyalty of Muslims to their own tribal community. The distinguished German orientalist Joseph van Ess states that after the death of the Prophet each Arab tribe had its own mosque.[23] No one was willing to pray behind an Imam in the collective Friday prayer who was not a Shykh of one's own tribe. This historical record is pertinent to the present and to the theme of this study, that is, Islam in the European diaspora. Go today to Berlin and you shall see Arab, Turkish, Pakistani, Bosnian, Iranian/Shia mosques where the faithful behave in this manner and thus maintain this exclusive tradition. This behavior is not consistent with Islamic tenets, because Islam is *not* derived from a patrilineal system. I refer to Islamic history and to religious doctrine to help us better understand the mechanism of ethnicization of Europe's Islamic community. The creation of divisions with quasi-tribal functions among Europe's Muslims also alienates them from the society that shelters them. This alienation imbues a sense of ethnic difference that relies on a fear of the other. It is most unfortunate that Jews serve in this process as a scapegoat. This explains the spread of anti-Semitism within the diaspora of Islam in Europe, combined with an anti-Americanism.

In early Islam, the three major people of Islamic history who constituted the *umma* were the Arabs, Iranians, and Turks. The order of Islam, the caliphate, was always Sunni and excluded Shi'i Muslims. This order was first Arab and then Ottoman-Turkish. After the abolition of the caliphate in 1924 a new pattern was introduced for Arabs, based on the model of the European nation. It is not the place here to study how nations and nationalisms emerged on the wrecks of the dissolution of the classical Muslim order of the caliphate. Some notes have to suffice. Basically the *umma* of the Ottoman Empire consisted of Arabs and Turks; it was replaced by the secular nation in the European sense represented by the emergence of a pan-Arab nationalism[24] and, in contrast to it, Turkish nationalism. Arab nationalism claims that all Arabs create one nation, and it dissociates Arabs from Turks and also from all other non-Arab Muslims (such as Iranians). The latter were not part of the dissolved Ottoman Empire. This pan-Arab nationalism prevailed until the 1967 Six Days' War. The Arab defeat in this war smoothed the way for political Islam, which is today also seen in the diaspora. This historical overview demonstrates that—beyond Europe—there is no one *umma*. It is subdivided into classical tribes, ethnic and sectarian communities, and into modern, only nominal, nations.

## Ethnicity, Diversity, and Pluralism

After having presented some major foundations, I return in this section to the core issue of the present study, that is, ethnicity in Europe. The remedy proposed is the pluralism of cultures and religions. Even though I cannot elaborate here, as already stated, on the concept of pluralist Euro-Islam, I cannot put aside "pluralism" altogether. The theory of democracy is based on diversity in a system of parties with different political orientations. Democratic pluralism acknowledges this diversity, but—aside from some postmodern views—it does not admit a contestation of values and rules of the political culture itself on which pluralist democracy rests. There is a core of civic values supposed to be shared by all parties involved, regardless of their diversity. In contrast, ethnicity is mostly based on the fault lines between communities defined in terms of "we" and "they." This meaning precludes combining the two concepts of ethnicity and pluralism into a notion of "ethnic pluralism."[25]

Is a pluralism of cultures and religions thinkable and feasible? This question is most pertinent to the debate on diversity in an age of global migration. In view of the exclusivist character of "ethnicity" and the perils it implies, above all cruelty, the proposed religious and cultural pluralism promises to lead out of this dead end. There are competing scenarios discussed in this study, either a cultural pluralism or a fragmentation that results in an ethnicity of fear. There seems to be no middle way between the two alternatives. With a commitment to pluralism, Europeans need to deliver what their civic model promises, and European Muslims must de-ethnicize Islam towards a shared goal of Europeanization.[26]

At issue is the introduction of pluralism as a framework for accommodating diversity. This concept contradicts cultural relativist multiculturalism. I share the criticism of Jacob Levy that multiculturalists overlook the "dangers of violence, cruelty and political humiliation."[27] These ugly features often accompany "ethnic politics" intertwined with "ethnic conflict." Young

Muslims targeting Jews, be it in Berlin or Paris, do not act on economic premises; they act on faith. The assaults are ethnically motivated.

In contrast to the real—basically ethnic—polarizing forces, I argue here for a vision of a Euro-Islam based on the acceptance of a religious pluralism. Democratization is the most viable option as an alternative to the ethnicization of Islam in Europe and its neighborhood.[28] In today's Europe, ethnically based strife seems facilitated by what has been described as a "multiculturalism of fear" (see reference in note 27.) In this essay I extend this to explain an analogous "ethnicity of fear." This scenario has already materialized in Iraq. I dare to state that what happened in Kosovo during the Balkan War and in Iraq since 2003 could—in a long-term perspective—also take place within Europe as well. There seem to be few in Europe, however, who are willing to admit to the threat in such comparative terms. The Balkans scenario of an ethnicity of fear has materialized on both sides, and it matters to Western Europe. What happened first in Bosnia, where Serbs butchered Muslim Bosnians, could be repeated elsewhere. The genocide was stopped only by the humanitarian intervention of the international community. In Kosovo Muslim Albanians took revenge on the Serbs and ousted most of them most violently from their homes in Kosovo, the cultural core of Serbia. Also in this case, these cruelties happened on an ethnic-religious basis in a behavior directed by hatred combined with a fear of the other. Therefore, Bosnia and Kosovo are cases of the ethnicity of fear, and they serve as a warning for Western Europeans. Indeed, if this alert is to be taken seriously, then the cruelties in the *banlieues* of Paris in 2005, and revived in 2007, ought not to be forgotten. This frightening scenario for Western Europe looms over Europe's future. It is in the common Muslim and European interest to openly discuss this issue, the phenomenon of the ethnicity of fear, and a common understanding of a pluralist solution.

Unlike Muslims of southeastern Europe, who are native-born Europeans, the Islamic Diaspora in Western Europe originates from a global migration. People of different cultures and religions emigrate and are compelled to live with their differences among their closest immigrant neighbors and within their host community. Those who embrace diversity under these conditions must recognize the conditions for a stable and peaceful society. Under these conditions, multiculturalism does not avert but rather encourages the ethnicization that is already taking place.

I acknowledge the importance of recognizing difference and diversity, but do so only while insisting on the general acceptance of a pluralism of cultures and religions based on shared civic values. The ethnicization of Islam in Europe is in conflict with this kind of civic Euro-Islamic pluralism proposed for Europe in the twenty-first century. The need for a peace strategy for twenty-first century Europe in a "global migration crisis"[29] compels us to consider two options: one is based on a cultural relativist multiculturalism in which ethnic groups are intrinsically in conflict with one another. The other is a cultural-religious pluralism based on a consensus. The vision of a non-ethnic Europeanized Islam that could become part of Europe aims to avert conflict and to dispel the misgivings of a disunited Europe.[30]

## Literary Reflections of Europe's Muslim Immigrants

Along with analyzing ideology and social-political difference from above, one must also seek ways to reveal the contemporary experience from below. This is best done with a sensitive reading of popular literature. In this section, I refer to two novels written by Muslim authors with immigrant backgrounds. The first is the British-Pakistani novelist Mohsin Hamid, whose father obtained a Stanford Ph.D. and who himself was educated at Princeton. Hamid complains about his fate in Europe thusly: "I am a British citizen, yet they [Europeans] refer to me as Pakistani novelist."[31] As a Muslim immigrant myself, I share with Hamid a similar experience: after an active life of forty-five years in Germany (I lived only eighteen years in my birthplace, Damascus) that includes a scholarly contribution of twenty-six books written in German to enrich the culture of that country, I am still viewed as a Syrian holding a German passport.

The other novelist is the Iraqi-German novelist al-Mozany.[32] He, too, voices similar complaints. The two novels and their concerns serve as a literary illustration of the issues dealt with in the present study. The two European-Muslim novelists Hamid and al-Mozany represent authentic Muslim voices in Europe. The novel *Mansur oder der Duft des Abendlandes* [Mansur or the fragrance of Europe] by the Muslim-Iraqi immigrant Hussain al-Mozany illustrates the themes of ethnicity and pluralism. It includes a most telling story not only highly pertinent to an inquiry into how Muslim immigrants come and how they live in Europe but also touching on the questions of this study. At issue is the increasing significance of Islam to Europe—be it as a faith or an ideology of Islamism. Al-Mozany's novel, based on his autobiographical story of life in Germany, illustrates this issue from the point of view of individuals caught in the inherent tensions. From the perspective of examining ethnic-constructed identity, al-Mozany puts Europeans and Muslim immigrants in unavoidable and deepening tension. Each fails to come to terms with the other, and their conflicts are notably intractable.

The novel's Iraqi-born hero, Mansur, manages to get to Germany to seek asylum and is hoping to make for himself a better life in the new land. However, he ends up in a ghetto-diaspora, not in the society he was seeking to join. The novel compellingly depicts the immigrant's perspective of German society as well as his Arab Muslim neighbors with whom he finds little in common. The author al-Mozany himself lived the essence of this story, and eventually has become a German citizen, a columnist, a successful novelist, and frequent contributor to multiple newspapers.

Despite all of these accomplishments, he is no more than a token Iraqi—like the author—not accepted as a German. To be sure, a German qualifies only by ethnicity; this is a primordial quality not to be obtained by an act of legal naturalization. No immigrant could ever achieve this goal in an ethnic-exclusive society. Therefore, there can be no integration on these grounds, as represented in the novel. Both the author and his novel's main protagonist fail to win acceptance as a member of the society that is obliged by law to host asylum-seekers, and which, nevertheless, does not welcome them. The German case is but one example in today's Europe. The French should not be self-congratulatory. Another contributor to this volume, Alec Hargreaves (see note 11), reveals duplicity and setbacks in contemporary France. The problem in the French case, as for much of Europe, is not inherent in the idea of "*laïcité*" or separation of state and religion in and of itself, but rather that this model, without active and common support, provokes a kind of social retreat from all sides. The ethnic-exclusive character of most European societies that claim to be otherwise hinders giving Muslim immigrants a shared European civic identity. Would it in Europe be possible to establish membership in a polity and society on truly color-, religion-, and ethnicity-blind citizenship? European claims of civic membership are hollow in the face of the reality revealed in such immigrant narratives.

The hero of al-Mozany's novel has no German name, and this is sufficient grounds for leaving him isolated. Mansur had the illusion that his light skin would help him to be viewed as a German. He ends up disillusioned; he learns that an ethnic immigrant can never become a German or a European in a society which never fully overcomes its ethnic nationalism. In the ghetto he lives as an alien among those alienated; his neighborhood is a community only in that all share a distrust of anyone they meet. Even though the protagonist comes to Germany as a persecuted Arab Muslim, he does not internalize the status ascribed to him in his new land as an ethnic Iraqi. He is continually reluctant to share the concerns of similarly persecuted non-Iraqi Arabs. To be sure, in Iraq there are Iraqi Sunnis and Shi'is who view their particular community as ethnically exclusive and who hardly share the constructed Iraqi nationality. Mansur's identity is constructed along these lines, and he is stranded in a society that claims to be European but essentially resembles the premodern society that he fled.

The theater of al-Mozany's novel is Germany, where Muslims live under the poor conditions of a fractured diaspora. The situation of exile reinforces the views of Mansur, and he increasingly deeply despises others who share his fate, including the many Syrians and other non-Iraqi Muslim Arabs around him. These peoples are ethnically distinct—at least this is the way they perceive themselves—and they discriminate against one another at times more viciously than happens in the host community. In short, they fail to deal properly with cultural diversity on all counts. An Iraqi is a Sunni or Shi'i in Baghdad, an Arab outside of the country, and a Muslim in the West. There are various levels of ethnic identification which become enacted as part of the process of exclusion. Could a pattern of ethnic-religious pluralism be the light at the end of this extremely dark tunnel of mutually reinforcing ethnic difference?

What do we learn from the novel reviewed here? European states operate according to laws of asylum and at times open their borders to millions of Muslims, but they do so against the will of their societies. This situation can only be changed if Europeans and Muslims (among the other ethnic non-European immigrants) are willing to change and to agree to common principles of citizenship and social cohesion.

## A Proposed Solution

In previous publications I have developed my views on the place of culture in tensions plaguing the European Muslim Diaspora. I have noted that different values and worldviews, if not accommodated, could generate tensions and lead to intractable conflicts.[33]

There are two distinct scenarios for an effective response to Europe's syndrome of an "ethnicity of fear." The first scenario develops from any politicization of the existing ethnic divides, and it leads to bloodletting.[34] What happened in Indonesia in 1965–66 and what is currently transpiring in Iraq could be repeated anywhere in the world: Europe, to be sure, is not immune nor has European Union legislation erected an effective defense. The above-mentioned Intifada of young, socially marginalized Muslims in the suburbs of Paris named *"banlieues de l'Islam"* of 2005 (and continued in 2007) should be read as such a warning sign. There is, however, little evidence that the signs have been properly read and the alert heeded. The upheaval was not only rooted in a social alienation but is compounded by politicized religion within immigrant communities.

The second scenario should be conceptualized as a common Euro-Islamic project. The aim must be a cooperative effort to instill political culture of religious and cultural pluralism. In a study completed at Cornell University I proposed that the communities involved establish their diversity on a shared core of common civic values within the framework of "Euro-Islamic Religious Pluralism for Europe."[35] Such a notion of pluralism is rooted in political diversity within a parliamentarian system of democracy, and is supported by an agreement on principles for the civil society. In the realm of politics, parties of the left, right, and center are expected to accept a negotiated political difference, not a religious or social one. There is a right to diversity, but not to one's own rules and versions of social facts. This gives rise to the pivotal question whether one could apply this notion of political pluralism to culture and ethnicity. Is it possible to view diverse cultural, ethnic, and religious communities living in one society as if they were political parties interacting with one another? The notion of a pluralism of cultures and religions suggests the feasibility of this model.

Muslim immigrants in Europe constitute a largely disenfranchised ethnic-social underclass. Europeans have proven reluctant to admit this in everyday as well as political and intellectual discussion. Unfortunately, Muslims compensate by reviving an inherited supremacist ideology. Muslims in Europe adopt this thinking and claim to be superior to "morally decadent" Europeans. When leaders of the Muslim Diaspora classify their host society as "morally decadent European/one of the unbelievers," they underline their unwillingness to integrate. There are Muslim preachers who use Friday sermons to incite this hatred (see note 3.) This form of Islamic supremacist preaching can be witnessed in some of the major mosques of Western Europe.

The global return of the sacred reaches Europe via the Islamic Diaspora. This is documented in *The Economist*'s special issue on religion. *The Economist* states in that issue, ironically, that "The White House (under George W. Bush) might be going to hell . . . , but Europe faces a worse nightmare: a continued descent into Godlessness, and then a takeover by Islam."[36] This sarcasm reflects how Muslims view Europe, and its future. The phenomenon of supremacist ideology is magnified by the rapid growth of the diaspora. In 1950 there were only eight hundred thousand Muslim immigrants in Western Europe. Today, the number is skyrocketing and currently exceeds twenty million. Add to this the twelve million Muslims of southeastern Europe, and projections point to a milestone around the year 2035 when the Muslim Diaspora in Europe is expected to reach fifty million.

Looking more closely at these numbers, the Muslim community in Europe is composed of diverse and at times rival subgroups (Turks, Arabs, Pakistanis, and so on). In Germany, the basic majority of the Muslim immigrants are Turks, but nearly one and a half million out of the four million total Muslims have a different origin. In France, since the Algerian war of independence most Muslims have been Maghrebi Arabs; and in the United Kingdom, since the era of decolonization, most Muslims have had family origins in South Asia. The recent wave of global migration has begun to rapidly change these traditions and has increasingly diversified each European Muslim community. As they become internally more diverse, Europe's twenty million Muslims live in neighborhoods that resist or are excluded from integrating into their nearest urban centers. Headlines have made well known the phenomenon of the Paris *banlieues*; in Germany, there are the analogous districts of Kreuzberg and Neukölln around Berlin, as well as smaller areas in Cologne and Hamburg. In these districts, Turks share the assumed Muslim space with Arabs (mostly Palestinian), and also with Kurds.

This leads to an array of subethnic tensions in which neighborhoods tend toward implosion. In Berlin in October and November 2007, Kurds, Turks, and Arabs waged violent attacks against one another in the streets of Neu-kölln. In the United Kingdom, South Asian neighborhoods have come to be labeled the foreign-sounding name of Londonistan.[37] Despite, or rather as a result of the violence within their neighborhoods, many European Muslims including the newest immigrants have been seduced by calls for a radical-ized version of an *umma* community of self-defense. The Islamic "we" that heralds a collective Islamic identity is increasingly and notably based in op-position to the European "they."

Because Muslim immigrants find little avenue for a European identity, some are compelled to view Europe as *dar al-Shahada*, as described by the Islamist Tariq Ramadan.[38] Such an ideological view reveals a reading of Eu-rope as an extension of *Dar al-Islam* [House of Islam], in other words, an extended area of the territoriality of Islamic civilization. This position lends support to what some characterize as "Islamic imperialism." It follows that the problem is not exclusively created by the majority European society: it is also a Muslim failing. Speaking personally, even though I find difficulty even today to be accepted as a German citizen beyond the legal status guaranteed by my German passport, I refuse to draw such unwarranted conclusions. There must be a Muslim response to ethnic exclusion other than to assert a morally superior, exclusive, and separate status.

One of the obstacles against cultural pluralism is the propaganda war cur-rently waged by some leaders of the European Islamic Diaspora. Islamists speak of a holocaust against Muslims and confuse discrimination with geno-cide. The allegation of a Muslim holocaust is a pure defamation. Their false comparison associates them with the worst of those who would deny the Holocaust. Their campaigning not only does great harm to the Islamic Diaspora in Europe but also makes European Jews apprehensive of the ex-pansion of the Islamic and Islamist community in Europe. In the 2004 Jew-ish World Congress held in Basel the issue of Islam in Europe took center stage. The fight against genocide and "ethnicity of fear" must be articulated with a grammar of humanism. It should not be instrumentalized for the gain of one community over another.

My argument is that the concept of Euro-Islam provides a vision of a Eu-ropeanized Islam as grounds for inclusion in the pursuit of a deethnicization of the Islamic Diaspora in Europe.[39] To make this happen, social inclusion has to be combined with establishing a variety of Islam compatible with an ethnicity-blind secular concept of Europe. On paper the civilizational identity of Europe is based on religion-blind citizenship, but as shown in this study, the realities in Europe do not fulfill this promise. Therefore, the requirements for a European Islam are not merely the business of Muslim immigrants but create also a challenge to Europeans as well. They, too, need to engage in a deethnicization of their identity to contribute to integration, and to support the same process among Muslims. This is not happening in Germany. Politicians do exactly the opposite of what is needed on both fronts: they promote German ethnicity (such as the *deutsche Leitkultur* [German dominant culture] of the Christian Democratic Union) and demand a united religion among Muslims, believing both will contribute to integration in society. The result is precisely the contrary.

To date one can continue to speak of the unsuccessful politics of integration in Europe. As an immigrant I fail to see any light at the end of the tunnel.[40] As shown above, the difference between the opposite extremes of multiculturalism and pluralism lies in dealing with diversity. A sharing of core values by Europeans and Muslim immigrants associated with a social and economic integration at the workplace (no migration into the welfare system) would be a positive response to the challenge. It could also contribute to creating for Muslim immigrants what one may call European citizens of the heart. It is in this context that I have developed elsewhere the concept of "Euro-Islam" that combines difference with commonality. Of course, it is important to note that this concept is not only rejected by Salafist leaders of the bulk of the Muslim community who are mostly Islamists, but also rebuffed by European multiculturalists, who disagree when limits are set to cultural difference.

Not all Islamist Imams who act in many mosques and faith schools (see note 3) in the European diaspora speak with candor, nor do they spell out their thinking in public, simply for tactical reasons. The positive Islamist reference to multiculturalism of "anything goes" is purely instrumental. There is every indication that Islamists are neoabsolutists who despise cultural relativism but nevertheless make full use of it in "battlefront Europe." There is an equal need to deter both Islamophobia and Islamism. I believe that a Euro-Islamic integration inspired by an inclusive approach limited to civic values and to the workplace promises to be the foundation for the best policy. Euro-Islam (see note 39) is compatible with democracy, because it rests on the basis of a reformist view of this religion, and presents in Europe a solution for Islam's predicament with cultural modernity. A Muslim contribution to a deethnicizing of the belonging to Islamic faith could amount to an embrace of cultural modernity.

## Conclusion

Democracy, individual human rights, pluralism, civil society, and the enlightenment culture of tolerance are the universal core values of cultural modernity,[41] but are no longer European in their validity. Today, a pluralism of religions could rest on these values that can be embraced by Muslim immigrants for becoming Europeans. This is the meaning of the notion "citizens of the heart" in a citizenry, which is not an ethnic community. There is "an intercivilizational conflict," but no essentialized "clash." A conflict can be resolved peacefully; a clash cannot. All cultures can change, and hence the notion of "developing cultures" also applies to Islam.[42]

With these perspectives the present study has dealt with Islam and ethnicity in Europe, while discerning a "multiculturalism of fear" that results from ethnic conflict. This formula is enhanced to an ethnicity of fear employed in the present inquiry. It is viewed as an alert. The study also addresses an inherent ethnic awareness of Europe cultivated by Western Europeans themselves. With some exceptions (Germany and Spain), most Western European societies claim an ethnicity-blind citizenship. The Intifada of 2005 in Paris was not without precipitating factors. It had its undercurrents in the suppression of dialogue as discussed by Alec Hargreaves elsewhere in this volume (see note 11). It was also spurred by the chain of assaults including the assassination of Theo van Gogh by a jihadist Islamist, the bombings in Madrid and London in 2005, and the conflict related to the outrage over the Danish cartoons of the prophet Muhammad.[43] To dissociate these acts from a notion of global terrorism conjured by the United States military campaigns, I emphasize my approach as expressed at the Club of Madrid to seek a democratic response to violence.[44] European civil society needs to become for European Muslims a non-ethnic shared home that replaces ethnic enclaves or parallel societies based on an imagined *umma*, and also the ethnic-exclusivist bellicose campaign born in the diasporic conditions.

In the present conflict-ridden situation, both parties need to engage in a double-track strategy of dialogue and security. European leaders must distinguish between Islam and Islamism, so that they can effectively strategize and support pro-democracy Muslims who are willing to stand against the Islamists.[45] European Muslims could jointly avert a jihadization and a shari'atization of Islam and promote instead a Euro-Islam in a European-Islamic project. No doubt there has been a positive change in recent years. For instance, Germany's new citizenship law for naturalization of non-ethnic German immigrants that was legislated in 2000 opens access to legal citizenship. However, the new legislation still exists alongside the still valid 1913 citizenship law determining true German descent based on ethnicity and blood lineage.

I conclude with a reference to a major German debate on the issue in 2004. In that year, the *Financial Times Deutschland* published a series of articles on the future of Germany with the title "Deutschland 2014." Twelve articles written by editors of the *Financial Times Deutschland* addressed a variety of themes including the German economy, health system, and primary and university education systems. Each of the articles was based on an interview with an expert on the chosen subject. I was chosen to be interviewed for the article on the subject of "Islam in Germany 2014." In the conversation with the editor, I drew two scenarios: one is positive, based on the integration of Muslim immigrants as citizens in law and of the heart, and the other, less optimistic, and expressed as a warning of the conditions that could lead to social unrest. I had no authority to determine the headline, and the article based on the interview with me was eventually published with the title "Muslim Children Without a Future Shall Take Revenge on Germany."[46] This was a shock even to me, and after the publication I was even accused of seeking to foment panic. It was, however, gratifying to receive dozens of mails, letters, and phone calls from young Muslims born in Germany to express their gratitude to me for having made public what they really feel. A year later, a similar editorializing took place in Paris. In 2005, following the riots in the suburbs of Paris, I was invited to participate in a ZDF-TV debate on this issue and was asked, "Could this happen in Germany?" I answered in the affirmative. With me in the studio was the mayor of the district of Berlin-Neukölln, and he added to my comment, "As long as the German welfare state continues to be generous the situation will continue to be calm." I note, however, that overlooking or denying root causes of the tension and alienation does not tend towards a resolution. The real solution has to be found with those who take responsibility for engaging in learning the origins and process of ethnicizing Europe and to seek common principles for an alternative. In Europe, currently, I find few who are able to freely engage positively in this debate.

The world of Islam is undergoing a radicalization, and that extreme position is entering the European community.[47] In the long term, these ethnicized conflicts could result in an intractable and contagious ethnicity of fear. This essay presents an alternative to develop thinking on a European Islam as a variety of a civic Islam. I end with the experience of a Western observer of the European arena. The former chief of the bureau of the *New York Times* in Berlin, Richard Bernstein, after living for four years in Europe ahead of returning to New York, wrote an editorial article as a farewell under the title "Tuscan Paradise," in which he describes European attitudes based on this "paradise" which is "wealthy, soignée, ecologically correct, [and] distant from vexing problems like Muslim immigration. . . . [In this Europe] crises seem especially distant."[48] It is disappointing to note that the true experience of what happens beyond, and within, the Tuscan orbit seems not to greatly interest observers of Europe. Ethnicity in today's Europe may be discussed at Stanford University and in such collections, but not in Europe's public discourse. Europeans seem to have learned only little from their shameful past, but I also continue to reject the identification of today's Muslims in Europe with the Jewish victims of the European Holocaust.[49] The scenario of an ethnicity of fear does not preclude the repetition of those who would instrumentalize anxiety for supremacist campaigns. It is all the more imperative that we engage proposals for positive integration as discussed in this essay.

NOTES

This study was completed first as a paper presented to the Stanford Conference on Ethnicity in Europe. The present essay has been extensively revised and extended. The final version was completed at the Center for Advanced Holocaust Studies in Washington, D.C., with a Senior Fellowship in Spring 2008. The earlier draft of this research paper was presented at the symposium sponsored at Stanford University by the Forum on Contemporary Europe and the Stanford Humanities Center, on "Ethnicity in Today's Europe" (November 7–8, 2007). I wish to express my gratitude to the chairs of the symposium, John Bender and Amir Eshel, and to Professor Davydd Greenwood at Cornell University for his valuable comments. The comments by Greenwood have helped develop both the seminar paper and the final essay. I am most grateful to Roland Hsu, the editor of this volume, for his guidance and support and for copyediting and abridging the essay. I also thank the Center for Advanced Holocaust Studies in Washington, D.C., for the fellowship.

1. For a contribution to the debate on this contentious issue, see Bassam Tibi, *Islamische Zuwanderung: Die gescheiterte Integration*, esp. chapters 3 and 4. The fate of this book, and its stifled reception, is recounted in George Lawery, "Europe's Failure to Integrate Muslims Called a Recipe for Civil War," *Cornell's Chronicles*, September 28, 2007: 7 ff. The article is based on an interview about my personal experience as an immigrant in Germany.

2. See the contributions to the reader edited by Anthony Smith and John Hutchinson, *Ethnicity*, including a text by Bassam Tibi, "Old Tribes and Imposed Nation-States in the Middle East," 174–179.

3. Hanif Kureishi, "Der Karneval der Kulturen," *Neue Zürcher Zeitung*, August 11, 2005.

4. This is the subject of the research project pursued at the Center for Advanced Holocaust Studies. The project has been published as: Bassam Tibi, "Public Policy and the Combination of Anti-Americanism and Anti-Semitism in Contemporary Islamist Ideology," *The Current* (Cornell University) 12(1) (2008): 123–146.

5. See: Matthias Küntzel, *Jihad and Jew-Hatred: Islamism, Nazism and the Roots of 9/11*; and Bassam Tibi, "Der djihadistische Islamismus, nicht der Islam ist die zentrale Quelle des neuen Antisemitismus," in *Antisemitismus und radikaler Islamismus*, ed. Wolfgang Benz and Juliane Wetzel, 43–69.

6. See: Donald Horowitz, *Ethnic Groups in Conflict*; and Stefan Wolff, *Ethnic Conflict*. In their book *Ethnic Conflict in World Politics*, Ted R. Gurr and Barbara Harff include in chapter 6 the Turkish immigrants in Germany as a subject for the study of ethnic conflict.

7. Leslie Lipson, *The Ethical Crises of Civilizations*, 63.

8. For more historical details see Bassam Tibi, "Krieg und Ethnizität im Islam," in *Krieg im Mittelalter*, ed. Hans-Henning Kortüm, 59–76.

9. Anthony Smith, *The Ethnic Origins of Nations*.

10. The classic on this subject is Reinhard Bendix, *Kings or People: Power and the Mandate to Rule*. On the difference between the ethnic German and the civic French concepts of the nation, see Bassam Tibi, *Arab Nationalism: Between Islam and the Nation-State*, 3rd ed., esp. chapters 6 and 7.

11. On Islam in France see the authoritative study by Alec Hargreaves, *Multi-Ethnic France*. On Islam in the United Kingdom see: Philip Lewis, *Islamic Britain*; and the recent provocative book *Londonistan* by Melanie Phillips.

12. Davydd Greenwood, "Castilians, Basques and Andalusians: True Ethnicity and False Ethnicity," in *Ethnic Groups and the State*, ed. Paul Bross, chapter 6, esp. page 202.

13. Davydd Greenwood, "Cultural Identities and Global Political Economy," *Indiana Journal of Global Legal Studies* 1(1) (Fall 1993): 101–117.

14. Davydd Greenwood, "Continuity and Change: Spanish Basque: Ethnicity as a Historical Process," in *Ethnic Conflict in the Western World*, ed. Milton Esmon, chapter 4, 81–102.

15. The Islamic Diaspora in Europe heralds a peaceful return of Islam to the old world. Muslims, however, are returning as underclass immigrants, not as jihad warriors. The nature of this "return" was the subject of a study at the University of Leiden in a project chaired by W.A.R. Shadid and P. S. van Koningsveld. The project papers were published in two volumes: vol. 1, *Religious Freedom and the Position of Islam in Western Europe*, and vol. 2, *Muslims in the Margin: Political Responses to the Presence of Islam in Western Europe*. Volume 2 includes the following contribution on the relevance of the Indian-Islam model (Muslims as a minority within a dual legal system) for Muslims living in Europe: Bassam Tibi, "Islam, Hinduism and the Limited Secularity in India: A Model for Muslim-European Relations in the Age of Migration?", 130–144.

16. Ted R. Gurr and Barbara Harff, *Ethnic Conflict in World Politics*. See also: Bassam Tibi, *Islamische Zuwanderung: Die gescheiterte Integration*, esp. chapters 3 and 4, on conceptualizing Muslim ghettos as ethnic parallel societies; Francis Fukuyama, "Identity, Immigration and Democracy," *Journal of Democracy* 17(2) (2006): 5–20; and Bassam Tibi, "Islam: Between Religious and Cultural Practice and Identity Politics," in *Conflicts and Tensions*, ed. Y. Raj Isar and Helmut Anheier, 221–231.

17. Shahram Akbarzadeh is the editor of the four-volume reader *Islam and Globalization*.

18. Shahram Akbarzadeh and Fethi Mansouri, eds., *Islam and Political Violence: Muslim Diaspora and Radicalization in the West*, 3.

19. Ibid., 9–10.

20. Ibid., 11.

21. On this tribal-ethnic identity pattern and its conflict with Islamic religious identity see Bassam Tibi, "The Simultaneity of the Unsimultaneous: Old Tribes and Imposed Nation States in the Middle East," in *Tribes and State Formation in the Middle East*, ed. Josef Kostiner and Philip Khoury, 127–152.

22. William Montgomery Watt, *Mohammed at Medina*, 144.

23. Josef van Ess, *Theologie und Gesellschaft im 2. und 3. Jahrhundert Hidschra: Eine Geschichte des religiösen Denkens im frühen Islam*, 6 vols., esp. vols. 1 and 4.

24. Bassam Tibi, *Arab Nationalism: Between Islam and the Nation-State*.

25. In the current practice of ethnic politics, "ethnic pluralism" is a contradiction in terms, because ethnic ideologies are based on an exclusive communitarianism. By contrast, pluralism is a combination of diversity with shared values, and it admits no

communal divide. On the values of pluralism and the unavoidability of conflict see John Kekes, *The Morality of Pluralism*.

26. Bassam Tibi, "Europeanizing Islam or the Islamization of Europe: Democracy vs. Cultural Difference," in *Religion in an Expanding Europe*, ed. Peter Katzenstein and Tim Byrnes, 204–224.

27. Jacob Levy, *The Multiculturalism of Fear*, 12.

28. This is the official foreign policy term of the EU for the Middle East, as discussed in Michael Emerson, ed., *Democratization in the European Neighborhood*, and the chapter by Bassam Tibi, "Islam, Freedom and Democracy," 93–116.

29. Myron Weiner, *The Global Migration Crisis*.

30. I develop this phrase drawing upon the argument in Arthur Schlesinger, *The Disuniting of America: Reflections on a Multicultural Society*.

31. On M. Hamid and his novel *The Reluctant Fundamentalist* see the report by Jane Perlez, "A Sympathetic Muslim Eye on America," *International Herald Tribune*, October 13–14, 2007, 2.

32. Hussain al-Mozany, *Mansur oder der Duft des Abendlandes*.

33. *International Herald Tribune*, August 17, 2007, 6. See also: Bassam Tibi, "Islam: Between Religious and Cultural Practice and Identity Politics," in *Conflicts and Tensions*, ed. Y. Raj Isar and Helmut Anheier, 221–231; and Fred Khuri, *Imams and Emir: State, Religion and Sects in Islam*.

34. *International Herald Tribune*, August 17, 2007, 6. Editorial on slaughtering the minority Yezids in Iraq. For details on the minority of the Yezids see Fred Khuri, *Imams and Emir: State, Religion and Sects in Islam*.

35. Bassam Tibi, "Euro-Islamic Religious Pluralism for Europe: An Alternative to Ethnicity and to Multiculturalism," in *The Current: The Public Policy Journal of the Cornell Institute for Public Affairs* 11(1) (Fall 2007): 89–103. For the development of this argument see Bassam Tibi, "The Pertinence of Islam's Predicament with Democratic Pluralism for the Democratization of Asia," in *Religion-Staat-Gesellschaft* 7(1) (2006): 84–117. See also the research conducted at Asia Research Institute at the National University of Singapore, in Anthony Reid and Michael Gilsenan, eds., *Islamic Legitimacy in a Plural Asia*, esp. Bassam Tibi, "In Pursuit of Democratic Pluralism," 28–52.

36. *The Economist*, November 3–9, 2007, published a cover story with the heading "The New Wars of Religion" that includes an 18-page special report on faith in politics. The report includes sections on Europe.

37. Melanie Phillips, *Londonistan*.

38. Caroline Fourest, *Brother Tariq: The Doublespeak of Tariq Ramadan*: and Paul Berman, "Who's Afraid of Tariq Ramadan? The Islamist, the Journalist, and the Defense of Liberalism," *The New Republic* 4 (June 2007): 37–63. On the sentiments related to the imperial conquests of Islam see Efraim Karsh, *Islamic Imperialism: A History*.

39. The concept of Euro-Islam was first presented in a paper in Paris in 1992,

subsequently published as Bassam Tibi, "Les conditions d'un Euro-Islam," in *Islams d'Europe: Intégration ou Insertion Communautaire*, ed. Robert Bistolfi and Francois Zabbal, 230–234. On the history of the concept with related references see the chapter "Euro-Islam" in Bassam Tibi, *Im Schatten Allahs: Der Islam und die Menschenrechte*, 491–529. Basic treatments of this concept include: Nezar AlSayyad and Manuel Castells, *Muslim Europe or Euro-Islam*, 31–53; and *Time Magazine*, special issue, "Islam in Europe," December 24, 2001, 49.

40. Bassam Tibi, "A Migration Story: From Muslim Immigrants to European Citizens of the Heart," *Fletcher Forum of World Affairs* 31(1) (2007): 147–168; and Tibi, "The Quest of Islamic Migrants and of Turkey to Become European," *Turkish Policy Quarterly* 3(1) (2004): 13–28.

41. Jürgen Habermas, *The Philosophical Discourse of Modernity*.

42. Lawrence Harrison, ed., *Developing Cultures*, 2 vols.

43. On the Madrid bombing and the conflict over the Muhammad cartoons see Bassam Tibi, *Die islamische Herausforderung*.

44. Paper included in Leonard Weinberg, ed., *Democratic Responses to Terrorism*, 41–61.

45. On this distinction between Islam and Islamism see Bassam Tibi, "Between Islam and Islamism," in *Redefining Security in the Middle East*, ed. Tami A. Jacoby and Brent Sasley, 62–82. On Islamism see Bassam Tibi, "The Totalitarianism of Jihadist Islamism and Its Challenge to Europe and to Islam," *Totalitarian Movements and Political Religions* 8(1) (2007): 35–54. On the transnational links and networks of the Islamist movement see: Bassam Tibi, *Political Islam, World Politics and Europe*, part 2 on Islamism, part 3 on Europe.

46. Astrid Maier, "Muslimische 'No Future' Kids werden sich an Deutschland rächen, mit Islamforscher B. Tibi," *Financial Times Deutschland*, August 12, 2004, 10. In December 2007 an investigative study commissioned by the German Ministry of the Interior was published (see the review in *Frankfurter Allgemeine Zeitung*, December 11, 2007, 4) that indicates that half of the young Muslims in the German Islamic Diaspora are susceptible to the appeal of jihadist Islamism. About 12 percent of these young Muslims born in Germany express approval for violence for religious ends. According to this same study, the majority of German Muslims express disapproval of terror but would agree that jihadists will be gratified by Allah for their martyrdom. I was interviewed live on this study by a German radio station but was interrupted before finishing discussion of this issue.

47. Shahram Akbarzadeh and Fethi Mansouri, eds., *Islam and Political Violence: Muslim Diaspora and Radicalization in the West*, esp. Bassam Tibi, "Jihadism and Intercivilizational Conflict: Conflicting Images of the Self and the Other," 39–64; and Marc Sageman, *The Leaderless Jihad*, esp. "Radicalization in the Diaspora," 71–88.

48. Richard Bernstein, "Tuscan Paradise and Beyond," *International Herald Tribune*, July 28, 2006, 2.

49. This comparison is challenged in Bassam Tibi, "Muslims: Foreigners—Today's Jews? Xenophobic Right-Wing Radicalism and the Fundamentalism of the Other," in *The Resurgence of Right-Wing Radicalism in Germany,* ed. Ulrich Wand, 85–102.

WORKS CITED

Akbarzadeh, Shahram, ed. *Islam and Globalization.* 4 vols. New York: Routledge, 2006.

———, and Fethi Mansouri, eds. *Islam and Political Violence: Muslim Diaspora and Radicalization in the West.* London: Tauris, 2007.

AlSayyad, Nezar, and Manuel Castells. *Muslim Europe or Euro-Islam.* Berkeley: Lexington Books and University of California Press, 2002.

Bendix, Reinhard. *Kings or People: Power and the Mandate to Rule.* Berkeley: University of California Press, 1978.

Berman, Paul. "Who's Afraid of Tariq Ramadan? The Islamist, the Journalist, and the Defense of Liberalism." *The New Republic* 4 (June 2007): 37–63.

Bernstein, Richard. "Tuscan Paradise and Beyond." *International Herald Tribune,* July 28, 2006, 2.

"Editorial." *International Herald Tribune,* August 17, 2007, 6.

Emerson, Michael, ed. *Democratization in the European Neighborhood.* Brussels: CEPS, 2005.

Ess, Josef van. *Theologie und Gesellschaft im 2. und 3. Jahrhundert Hidschra: Eine Geschichte des religiösen Denkens im frühen Islam.* 6 vols. Berlin: Walter de Gruyter, 1991–.

Fourest, Caroline. *Brother Tariq: The Doublespeak of Tariq Ramadan.* New York: Encounter Books, 2008.

Fukuyama, Francis. "Identity, Immigration and Democracy." *Journal of Democracy* 17(2) (2006): 5–20.

Greenwood, Davydd. "Castilians, Basques and Andalusians: True Ethnicity and False Ethnicity." In *Ethnic Groups and the State,* ed. Paul Bross, chapter 6. London: Croom Helm, 1985.

———. "Continuity and Change: Spanish Basque. Ethnicity as a Historical Process." In *Ethnic Conflict in the Western World,* ed. Milton Esmon, chapter 4. Ithaca, NY: Cornell University Press, 1977.

———. "Cultural Identities and Global Political Economy." *Indiana Journal of Global Legal Studies,* 1(1) (Fall 1993): 101–117.

Gurr, Ted R., and Barbara Harff. *Ethnic Conflict in World Politics.* Boulder, CO: Westview Press, 1994.

Habermas, Jürgen. *The Philosophical Discourse of Modernity.* Cambridge, MA: MIT Press, 1989.

Hamid, M. *The Reluctant Fundamentalist.* Orlando, FL: Harcourt, 2007.

Hargreaves, Alec. *Multi-Ethnic France.* New York: Routledge, 2007.

Harrison, Lawrence, ed. *Developing Cultures*. 2 vols. New York: Routledge, 2006.

Horowitz, Donald. *Ethnic Groups in Conflict*. Berkeley: University of California Press, 1985.

"Islam in Europe." *Time Magazine*, special issue, December 24, 2001.

Jacoby, Tami A., and Brent Sasley, eds. *Redefining Security in the Middle East*. Manchester: Manchester University Press, 2002.

Karsh, Efraim. *Islamic Imperialism: A History*. New Haven, CT: Yale University Press, 2006.

Kekes, John. *The Morality of Pluralism*. Princeton, NJ: Princeton University Press, 1993.

Khuri, Fred. *Imams and Emir: State, Religion and Sects in Islam*. London: Saqi Books, 1990.

Küntzel, Matthias. *Jihad and Jew-Hatred: Islamism, Nazism and the Roots of 9/11*. New York: Telos, 2007.

Kureishi, Hanif. "Der Karneval der Kulturen." *Neue Zürcher Zeitung*, August 11, 2005.

Lawery, George. "Europe's Failure to Integrate Muslims Called a Recipe for Civil War." *Cornell's Chronicles*, September 28, 2007.

Levy, Jacob. *The Multiculturalism of Fear*. New York: Oxford University Press, 2000.

Lewis, Philip. *Islamic Britain*. London: Tauris, 1994.

Lipson, Leslie. *The Ethical Crises of Civilizations*. London: Sage, 1993.

Maier, Astrid. "Muslimische 'No Future' Kids werden sich an Deutschland rächen, mit Islamforscher B. Tibi." *Financial Times Deutschland*, August 12, 2004, 10.

Mozany, Hussain al-. *Mansur oder der Duft des Abendlandes*. Leipzig: Reclam, 2002.

"The New Wars of Religion." *The Economist*, November 3–9, 2007.

Perlez, Jane. "A Sympathetic Muslim Eye on America." *International Herald Tribune*, October 13–14, 2007, 2.

Phillips, Melanie. *Londonistan*. New York: Encounter Books, 2006.

Reid, Anthony, and Michael Gilsenan, eds. *Islamic Legitimacy in a Plural Asia*. New York: Routledge, 2008.

Sageman, Marc. *The Leaderless Jihad*. Philadelphia: Pennsylvania University Press, 2008.

Schlesinger, Arthur. *The Disuniting of America: Reflections on a Multicultural Society*. New York: W.W. Norton, 1998.

Shadid, W.A.R., and P. S. van Koningsveld. *Volume 1: Religious Freedom and the Position of Islam in Western Europe. Volume 2: Muslims in the Margin: Political Responses to the Presence of Islam in Western Europe*. Kampen, Netherlands: Kok Pharos, 1995 and 1996.

Smith, Anthony. *The Ethnic Origins of Nations*. New York: Basil Blackwell, 1986.

———, and John Hutchinson, eds. *Ethnicity*. Oxford: Oxford University Press, 1996.

Tibi, Bassam. *Arab Nationalism: Between Islam and the Nation-State*. 3rd ed. New York: St. Martin's Press, 1997.

———. "Between Islam and Islamism." In *Redefining Security in the Middle East*, ed. Tami A. Jacoby and Brent Sasley, 62–82. Manchester: Manchester University Press, 2002.

———. "Der djihadistische Islamismus, nicht der Islam ist die zentrale Quelle des neuen Antisemitismus." In *Antisemitismus und radikaler Islamismus*, ed. Wolfgang Benz and Juliane Wetzel, 43–69. Essen: Klartext Verlag, 2007.

———. *Die islamische Herausforderung*. Darmstadt: Primus, 2007.

———. "Euro-Islamic Religious Pluralism for Europe: An Alternative to Ethnicity and to Multiculturalism." *The Current: The Public Policy Journal of the Cornell Institute for Public Affairs* 11(1) (Fall 2007): 89–103.

———. "Europeanzing Islam or the Islamization of Europe: Democracy vs. Cultural Difference." In *Religion in an Expanding Europe*, ed. Peter Katzenstein and Tim Byrnes, 204–224. Cambridge: Cambridge University Press, 2006.

———. *Im Schatten Allahs: Der Islam und die Menschenrechte*. Munich: Ullstein Verlag, 2003.

———. "In Pursuit of Democratic Pluralism," In *Islamic Legitimacy in a Plural Asia*, ed. Anthony Reid and Michael Gilsenan, 28–52. New York: Routledge, 2008.

———. "Islam, Freedom and Democracy." In *Democratization in the European Neighborhood*, ed. Michael Emerson, 93–116. Brussels: CEPS, 2005.

———. "Islam, Hinduism and the Limited Secularity in India: A Model for Muslim-European Relations in the Age of Migration?" In *Muslims in the Margin: Political Responses to the Presence of Islam in Western Europe, Volume 2*, ed. W.A.R. Shadid and P. S. van Koningsveld, 130–144. Kampen, Netherlands: Kok Pharos Publishing House, 1996.

———. "Islam: Between Religious and Cultural Practice and Identity Politics." In *Conflicts and Tensions*, ed. Y. Raj Isar and Helmut Anheier, 221–231. London: Sage, 2007.

———. *Islamische Zuwanderung: Die gescheiterte Integration*. Munich: Deutsche Verlagsanstalt, 2002.

———. "Jihadism and Intercivilizational Conflict: Conflicting Images of the Self and the Other." In *Islam and Political Violence: Muslim Diaspora and Radicalization in the West*, ed. Shahram Akbarzadeh and Fethi Mansouri, 39–64. London: Tauris, 2007.

———. "Krieg und Ethnizität im Islam." In *Krieg im Mittelalter*, ed. Hans-Henning Kortüm, 59–76. Berlin: Akademie Verlag, 2001.

———. "Les conditions d'un Euro-Islam." In *Islams d'Europe: Intégration ou Insertion Communautaire*, ed. Robert Bistolfi and Francois Zabbal, 230–234. Paris: Editions de l'Aube, 1995.

———. "A Migration Story: From Muslim Immigrants to European Citizens of the Heart." *Fletcher Forum of World Affairs* 31(1) (2007): 147–168.

————. "Muslims: Foreigners—Today's Jews? Xenophobic Right-Wing Radicalism and the Fundamentalism of the Other." In *The Resurgence of Right-Wing Radicalism in Germany*, ed. Ulrich Wand, 85–102. New York: Humanities Press, 1993.

————. "Old Tribes and Imposed Nation-States in the Middle East." In *Ethnicity*, ed. Anthony Smith and John Hutchinson, 174–179. Oxford: Oxford University Press, 1996.

————. "The Pertinence of Islam's Predicament with Democratic Pluralism for the Democratization of Asia." *Religion-Staat-Gesellschaft* 7(1) (2006): 84–117.

————. *Political Islam, World Politics and Europe*. New York: Routledge, 2008.

————. "Public Policy and the Combination of Anti-Americanism and Anti-Semitism in Contemporary Islamist Ideology." *The Current* (Cornell University) 12(1) (2008): 123–146.

————. "The Quest of Islamic Migrants and of Turkey to Become European." *Turkish Policy Quarterly* 3(1) (2004): 13–28.

————. "The Simultaneity of the Unsimultaneous: Old Tribes and Imposed Nation States in the Middle East." In *Tribes and State Formation in the Middle East*, ed. Josef Kostiner and Philip Khoury, 127–152. Berkeley: University of California Press, 1990.

————. "The Totalitarianism of Jihadist Islamism and Its Challenge to Europe and to Islam." *Totalitarian Movements and Political Religions* 8(1) (2007): 35–54.

Wand, Ulrich, ed. *The Resurgence of Right-Wing Radicalism in Germany*. New York: Humanities Press, 1993.

Watt, William Montgomery. *Mohammed at Medina*. Oxford: Oxford University Press, 1977.

Weinberg, Leonard, ed. *Democratic Responses to Terrorism*. New York: Routledge, 2008.

Weiner, Myron. *The Global Migration Crisis*. New York: HarperCollins, 1995.

Wolff, Stefan. *Ethnic Conflict*. New York: Oxford University Press, 2006.

# CHAPTER EIGHT

## Germans and Jews in Turkey

*Ethnic Anxiety and Mimicry in the Making of the European Turk*

KADER KONUK

Commenting on international tensions after the war that was supposed to end all wars, Albert Einstein reflected on how Europe now perceived him: "By an application of the theory of relativity to the taste of readers, to-day in Germany I am called a German man of science and in England I am represented as a Swiss Jew. If I come to be regarded as a *bête noire*," he went on, "the descriptions will be reversed, and I shall become a Swiss Jew for the Germans and a German man of science for the English!"[1] With his usual concision Einstein pointed out the interchangeability of Jewish, Swiss, and German affiliations at a time of shifting European relationships and rising anti-Semitism. But the physicist's 1919 statement in the London *Times* would prove sadly prescient, for within two decades he would indeed become a German *bête noire* and be forced to leave Europe, ultimately becoming an American citizen. We can think of Einstein's comment as an aphorism for this essay. Focusing on the shifting status of the transnational scholar, this essay explains how the very scholars that were labeled un-German and degenerate by the Nazis came to be construed as "European men of science" by the Turkish reformers. To go one step further, I suggest here that Turkey's Europeanization necessitated the utilization but simultaneous disavowal of the émigrés' Jewishness.

Émigrés to Turkey in the 1930s who were respected as European scholars said that Turkey was "unscathed by the Western plague"—a country untouched by either fascism or anti-Semitism. This image was promulgated by émigrés like Philipp Schwartz, who had close contact with Turkish officials and negotiated the hiring of émigré scholars through the Notgemeinschaft deutscher Wissenschaftler im Ausland [Aid Organization for German Academics Abroad]. Schwartz told the minister of education, Reşit Galip, that the arrival of Europeans in Turkey would compensate for the shameful expulsion of scholars from Germany.[2] This positive rhetoric has been handed down to us in the present. As a result, many people ranging across the entire confessional and political spectrum now view Turkey as the official savior of some of Germany's exiled scholars. It is estimated that approximately eight hundred German professionals and their families found a haven in Turkey.[3] Most of the scholars, architects, musicians, economists, and scientists were hired by the government to facilitate the Westernization of Turkish culture, specifically the modernization of Turkish universities that was launched in 1933. If we take a critical look at the status of Turkish and German Jews between 1933 and 1945, we find, however, that Turkey as a place of exile was by no means immune to the kinds of bigotry, racism, and anti-Semitism that then benighted Western Europe. Even if the Turkish government did not pursue fascist and expansionist goals, racialist discourse was widespread and public debate about the loyalty of Jewish Turks to the new nation was common currency. By the same token, Turkey did not commit itself to saving Jews from rising anti-Semitism in Europe—not even to saving all Jewish scholars who were willing to continue their work in the interest of its modernization project.

It is perhaps not a surprise that today, at a time when Turkey tries to emphasize its European qualities, anxieties about what it means to be Turkish are coming to the surface. Such anxieties—as exemplified by Article 301 of the Turkish Penal Code which prohibits the act of "insulting the Turkish nation"—inhibit the country's capacity to face its history and critically review the relationship between Muslims and non-Muslims in Ottoman and

Turkish history.[4] International debates focus predominantly on the status of Armenians and the official recognition of the Armenian genocide, which is seen as a potential litmus test for Turkey's entry into the European Union. Against the notion of Turks as perpetrators of the Armenian genocide, however, stands the image of Turks as saviors of Jews during the Holocaust. This image is promulgated by, for example, the recent biography of Behiç Erkin, the Turkish ambassador to France, who is said to have saved thousands of Turkish Jews in France from deportation to concentration camps between 1942 and 1943.[5]

As I argue here, the claims made on behalf of Erkin cannot entirely be supported by material preserved in German archives. Nonetheless, Turkish authorities use the biography of Erkin to stress certain salutary qualities of Turkey; they promote its civilized character over and against Germany's barbaric past and attempt to demonstrate Turkey's Europeanness via its role in helping Jews survive the Holocaust. Above all, however, such narratives paper over Turkish anti-Semitism and the country's past atrocities against Greeks, Armenians, and Kurds. My contention is also that these one-sided stories celebrating Turks as saviors of Jews from the Holocaust tend to obscure the insecure status of Jews within Turkish society. Contrary to these official narratives about the history of German Jewish emigration to Turkey, I argue that humanitarian reasons were in fact *not* the principal motivation for hiring Jewish scholars. Hence the aim of this essay is to analyze the story of German Jews surviving the Holocaust in a Muslim-dominated society while critically reviewing the function of ethnoreligious difference for the project of Turkish nation-building.

. . .

Turkey's desultory attitude toward imperiled Jews is evident from a letter written by Einstein in September 1933. Communicating with the prime minister, İsmet İnönü, Einstein made the unusual offer of forty highly skilled and experienced "professors and doctors from Germany," who would be willing to work in Turkey "for a year without any remuneration in any of your institutions, according to the orders of your government." Although it came from a person as eminent as Einstein and implied no financial burden for the Turkish government, the offer was firmly declined.[6] As the honorary president of the Union des Sociétés OSE, the Paris-based Jewish organization, Einstein tried to act as a mediator between his needy colleagues and the Turkish government.[7] İnönü declined Einstein's offer implying that it contravened Turkish laws:

> Although I agree that your proposal is very attractive, I have to inform you that I see no possibility to make this suggestion compatible with the laws and regulations of our country. As you surely know, distinguished Professor, we have already engaged under contract more than forty professors and physicians who have the same qualities and the same capacities, and most of whom are under the same political conditions as those who are the object of your letter. These professors and doctors have agreed to work here in conformity with the current laws and regulations. At present, we are trying to finalize a delicate mechanism, namely an organization comprising members who are very different by their origins, cultures, and languages. This is why at present, under the circumstances in which we are, it will unfortunately not be possible for us to hire a greater number of these gentlemen.[8]

This rejection seems anomalous when we consider that Turkish institutions continued to hire German émigrés, most of Jewish background, through other channels. But unlike the Zürich-based Notgemeinschaft, the Union des Sociétés stood specifically for the protection of Jews, something that the organization's letterhead made clear.[9] It seems likely that the prime minister, İnönü, did not want to set a precedent by hiring German scholars at the instigation of a patently Jewish organization. Possible explanations for the rejection of the offer include the ambiguous place of Jews within the young Turkish Republic, where measures had already been introduced to discourage the public use of Ladino. This was compounded by a twofold assimilatory policy instituted in 1923: the country required its citizens—regardless of ethnic or religious background—to conform to a unified Turkish culture and language. At the same time, the government implemented an equally assimilatory Westernization project that was designed to achieve cultural recognition from the heart of Europe: national powers like France, Germany, and Britain were supposed to confer legitimacy on the incipient Turkish state.

In examining the official rhetoric surrounding Turkey's minority populations and its relations with foreign states, we find that the period of Turkish renewal between 1923 and 1946, that is, between the foundation of the republic and the end of the humanist reform, was characterized by three dominant tropes—concerning the mimic, *dönme*, and eternal guest.[10] This essay explores how these tropes were used in interconnected ways to characterize

Jewishness, Turkishness, and Europeanness within public discourse. The tropes had powerful cultural resonances in Turkey, resonances that echo to this day. As the historian Rıfat Bali points out, the notion of the eternal guest evoked the Sephardic Jews who had migrated to the Ottoman Empire at the end of the fifteenth century; the term *dönme* originated with the conversion of Ottoman Jews to Islam in the seventeenth century but continues even now to denote a sense of falseness and betrayal. While the figure of the mimic was an anti-Semitic trope used by the Nazis, it also occupied its own distinct place within late Ottoman and modern Turkish discourses of Westernization. Interestingly, and notwithstanding its Nazi associations, the mimic remains a powerful trope for signifying the failed process of Europeanization in present-day Turkey. By mapping a genealogy of these tropes, we learn something about the price of Turkish modernity—what was concealed, suppressed, and appropriated; we also learn something about discursive continuities between Turkish modernity and the global postmodern.

## Creating New Historical and Racialist Narratives: The Dönme and the Mimic

In the 1990s, civic leaders in Turkey organized a series of public events to commemorate the arrival of Sephardic Jews in the Ottoman Empire after their expulsion from Spain and Portugal at the end of the fifteenth century. At the quincentennial commemoration civic leaders drew parallels between the Sephardic Jews, who had introduced the Ottomans to new technologies like book printing, and the German Jews, who in 1933 pioneered new methodologies in a broad variety of disciplines.[11] The tendency to draw such links points to the current fad for historical analogy, a fad that sees the past as a fecund repository for lessons in the present. During the 1930s, in contrast, Turkish authorities in charge of hiring émigré scholars refrained from drawing similar comparisons: no links seem to have been made between the flight of the Jews from the Iberian Peninsula to the Ottoman Empire and the flight of Jews from Nazi Germany to modern Turkey. The then Turkish minister for education, Reşit Galip, invoked an alternative historical analogy, one that emphasized both comings and goings and a different set of historical figures. He construed the arrival of academic émigrés from Europe in 1933 as a compensation for the Byzantine scholars who had fled Constantinople after its surrender to the Ottomans in 1453. In contrast to the rhetoric surrounding the quincentennial celebrations in the 1990s, which highlighted the shared Jewishness of exiles separated by five hundred years of history, it did not seem to matter in 1933 that a significant number of the imported scholars were German-Jewish. Indeed, as I show in this essay, Turks initially welcomed the scholars as Europeans and not as Jews.

One ought not to conclude from this, of course, that Turkey was free of racism and anti-Semitism during the 1930s. In fact, the year 1934 saw thousands of Jewish Turks fleeing anti-Semitic attacks in Thrace. And although generally frowned upon by the Turkish government, anti-Semitic propaganda was disseminated by journals like *Milli İnkilap* [National Revolution][12] and by writers like Nihal Atsız, who promoted Turanism, a racial movement that promulgated the unification of the Turkic people. Anti-Semitic rhetoric also circulated within the Turkish academy. We see this in a lecture delivered at Istanbul University in 1936 by prominent historian Şemseddin Günaltay. The lecture exemplifies the ways in which tropes like the mimic and *dönme* were used to characterize the modern European Turk. I will argue that these tropes point to profound anxieties about the stability of Turkishness as a marker of racial identity.

Şemseddin Günaltay's lecture titled "The Homeland of the Turks and the Question of Their Race" specified the supposed racial origins of Turks. Contesting the thesis put forth by Western Orientalists that Turks and Mongolians belong to the self-same "yellow race," Günaltay disavowed the "yellowness" of Turks and reclassified them as "white." According to the historian, the original homeland of the Turks was not Mongolia—as generally assumed—but Turkistan, which he referred to as the "cradle of the Neolithic age."[13] Going even further, Günaltay construed a racial relationship between the ancient Sumerians and modern Turks.[14] While Günaltay's thesis seems improbable to us today—unsupported by either historical or scientific evidence—it is important to remember that this was not just the singular opinion of a conjectural racialist historian. Such views were in fact quite common. What lent real weight to Günaltay's claims, however, was his status as both a highly visible member of the Turkish parliament and a renowned scholar who would later preside over Türk Tarih Kurumu [Institute for Turkish History]. The newly founded institute would set about creating a new historical narrative for Westernized Turkey.[15] And it was claims like Günaltay's that constituted the new *millî tarih tezi*, the "national history thesis" promulgated by the institute.[16]

Günaltay's "Homeland of the Turks and the Question of Their Race" can, in other words, be seen as indicative of the kinds of racial anxieties circulating in Turkey in the decade preceding the outbreak of the Second World War. These anxieties were manifest in anti-Semitic tropes that underscored the lecture's rhetoric. Günaltay seized on Reşidüddin, the thirteenth-century Jewish-born Persian historian, whom he criticized for equating Turks with Mongols. Turks did *not* originate in Mongolian Central and East Asia, Günaltay countered; this was, apparently, corroborated by Ottoman as well as European Orientalist scholars.[17] Günaltay proposed that rather than being of the "yellow race," Turks were of the "Alpine type." In order to make his point and discredit the earlier historian, Günaltay reminded his audience of Reşidüddin's Jewish heritage and invoked the figure of the Jewish imposter. He suggested that Reşidüddin's thesis about the relationship between Turks and Mongolians was nothing more than an act of *mehareti kalemiyet*, "skillful writing" (that is, fabrication). This, he said, casting aspersions about the thirteenth-century Persian, was just the kind of writing that came easily to a *dönme*—or "crypto-Jew."[18]

Günaltay's use of the word *dönme* warrants some attention. The root of the noun *dönme* is *dönmek*, the verb "to turn." But *dönme* also means "to convert," and it is this sense of the word that is of particular interest to us here. Historically, this term was applied to a community in Saloniki that converted from Judaism to Islam, following the example of Sabbatai Sevi, a messianic rabbi who was forced to renounce Judaism in 1666.[19] The nature of this conversion remains ambivalent to this day since *dönme* developed a form of religious practice that combined elements of both Islam and Judaism. The polydenominational character of their beliefs has meant that *dönme* have been difficult to classify, a fact that has always been exploitable for political ends. In 1924, when Turkey and Greece agreed to exchange their respective Muslim and Christian populations, *dönme* were deemed Muslim and consequently deported from Greece to Turkey. In Turkey, on the other hand, *dönme* were not necessarily seen as Muslims, and their status within the new republic remained controversial.[20] In the intervening period, the *dönme* often came to be thought of as people who pretended to be Muslim yet secretly practiced Judaism.[21] Even today, *dönme* continue to be associated with the proverbial Trojan horse—a danger posed by something that is not what it seems to be. Thus we find that the trope often appears in political discourse to signify conspiracy and betrayal.[22]

Günaltay's revision of the place of Turks within a racial hierarchy illustrates how notions of Turkishness, Jewishness, and Europeanness were linked in modern Turkey. It was by labeling historian Reşidüddin a deceitful Jew that Günaltay opened the possibility for constructing Turks as both white and European. We can only speculate about Günaltay's personal motivations for insisting on Turkish whiteness and Europeanness, and scapegoating *dönme* as untrustworthy crypto-Jews. But if we see Günaltay as symptomatic of a broad current within Turkish thought, we can say that his comments illustrate the profound racial and cultural anxieties aroused by Turkey's rapid process of secularization and Westernization.[23] Günaltay explicitly discouraged his audience from subscribing to Reşidüddin's claims; his audience was instructed instead to follow the guidelines of the new Türk Tarih Kurumu, Institute of Turkish History. Following the institute's guidelines would, he assured them, contribute to a "high Turkish culture," as he called it, and prevent Turks from indulging in base imitation.[24] In making this claim, Günaltay addressed two occult fears. The first, as I have said, was the kind of fear posed by deception and inauthenticity. Günaltay's other fear concerned the question of imitation: Turks were cautioned about those who pretended to be like them; at the same time, they themselves were to avoid pretending to be something they were not. To convert, he seemed to say, was as bad as to imitate superficially.

To further our investigation into concepts of imitation and authenticity in modern Turkey, it is worth considering Homi Bhabha's insights into the politics of appropriation. Bhabha developed this theoretical term to characterize power relations in British India. Mimicry, he argues, is one of the most effective strategies for establishing colonial power. Crucial for Bhabha is the inherent ambivalence of mimicry, since it produces something that is *"almost the same, but not quite."*[25] The difference between the colonized who is Anglicized and the English colonizer was, according to Bhabha, a difference that could be exploited in order to maintain British control over the colony. Indeed, such difference might explain the continued influence of British culture in postcolonial India. Without equating colonial strategies in British India with Turkey's self-imposed appropriation of Western

European culture, there are nonetheless instructive parallels to be drawn. Bhabha's insights help us understand the anxieties that were triggered by the Europeanization of Turkey, for his notion of mimicry highlights the difference between representation and repetition. Translated into the Turkish context, Bhabha's notion of mimicry highlights the difference between the European who stands for Europe and the Europeanized Turk who is thought capable of merely aping that which is European.

As I have suggested, we see evidence of these anxieties in Günaltay's lecture when the historian specifically cautions his audience against superficial imitation and the dangers of unsuccessfully copying Europe. Nor was Günaltay the only one to express such sentiments; other Turkish reformists, too, warned against the kind of superficial reproduction that would result only in hypocrisy.[26] To sum up, we can distinguish two distinct tropes in Günaltay's lecture: first, the figure of the *dönme* as the Trojan horse—someone who tries to subvert the national community by infiltrating it under a false guise—and second, the mimic, who is too superficially Europeanized to effectively transform Turkish society. Such rhetoric was in keeping with the general tenor of public discourse in Turkey at the time. What lent provocation to the lecture was, however, the fact that Günaltay was speaking not only to a home-grown audience of Turkish scholars and students in 1936: included among his listeners were the German-Jewish scholars recently hired at Istanbul University. These émigrés were the very scholars who had been stigmatized in Germany on the grounds that they subverted German culture. Paradoxically, these scholars were considered instrumental in overcoming the opposition between Orient and Occident and were thought capable of rendering Turks more than just mimics of the West. The paradoxical relationship among notions of Jewishness, Europeanness, and Turkishness was rendered more intricate by virtue of the fact that German émigrés were construed as exemplary Europeans in Turkey. Creating a "high Turkish culture" was to take place via the European scholar, who was in many cases a Jewish-German émigré.

## The German-Jewish Émigré as the Exemplary European

At this juncture, it is worth reviewing the contradictory attitudes toward Turkey's religious and ethnic minorities. In the initial years of their academic appointments, German Jews were not officially identified as Jews. At the same time, Turkey's indigenous Jews were subject to ongoing public discussion about their loyalty to the republic. In the 1920s, Turkish citizenship had indeed been extended to everyone irrespective of religious affiliation, but in cultural terms Jews and Armenians were never fully acknowledged as Turks. In the case of Greeks, it was agreed that more than one million Orthodox Greeks should be deported from Turkey to Greece in exchange for the nearly half a million Muslims who lived in Greece. Kurds, Arabs, Azeris, Laz, and numerous other predominantly Muslim communities were consequently subordinated and homogenized under the ethnic category "Turk." The remaining Armenian and Jewish communities—seen as resistant to assimilation—were subjected to wide-ranging "Turkification" measures of the early republic.

As I pointed out earlier, an assimilationist campaign was instituted in 1928 in an effort to force Turkish Jews to forego Ladino for Turkish.[27] This was intended to establish the secular basis for Turkish citizenship and so achieve a kind of isomorphism among culture, nation, and geography. And indeed, some leading members of the Turkish-Jewish community like Moiz Kohen, who took the Turkish name Munis Tekinalp, subscribed to this assimilationist platform. Yet these assimilationist strategies notwithstanding, truly inhabiting Turkishness seems to have been ultimately reserved for Muslim citizens alone.[28] Put another way, we can say that the boundaries of the ethnic Turk came to be drawn along strictly religious lines.[29] Marc Baer is generally correct in pointing out that minorities were "purified from the body politic" during the 1920s and 1930s, and that "extraneous elements" became "parasites."[30] This did not, however, apply to the hundreds of Jewish Germans and their families who migrated to Turkey in the 1930s. When German Jews were hired for the Europeanization reforms, they were not seen as parasites. To the contrary, they were seen as facilitators of progress and as a means of bridging the gap between Western Europe and Turkey.

This differentiation takes us one step closer to understanding why German-Jewish scholars were greeted in Turkey not as Jews—or Germans, for that matter—but as Europeans. Of course I do not mean to imply that Turkey ought to have explicitly acknowledged their Jewishness. Letters, memoirs, and archival sources show that conditions in Turkey made it possible for Jewish émigrés to continue identifying as German scholars, something they had been effectively denied by the Nazis, who categorized and persecuted them precisely as Jews. As the Romance scholar Leo Spitzer put it in one of his letters, the tight-knit German academic community in Istanbul provided the context for pursuing a somewhat "German life."[31] It is thus perhaps unsurprising that Turks tended to see the émigrés as representatives of Europe. We find this expressed in many guises. Erol Güney, a newspaper correspondent who studied philosophy at Istanbul University with Hans Reichenbach, said about the émigré Herbert Dieckmann, a Diderot specialist, that "he personified for me the perfect type of European intellectual, not a German, a French, a British, but a 'real' European, much before Europe started on its long and difficult period toward unity."[32]

We see this, too, in the case of the Orientalist scholar Hellmut Ritter, who had been dismissed as a homosexual from Hamburg University in 1926 and found refuge in Istanbul that same year. Fruitless efforts to secure another professorship in Germany brought Ritter to write:

> The Turks are utterly uninterested in my past, what I stand for here—whether one wants to acknowledge this in Germany or not, regardless whether I do or don't—in the eyes of the Turks I don't stand for the German Orientalist tradition, but rather that of Europe.[33]

My point, then, is not to criticize the Turkish authorities for having failed to publicly acknowledge the fact that many of the émigrés had been vilified as Jewish, communist, or homosexual in their home countries. Rather, I want to shed some light on Turkish immigration policy at this time and explain why the exiles' shared Europeanness was so strongly emphasized over the reasons that led to their persecution in the first place. As I pointed out earlier, Galip, the Turkish minister for education, did not draw explicit comparisons between two historical moments of exodus, namely, the flight of the Sephardic Jews in the fifteenth century and the German Jews of his own day. It would have been logical to compare the two, given the rich contribution made by the Sephardic Jews to intellectual and cultural life in the Ottoman Empire.[34] Galip and other Turkish officials did not of course explain why this resonance went unremarked. We can, however, indulge in some conjectural history and speculate why it is that past analogies are mobilized at some historical moments and not at others. My suggestion is that it did not then suit the Turkish authorities to stress the scholars' Jewishness. Drawing attention to this fact would have meant informing the Turkish public that

Jewish Germans had been forced to leave their homes because they had been denied full rights as German citizens. At a time when Turkey was preoccupied with its own questions about assimilation and religious minorities, highlighting the general failure of mimetic and assimilationist projects was a topic that seemed too hot to handle.

For their part, the Nazis continued to construe Jews as Orientals and mimics—something a 1935 report to the Foreign Office in Berlin makes clear: "Due to their racial characteristics these people [Jewish émigrés] can adapt to the Turkish mentality particularly well and learn the country's language very quickly."[35] In this statement, racialist stereotyping goes hand in hand with notions of deceitful assimilation and mimicry. To my knowledge, the Turkish ministry for education did not take a clear stance against the Nazi pronouncements about Jews. As I have explained, however, it would not have been strictly within its own interests to do so. Until the war, many if not most Jews living in Germany had defined themselves first and foremost as assimilated Germans. That their assimilation collapsed—or rather was so rapidly and effectively quashed by the Nazis—must have raised a specter. Indeed, doubts about the viability of assimilation extended not only to Turkey's religious minorities but to Turkey as a whole. We must remember, after all, that Turkish officials were concerned with assimilating Turkey's citizens to a unified language and culture. At the same time, the country as a whole looked to Western Europe for its model. To question assimilation, then, was to question whether appropriating and disseminating European knowledge would ever effectively transform Turks into Europeans. It would have meant asking whether Turks, like Jews, were bound to remain Orientals in the eyes of Western European Christians. And finally, it would have meant acknowledging that the act of adjudication was something that lay within the power of Western Europeans. It would not be left to the Turks themselves to determine whether they were European.

### Erich Auerbach as the Eternal Guest

So far we have concentrated primarily on the firsthand accounts of émigrés and their Turkish hosts, but we learn something, too, from foreign travelers to Turkey. Swiss travel writer and journalist Annemarie Schwarzenbach, passing through Istanbul in 1933, made trenchant observations about the status of Europeans:

> The Europeans are fearful in this country. None of them is at home; passing years don't change this. They are given weighty tasks; they accomplish them without the success satisfying them. . . . They have pretty houses, tennis courts, a club, good horses. They also own this and that and live in a country that believes in the future and the benefits of reason, civilization, and progress, things that are so undervalued in Europe. The country is governed by a group of intellectually superior men, by honest democrats, who know no other goal than enfranchising their people as quickly as possible. And the Europeans who are appointed to assist in accomplishing this task may well believe that they will soon be superfluous. No one doubts the country or the people. But everyone has doubts about his own task. That is the fear.[36]

From her we also learn something about the transitory character of the exile condition—something that Bertolt Brecht expressed in his poem about the duration of exile: "Schlage keinen Nagel an die Wand, wirf den Rock auf den Stuhl" [Do not pound a nail in the wall, throw your coat on the chair]. The émigrés in Turkey faced a kind of planned redundancy and could not settle, since their own superfluity was built into the Westernization reforms. Once the Westernization process was deemed complete, the country would have no further need for their services. Thus, although they were regarded as necessary instructors in Western-style architecture, literature, music, and the natural sciences, their university contracts were initially limited to three years. Someone like Leo Spitzer could immigrate to the United States with the prospect of spending the rest of his life there, yet the German scholars who remained in Turkey could neither be sure about their employment prospects nor predict the outcome of the Westernization reforms.

The precariousness of life in Turkey helps explain Erich Auerbach's attitude to his host country. The Romance scholar who had been dismissed by the Nazis on racial grounds from his position as professor at the University of Marburg and emigrated to Istanbul in 1936 summed up the tribulations of living in the foreign port: "The conservatives distrust us as foreigners, the fascists as émigrés, the antifascists as Germans, and anti-Semitism exists, too."[37] Auerbach's typology provides some indication as to the complex sociopolitical climate that prevailed at the time. In the first instance, he refers to conservative, reform-leery Turks; second, to the organized network of Istanbul Nazis who tried to curtail the activities of the German émigrés; and third, to the antifascist émigrés. Anti-Semitism, so his letter implies, crisscrossed all three of these circles. The challenge for Auerbach and other Jewish scholars stemmed, in other words, from their confrontation with various politically motivated groups in Turkey, each of which competed vigorously over the direction of the reforms.

If the Turkish ministry for education had an investment in the émigrés as scholars who lacked any explicit national agenda, other groups in Turkey did not necessarily perceive them in quite such politically neutral terms. Istanbul University is a case in point. In order to ensure—as if this would have been necessary—that Auerbach abstain from German propagandizing, his employment contract, dated 1936, stipulated the following terms: "Mr. Auerbach commits himself to abstaining from political, economical, and commercial activities and hence from activities serving the propaganda of a foreign government. He is not allowed to accept any other position in foreign institutions or establishments."[38]

In other words, privileges in the host country were contingent upon the émigrés agreeing to suspend any national agenda of their own. Caught between a country that no longer wanted them and a country that wanted them only conditionally and for an indeterminate, but potentially limited, period of time, we can think of them as perpetual guests. Auerbach and his colleagues may not have been officially compared with the Sephardic Jews discussed earlier, but their status in Turkey was a comparable one. Rıfat Bali argues in this regard that Sephardic Jews were perceived as guests whose loyalty to Turkey was constantly under suspicion. The notion of the Jew as guest is, Bali argues, reaffirmed in the declarations of gratitude and indebtedness that contemporary Jews express to the Turks even half a millennium after their original flight from the Iberian Peninsula.[39] This is not the place to compare notions of Jewishness in Europe and the Ottoman Empire, but it is worth considering that the idea of the "eternal guest" in the Ottoman Empire and Turkey parallels that of the Jewish "eternal wanderer" in Christian thought.[40] The *dönme*, on the other hand, parallels the figure of the mimic in European discourses.

Considerable scholarly attention has been devoted to the figure of the wandering Jew. Galit Hasan-Rokem and Alan Dundes, for example, see this trope as having always been a "pivotal reflection of Jewish-Christian relationships."[41] Rather than interpreting the wandering Jew as part of a Christian legend, Edward Timms, on the other hand, examines the trope within a specifically German context and shows its transformations from its first appearance around 1600 to its appropriation by the Nazis in the early twentieth century.[42] Elizabeth Grosz, yet again, regards the Jew as a trope of "alterity, occupying the position of *perennial other* for millennia."[43] There is room for further research into the construction of Jewishness in the Ottoman period. Such a study would likely provide insights into the nature of Jewish-Muslim relationships and map the transition from Jews as *millet* [nation] during Ottoman times to their reclassification as a minority community based on a shared religion in the twenty-first century.[44] Thanks to Rıfat Bali's and Avigdor Levy's work, however, we can assume that the "lingering sense of Jewish insecurity and feeling of 'apartness'"[45] stemmed, at least in part, from the social status of Sephardic Jews as guests residing in a Muslim world.

We find evidence of this point in the Turkish policies toward Jewish refugees from 1933 on. Before the outbreak of the war, Turkey was regarded as a transit country for Europe's Jews; thousands of refugees migrated to Palestine via Turkey, giving Istanbul the character of something of a waiting room. Yet it is a little-appreciated fact that Jewish refugees were not generally welcome to stay. This became clear when, in response to the Jewish flight from Nazi Germany in early 1939, Prime Minister Refik Saydam declared emphatically that Turkey was not going to provide refuge to Jews. He conceded that there were Jews among the people brought in to serve the country's national and administrative needs. Provision was made for their family members to enter Turkey so that these people could, as he put it, "work with comfortable minds." However, he stipulated that these family members could not seek employment.[46] This shift in Turkish policies vis-à-vis Jewish émigrés also meant that Turkish consulates in Germany started to require proof of Aryan descent as a precondition for granting an entry visa to Turkey.[47] The fact that many of the German scholars who had emigrated to Turkey were Jewish was by now part of the public consciousness.

The newspaper *Yeni Sabah* reported in the summer of 1939 that German Jews in Turkey were being stripped of their citizenship by the German authorities.[48] While closing Turkish borders to other German Jews by requiring certificates of Aryan descent, Turkish authorities now granted citizenship to many of the émigrés who were already employed. Hence, the immigration of greater numbers of Jews to Turkey was impeded, but the conditions for earlier émigrés who had become stateless were improved. In contrast to most of his fellow émigrés, however, Erich Auerbach seems to have been the only Jewish émigré not to apply for Turkish citizenship in 1939.[49] Doing so would have solved his legal predicament, but for some unknown reason, he chose to remain stateless. For other Jewish refugees trying desperately to find a safe haven from fascism, no such choice was available: the Turkish borders simply remained closed.

Contrary to what we might expect, acquiring Turkish citizenship did not seem to greatly impact the émigrés' social status. With or without Turkish citizenship, émigrés were regarded as privileged guests. While being a guest has its undoubted advantages—including special treatment and high social status—it also has its obligations and restrictions. Under the pressure of showing loyalty to the host country, émigrés tended to withhold substantive critique of the modernization reforms. They did not, for instance, expose any of the difficulties they faced at the university, nor were they vocal about their dealings with Turkish authorities. Indeed, Auerbach rarely commented on Turkey in public, and the country occupies a marginal place in his published work. That he harbored a secret critique is, however, evident from his private correspondence with friends and colleagues in Western Europe. Today, this correspondence provides us with insights into Auerbach's views on Turkish modernization and his own role in this process. It is here, in the private letters, that we find him critically assessing the country's reform measures, its nationalist politics, and its anti-Semitism.[50]

His 1938 letter to his former assistant, Freya Hobohm, for example, expresses concern about Turkey's attempt to reinvent itself as a European nation by severing itself from its own roots.[51] Auerbach could follow the logic that lay behind erasing the Ottoman cultural tradition in order to secularize the republic. By the same token, he remained critical of Turkey's official policy of renouncing its Ottoman heritage.[52] Such political decisions, Auerbach wrote to Walter Benjamin in 1936 (and reiterated in a 1952 essay "Philologie der Weltliteratur" [Philology of world literature]), contributed to the loss of historical consciousness and the standardization of culture.[53] While he may have felt safe expressing such views to his former assistant in Germany, Auerbach never said as much to his Turkish audiences. In fact, it is clear that Auerbach felt censored. In a letter to another former assistant, Martin Hellweg, discussing the progress of Turkish educational reform, Auerbach stated explicitly that he could not express in public what he held to be true.[54]

My analysis shows that the Turkish reformers expected the émigrés to behave like people without a nation: as such, they were thought capable of more readily implementing Turkey's new national agenda. Yet Auerbach's personal correspondence suggests something else: in this transnational encounter, German Jews were denationalized and secularized so as to stand for the idea of Europe. An excerpt from Auerbach's 1946 letter to Werner Krauss, his former colleague in Marburg, shows what was expected of intellectual émigrés in Turkey. Auerbach explained why the postwar position he was offered at Berlin's Humboldt University was unsuitable, and he reflected on how working in Turkey had affected his political stance:

> I am, after all, a typical liberal. If anything, the very situation which the circumstances offered to me has but strengthened this inclination. Here I am enjoying the great liberty of *ne pas conclure*. More than in any other situation, it was possible for me to remain free of any commitment. It is exactly this attitude of somebody who does not belong to any place, and who is essentially a stranger without the possibility of being assimilated, which is desired and expected from me.[55]

The letter illuminates more than just the reasons for Auerbach's reluctance to commit to Humboldt University, then located in Soviet-occupied East Berlin; it tells us something about his social status in modern Turkey. And, coming from an assimilated German Jew expelled from his native country, his words seem rather poignant. Instead of seeking, or being called upon, to assimilate, he understood his prescribed task in avowedly unassimilationist terms. He felt that it was necessary to conserve and embody his European identity as a model for the upcoming generation of Turkish students and scholars. Moreover, he understood that Turks wanted him to remain what I have referred to as the eternal guest. This, in itself, made cultural assimilation undesirable, if not impossible. Without speculating about Auerbach's private motivations and inner thoughts, I wish to emphasize exactly how narrow was the range of choices then at his disposal. It was the very failure to assimilate in Turkey that ensured Auerbach's safety and social status during the war. His comfortable and stimulating life in Istanbul was contingent on his continued commitment to transmitting European scholarship. The pact that Auerbach implicitly struck with Turkey was, in other words, dependent upon preserving—not eliminating—difference. Accepting this condition and personifying the European intellect was what allowed Auerbach to survive the Holocaust.

After the end of the war, Auerbach was once again offered Turkish citizenship. The offer by Turkish authorities had nothing to do with Auerbach's relationship to the place in which he now lived; in fact, Auerbach is known not to have spoken much Turkish. Writing to Werner Krauss, Auerbach conceded that Turkish citizenship would allow him to travel, but he thought that accepting such an offer would be dishonorable if one planned to leave the country.[56] To be sure, Auerbach's legal status would have been at least temporarily clarified by becoming a Turkish citizen. Nonetheless, he decided to take a risk and wait for the possibility of emigrating once more. It is in this light that we understand Auerbach's words in a letter to Martin Hellweg: "We did not become Turks, not even legally; now we are Germans without passports again, and everything is provisional."[57] Declining Turkish citizenship and hence the possibility of a lifelong commitment to Turkey, Auerbach finally took leave from Istanbul University in 1947. Without the security of an academic position, but with *Mimesis: Dargestellte Wirklichkeit in der abendländischen Literatur* among his papers—his magnum opus, which had been published in Bern the previous year—Erich Auerbach and his wife, Marie, moved to the United States. Family reasons—his son was a graduate student at Harvard—and the hope of better working conditions at an internationally acclaimed institution undoubtedly played a role in this decision. It is likely, however, that the vulnerable status of Jews in Turkey, especially between 1939 and 1943, also impacted his decision to leave. The section that follows highlights the changes in Turkish attitudes toward European and Turkish Jews and discusses the political, cultural, and academic conditions during Auerbach's tenure in Turkey.

## The Inassimilable Turkish Jew

As I have already suggested, the Turkish government enabled German-Jewish intellectuals to live and work under respectable conditions at Turkish institutions, yet it applied a contradictory policy to other Jews fleeing the Holocaust after 1939. Among those trying to escape deportation were thousands of Jews who were, or had once been, citizens of the Ottoman Empire and the new Turkey. Now trapped in Nazi-occupied territories, many tried to find ways of escaping to Turkey or using Turkey as a transit point. Thanks to the intervention of Turkish ambassadors and consuls like Selâhattin Ülkümen on the island of Rhodes or Behiç Erkin and Necdet Kent in France, an unknown number of Jews in Europe managed to escape deportation or were released from concentration camps because they could prove their Ottoman or Turkish citizenship. Behiç Erkin's grandson, Emir Kıvırcık, asserts that in France alone some twenty thousand Jews were thereby rescued from deportation.[58] Such claims seem exaggerated, and the numbers need to be verified by a comparative analysis of archival sources. German records of the period indicate that there were an estimated five thousand Turkish Jews living in occupied territories. It is not clear from sources in the political archive in Berlin whether all of these people were saved.[59]

In fact, Corinna Görgü Guttstadt argues that between 1938 and 1945 Turkey intended exactly the opposite: rather than meaning to save people, it deliberately deprived "several thousand of its Jewish nationals living abroad of their citizenship."[60] While this may be true, files in the Berlin political archive show that a number of Turkish ambassadors and consuls in Nazi-controlled territories did attempt to protect not all, but at least some, of their citizens. Nazis at the 1942 Wannsee Conference had decided behind closed doors that all European Jews, including those in Turkey, were to be subject to the "final solution." Turkish authorities would later argue that Turkey did not differentiate between Jewish Turks and non-Jewish Turks and, on these grounds, tried to get some of their Jewish citizens out of France and other countries controlled by the Germans.[61]

Yet this stance did not cohere, as Guttstadt demonstrates, with internal Turkish policies at the time, nor can it be said that Turkish authorities exhausted all avenues for saving their own nationals. Indeed, the government's dealings with the Nazis seemed at times rather too cozy. In 1943, the Turkish embassy in Berlin negotiated with the Nazi Foreign Office over the timing of the transfer of Turkish Jews to Turkey. At this meeting, the Turkish representative said that his government wanted to "avoid the mass immigration of Jews, particularly of those Jews who had correct Turkish papers but have not had any contact with Turkey for decades."[62] It seems clear from this that the Turkish authorities in Germany and those in the Nazi-occupied territories were interested neither in protecting all their citizens[63] nor in treating Jewish and Muslim Turks equally.

In 1942, anti-Semitism in Turkey reached a critical level. *Struma*, a ship carrying almost eight hundred Jewish refugees from Romania, arrived near the Istanbul coast and waited for ten weeks for permission to proceed to Palestine. The ship was denied access to the Mediterranean by the British, who refused to issue visas, while the Turks allowed only a few refugees to disembark in Istanbul. Eventually, the Turks towed the crippled ship through the Bosporus to the Black Sea where it was set adrift and later attacked by the Soviets. All but one passenger was killed.[64] After the tragedy and in defense of Turkey's decision, Prime Minister Saydam declared that "Turkey can not be a homeland for those who are unwanted elsewhere." This statement effectively put a stop to the immigration to Palestine via Turkey.[65] In addition, he dismissed Jewish journalists employed at the Turkish news agency *L'Agence Anatolie*.[66] It should be noted that Saydam's statement was made after the fate of the European Jewry had already been decided at the Wannsee Conference. Turkey's refusal to help Jewish refugees that same winter can be interpreted as preempting Turkey's own anti-Jewish legislation.[67]

Faced with economic difficulties in 1942, the Turkish government introduced a capital tax that discriminated between Muslims, non-Muslims (*gayrimüslim*), *dönme*, and foreigners (*ecnebi*). The new tax applied mostly to non-Muslim minorities, and as a result of the regulations introduced to "Turkify" the economy, Turkish Jews lost a significant amount of property.[68] More than fourteen hundred non-Muslims who were unable to pay the required tax were forced to work in a labor camp in Aşkale, near Erzurum.[69] Unlike Turkish Jews, German Jews were not treated as non-Muslims. Rather, they were classified as foreigners under the tax regulation and were hence subject to a lower tax rate than "regular" non-Muslims.[70] The debate over whether *dönme* ought to be considered Jews or Muslims was revived in the increasingly anti-Semitic atmosphere of the early 1940s. It was decided that *dönme* should pay double the taxes paid by Muslims, but not as much as Jews.[71] We can conclude from this that, however they may have been thought of before, by the middle of the war Turkish Jews were clearly set apart as an inassimilable ethnoreligious community. The popular anti-Semitic mobilization during this time can be seen in leading national newspapers that published cartoons depicting big-nosed Jews as shameless profiteers.[72]

There were widespread doubts about the loyalty of Turkish Jews to the republic. As part of the debate surrounding the new capital tax, leading journalist Nadir Nadi wrote that if non-Muslims wanted to prove they were Turks, they must either sacrifice their wealth for the good of the nation or leave the country.[73] Similar reasoning underscored statements made in a university lecture given by a Turkish army major in 1943. He blamed Turkish Jews for ignoring "the commands of the nation who had given them refuge [450 years earlier!]. We are not Germans to crush them beneath our feet," he went on. "But the faith in our Government tells us that slowly but surely we will reach our end. Then, only then, will this country be ours."[74]

This exceedingly low tolerance for Jews in Turkey was also apparent to Helmuth James von Moltke, the founder of the Kreisau resistance group against Hitler who visited the country in 1943 in order to prepare a peace plan with the Allies.[75] On his two brief visits to Istanbul, Moltke met members of the émigré community, including the economist Alexander Rüstow, who had a close collegial relationship with Auerbach, and the agriculturist Hans Wilbrandt. Moltke provided Rüstow and Wilbrandt with a detailed memo about the situation in Germany and the uprising in the Warsaw Ghetto. The two émigrés functioned as mediators between Moltke and the U.S. secret service.[76] What is interesting for our purposes is that Moltke perceived Istanbul as a racially segregated city. In a letter to his wife, Freya von Moltke, in July 1943, Helmuth James von Moltke wrote:

> Everyone is highly conscious of race. Zita, Leverkühn's employee, is Greek. She does not speak to Turks. The Jews are complete outcasts here; they are addressed with the familiar Thou and no one shakes hands with them or offers them a chair, even if they are rolling in money and are thoroughly Europeanized. Levantines are children of mixed marriages with Italians or Greeks. Also, the child of a German and a Greek mother is Levantine, and is socially subordinate to Turks. It is all very strange.[77]

Moltke's impressions of everyday life in Istanbul are expressed in language that is inflected by Nazi racialist discourse—the references to "outcasts" and "mixed marriages" do not match the specificity and language of Turkish racism at the time. Nonetheless, the letter inadvertently points to the anomaly that is at the heart of this essay: Turkish Jews were ostracized, notwithstanding their Western European roots and habitus, even while German Jews helped Europeanize the nation. What linked both German and Turkish Jews, however, was the constant reminder of their precarious circumstances.

In the last two years of the war, matters started improving. When Auerbach reviewed his own situation during this time in a letter to Martin Hellweg after the war, he wrote: "Against all odds, we were well; the new regime did not penetrate the Bosporus; that really says it all. We lived in our apartment and didn't suffer anything worse than minor troubles and fear: until the end of 1942 things looked really bad, but then the cloud slowly lifted."[78] Indeed, after the labor camps for non-Muslim minorities were closed and the unpaid capital tax debts were dissolved in 1943, anti-Semitism diminished in intensity.[79] During the single-party regime, President İsmet İnönü had managed to keep Turkey out of the war—the First World War had served as a lesson in defeat. In 1944, however, Turkey stopped delivering the all-important chromite and severed diplomatic relationships with Nazi Germany. In February 1945, Turkey finally declared war on Germany.

## Conclusion: The Mock European

In late Ottoman discourses that negotiated notions of authenticity and inauthenticity, the figures of the *züppe* and the *kukla*, the Europeanized dandy and the puppet, were popular tropes delimiting socially acceptable levels of Westernization. The years of Auerbach's exile in Turkey were, on the other hand, informed by transnational cross-identifications and deep concerns about Turkey's Europeanness. Figures of Jewishness like the disloyal *dönme* and the eternal guest shaped Turkish ideas about home, belonging, and the national character. For their part, the Nazis created an image of Jews as inauthentic mimics and used this as one of the grounds for their expulsion and extermination. Turks, on the other hand, used the trope of the mimic as a corrective in the Europeanization debates of modern Turkey. *Taklitçiik*, mimicry, once a word that meant both to "imitate" and "ridicule," lost its subversive connotation during the course of the Europeanization reforms.[80] Not only was imitation disassociated from subversive mockery, but a distinction was introduced between the Turkish mimic and the genuinely European Turk.

Today, the struggle over what it means to be European and what it means to be Turkish has become more intense than ever. In a 2005 interview, Nobel Prize-winning author Orhan Pamuk said that "conservatives, Islamists or anti-Westerners" who resent Turkey's Westernization "call us liberal secularists 'mock Europeans' and imitators. I don't buy this. Turkey has Westernized and modernized in its own way—outside of Europe. We are already way beyond being 'mock Europeans.'"[81] Irrespective of whether one agrees with Pamuk's point about a successful Turkish brand of Western identity, his statement shows that the Turk as mock European remains a powerful anti-Turkish trope that can be mobilized for various political ends. Despite Turkey's accelerated process of Westernization in the twenty-first century and its role as Europe's political ally in the Muslim world, the gap between the European and the Europeanized seems as unbridgeable as ever. Moreover, the fact that Turkey's Muslims and non-Muslims are still divided leads us to question the success of secularism in Turkey.

What remains interesting for both Germany and Turkey today are the implications of this for these countries' respective definitions of nationhood and citizenship. In light of today's ongoing debate about the relationship between migrants and European natives, the case of Jewish Germans in Istanbul also suggests something about models of integration and assimilation, and the historicity of these models. The benefits of cultural assimilation generally go unquestioned in European countries of immigration: Western European countries insist that migrants modulate or even suspend their indigenous cultural practices in favor of those of the host country. Auerbach's example shows, however, that the exact converse, namely preserving difference, was regarded as necessary for promoting the national project in Turkey. This is an interesting counterpoint to the policy as a result of the reverse route of migration in the postwar period. In the case of Turkish immigration to West Germany, assimilation—implying a kind of cultural mimesis—has become mandatory. That this was not always the case is evident from the changing terminology. The status of migrants from Turkey shifted from temporary, underprivileged "guest workers" in the 1960s to that of "foreigners" in the 1970s. This shift has been accompanied by an obligation to integrate into German society. Yet, assimilation has not always been (and perhaps has never been) quite the happy answer to national belonging that it is claimed to be. Against the models of eternal guest, mimic, and *dönme*, guest worker and foreigner, I propose disassociating national belonging from both religion and ethnicity.

NOTES

Part of this essay has been published in Kader Konuk, "Eternal Guests, Mimics, and *Dönme*: The Place of German and Turkish Jews in Modern Turkey," *New Perspectives on Turkey* (37) (2007). For an extended version of this chapter, see my forthcoming *East West Mimesis: German-Jewish Exile and Secular Humanism* (Stanford University Press). I would like to thank Vanessa Agnew for her invaluable input in my work. For the feedback I received on earlier drafts of this chapter I also thank Galit Hasan-Rokem, Erol Köroğlu, and Zafer Yenal.

1. Albert Einstein, "Einstein on His Theory: Time, Space, and Gravitation," *The Times*, November 28, 1919, 14.

2. "ein von der westlichen Pest unberührtes Land." On behalf of the Notgemeinschaft, Schwartz led successful negotiations with Galip in Ankara in July 1933, discussing the conditions of employment of German academics at Turkish universities; Philipp Schwartz, *Notgemeinschaft: Zur Emigration deutscher Wissenschaftler nach 1933 in die Türkei*, 45.

3. Jan Cremer and Horst Przytulla, *Exil Türkei: Deutschsprachige Emigranten in der Türkei 1933–1945*, 27.

4. Before the amendments made in April 2008, the phrase was "insulting Turkishness."

5. Emir Kıvırcık, *Büyükelçi*; see also Stanford J. Shaw's study of Turkey as the savior of Jews, *Turkey and the Holocaust: Turkey's Role in Rescuing Turkish and European Jewry from Nazi Persecution, 1933–1945*; and Duygu Güvenç, "Turkey Battles Genocide Claims in Hollywood," *Turkish Daily News*, February 13, 2007.

6. Arnold Reisman, "Jewish Refugees from Nazism, Albert Einstein, and the Modernization of Higher Education in Turkey (1933–1945)," 264.

7. For the interpretation of archival material regarding this case see Rıfat Bali, *Sarayın ve Cumhuriyetin Dişçibaşısı Sami Günzberg*, 89–107.

8. Gad Freudenthal and Arnold Reisman translated İnönü's letter from French to English in Arnold Reisman, "Jewish Refugees from Nazism, Albert Einstein, and the Modernization of Higher Education in Turkey (1933–1945)," 266–267.

9. The letterhead stated the purpose of the OSE as "Pour la protection de la santé des populations juives."

10. For an article on the humanist reform see Kader Konuk, "Erich Auerbach and the Humanist Reform to the Turkish Education System," *Comparative Literature Studies* 45(1) (2008):74–89.

11. For publications that locate the flight of Sephardic Jews and the emigration

of German Jews to Turkey within a common context of expulsion, see: Rıfat N. Bali, *Cumhuriyet Yıllarında Türkiye Yahudileri: Bir Türkleştirme Serüveni*; Avner Levi, *Türkiye Cumhuriyeti'nde Yahudiler*; Stanford J. Shaw, *Turkey and the Holocaust: Turkey's Role in Rescuing Turkish and European Jewry from Nazi Persecution, 1933–1945*.

12. Avner Levi, *Türkiye Cumhuriyeti'nde Yahudiler*, 103.

13. Şemseddin Günaltay, "Açış Dersi: Türklerin Ana Yurdu ve Irki Mes'elesi," *Üniversite Konferansları 1936–1937*, İstanbul Üniversitesi Yayınları (50): 13.

14. "Kafaları, bedeni teşekkülleri, iltisaki dilleri Türklerin aynı olan Sümerler." Ibid., 10.

15. Günaltay's lecture indicates the direction that the study of Turkish history took in the 1930s. For a discussion of Atatürk's nation-building project that draws on Benedict Anderson's theoretical framework, see Alev Çınar, *Modernity, Islam, and Secularism in Turkey: Bodies, Places, and Time*. The Institute for Turkish History was inaugurated in 1931.

16. The decoupling of Turkish from Ottoman history was justified by the fact that, so far, Ottoman history was occupied with the genealogy of the sultans and military achievements. In contradistinction, Turkish history was to be concerned with the history of the people. The debate about the disassociation of Turkish and Ottoman history is one that has broad implications today in view of Turkey's refusal to accept the Armenian genocide as historical legacy—it is one of the most important questions for Turkey's joining the European Union.

17. The Persian historian Reşidüddin's name is also transliterated as Rashid ad-Din Tabib, Rashid al-Din, or Rashiduddin. Günaltay refers here to the French eighteenth-century sinologist Joseph de Guignes. Günaltay, "Açış Dersi," 1.

18. "Bu mehareti göstermek, bir yahudi dönmesi olduğu rivayet edilen Reşidüddin için müşkül bir iş olamazdı." Ibid., 4.

19. The *dönme* can be compared to, but are not to be equated with, the *conversos* in fifteenth-century Spain. Sabbatai Sevi (Shabbatay Tzevi) declared himself the Jewish Messiah and planned to depose the Ottoman sultan. While imprisoned in Istanbul, he converted to Islam. Hundreds of his followers, particularly in Saloniki, also decided to convert to Islam.

20. Marc Baer, "The Double Bind of Race and Religion: The Conversion of the Dönme to Turkish Secular Nationalism," *Comparative Study of History and Society* 46(4) (2004): 682–708.

21. For a brief history of Sabbatai Sevi's and his followers' apostasy, see Avigdor Levy, *The Sephardim in the Ottoman Empire*, 84–89. Levy points out that the sect is referred to by Jews as *minim* [sectarian] and by Muslims as *dönme*. For a lengthier discussion of the term, see Abdurrahman Küçük, *Dönmeler (Sabatayistler) Tarihi*, 181–204. For a comprehensive discussion of the Sabbataian sect in the twentieth century see: Baer, "The Double Bind of Race and Religion"; and Ilgaz Zorlu, *Evet, Ben Selanikliyim: Türkiye Sabetaycılığı*.

22. In their dictionary of popular political terms, Aslandaş and Bıçakçı establish

that the term *dönme* is used to signify a person with a hidden agenda who acts like a Trojan horse. See Alper Sedat Aslandaş and Baskın Bıçakçı, *Popüler Siyasi Deyimler Sözlüğü*, 196–198. Yalçın Küçük and Soner Yalçın have, in recent years, mobilized the term *dönme* to serve their reactionary political agenda. See, for example, Yalçın Küçük, *İsimlerin İbranileştirilmesi:Tekelistan-Türk Yahudi İsimleri Sözlüğü*.

23. Abdurrahman Küçük argues that at times of political crisis, the idea of the *dönme* as a member of a conspiracy group is remobilized in Turkey. See Küçük, *Dönmeler (Sabatayistler) Tarihi*, 441 ff.

24. Günaltay, "Açış Dersi," 13.

25. Homi K. Bhabha, *The Location of Culture*, 122.

26. By way of alternative, means of becoming a part of Europe were suggested. In 1925, the radical reformist Abdullah Cevdet even suggested that intermarriages and the "mixing of blood" would pave the way to Turkey's Europeanization. For this purpose, he proposed encouraging Italian and German immigration to Turkey. Tarık Z. Tunaya, *Türkiyenin Siyasi Hayatında Batılılaşma Hareketleri*, 81. Abdullah Cevdet's vision of improving the "Turkish race" through hybridizing, however, did not find any support.

27. For an analysis of the "Speak Turkish" campaign see Bali, *Cumhuriyet Yıllarında Türkiye Yahudileri:Bir Türkleştirme serüveni*, 131–158. This campaign was initiated by a group of law students at Istanbul University. See Yelda, *Istanbul'da, Diyarbakır'da Azalırken*, 204.

28. Seyla Benhabib suggests that the effects of the "Speak Turkish" campaign of the 1920s lasted far into the 1950s and 1960s. Her own efforts to speak Turkish without an accent in public were an outcome of a "leveling and stupefying nationalism and patriotism." Seyla Benhabib, "Traumatische Anfänge, Mythen und Experimente: Die multikulturelle Türkei im Übergang zur reifen Demokratie," *Neue Zürcher Zeitung*, November 26, 2005, 71.

29. Marc Baer argues that a distinction was made between "Turks, members of a primordial nation, and Turkish citizens, members of the Turkish nation-state." Baer, "The Double Bind of Race and Religion," 694.

30. Ibid., 704.

31. Letter to the Romance philologist Karl Vossler, dated December 6, 1936, quoted in Hans Ulrich Gumbrecht, *Vom Leben und Sterben der großen Romanisten: Carl Vossler, Ernst Robert Curtius, Leo Spitzer, Erich Auerbach, Werner Krauss*, ed. Michael Krüger, Edition Akzente.

32. Quoted in Arnold Reisman, *Turkey's Modernization: Refugees from Nazism and Atatürk's Vision*, 393.

33. "Die Türken sind für meine Vergangenheit schlechterdings uninteressiert, ich vertrete hier, mag man das in Deutschland wissen wollen oder nicht, gleichviel ob ich will oder nicht will, in den Augen der Türken nicht die deutsche Orientalistik, sondern die Europas." Ritter to Kahle, March 10, 1933: Thomas Lier, "Hellmut Ritter in Istanbul 1926–1949," *Die Welt des Islams* 38(3) (1998): 347.

34. Avigdor Levy argues that Iberian Jewish culture "was transplanted to, and revitalized on, Ottoman soil," in Levy, *The Sephardim in the Ottoman Empire*, 37. See also Avigdor Levy, *The Jews of the Ottoman Empire*, 37–39.

35. Report of the NSDAP Auslands-Organisation Hamburg to the Foreign Office Berlin, January 8, 1935: "Vermöge ihrer Rasseeigentümlichkeit können sich diese Leute besonders gut der türkischen Mentalität anpassen und erlernen sehr schnell die Sprache des Landes." Politisches Archiv des Auswärtigen Amts, "Auswärtiges Amt Abteilung III, Akte Deutsche [Experten ?] in der Türkei 1924–36, R 78630."

36. Translated excerpt from Annemarie Schwarzenbach, *Winter in Vorderasien*, 22.

37. "Die Reaktionäre misstrauen uns als Ausländer, die Fascisten als Emigranten, die Antifascisten als Deutschen, und Antisemitismus gibt es auch." Erich Auerbach, May 27, 1938. I am grateful to Martin Vialon and Karlheinz Barck for making the letter available to me. "Dass 'man' uns von hier vertreiben wird, wenn man die Macht dazu hat, steht fest, und dann werden auch hier die Feinde nicht fehlen. Im Grunde haben wir natürlich viele, obgleich sie zur Zeit schweigen." Erich Auerbach, "Letter to Johannes Oeschger 27 May 1938," *Nachlass Fritz Lieb, Universitätsbibliothek Basel (Handschriftenabteilung)*.

38. "Monsieur Auerbach s'engage à s'abstenir de toute activité politique économique et commerciale et ainsi que toute activité ayant pour but de faire la propagande d'un gouvernement étranger. Il ne peut accepter aucune fonction dans des institutions ou établissements étrangers." Istanbul University, "Chaire de Philologie Romane à la Faculté des lettres, 11.12.1936," in *Erich Auerbach Nachlaß, Zugehörige Materialien* (Literaturarchiv Marbach).

39. Bali, *Cumhuriyet Yıllarında Türkiye Yahudileri*, 513 ff.

40. My thanks go to Galit Hasan-Rokem for clarifying this distinction in my work.

41. Galit Hasan-Rokem and Alan Dundes, *The Wandering Jew: Essays in the Interpretation of a Christian Legend*, vii.

42. Edward Timms, *The Wandering Jew: A Leitmotif in German Literature and Politics*.

43. Elizabeth Grosz, "Judaism and Exile: The Ethics of Otherness," in *Space and Place: Theories of Identity and Location*, ed. Erica Carter, James Donald, and Judith Squires, 61.

44. For an essay investigating the changing social structures for Jews in the Ottoman and republican period see Riva Kastoryano, "From *Millet* to Community: The Jews of Istanbul," in *Ottoman and Turkish Jewry: Community and Leadership*, ed. Aron Rodrigue.

45. Avigdor Levy also maintains in this context that in 1892, at the fourth centennial celebration of the settlement of Sephardic Jews in the Ottoman Empire, "sentiments of gratitude were sincere." Levy, *The Sephardim in the Ottoman Empire*, 124. Levy points out that by the mid-sixteenth century, "Ottomans came to regard the Jews in a class by themselves and as playing a special role in the processes

of empire-building." Levy, *The Sephardim in the Ottoman Empire*, 66. In the 1920s, Mehmed Karakaşzade Rüşdü, a Turkish nationalist of *dönme* origin, reinterpreted the motif of the host and the guest and developed "the host and the parasite motif, which was current at the time: the Turks are the unwitting host to a dangerous parasite that can destroy them." Baer, "The Double Bind of Race and Religion," 697.

46. "Başvekil Refik Saydam'ın gazetecilerle hasbıhali," *Vakit*, January 27, 1939. Cited in Douglas Frantz and Catherine Collins, *Death on the Black Sea: The Untold Story of the Struma and World War II's Holocaust at Sea*, 138–139. Refik Saydam announced that if "they happen to have sisters or families or close relatives in other countries who would wish to come to our country, we would welcome them to enable the experts to work with comfortable minds."

47. On January 23, 1939, the German embassy in Ankara informed the Foreign Office in Berlin that the Turkish government wanted to avoid the settlement of a greater number of Jewish emigrants in Turkey. Along with this, the embassy passed on the information about the proof of Aryan descent now required at Turkish consulates. Politisches Archiv des Auswärtigen Amts, "Konstantinopel / Ankara, # 539, Akte Judentum 1925–1939." Hellmut Ritter's brother writes in his travel diary in July 1939, too, that he has to verify his Aryan descent to Turkish authorities. Karl Bernhard Ritter, *Fahrt zum Bosporus: Ein Reisetagebuch*, 151.

48. "Şehrimizdeki Alman Musevileri Almanlıktan çıkardılar," *Yeni Sabah*, August 12, 1939. Cited in Bali, *Cumhuriyet Yıllarında Türkiye Yahudileri*, 337.

49. Politisches Archiv des Auswärtigen Amts, "Akten des Generalkonsulats Istanbul, # 3989, Paket 28, Akte 2 Istanbul Emigranten." Toepke's report is dated October 9, 1939; he wrote "Anträge auf Einbürgerung haben sämtliche Juden und Mischlinge gestellt mit Ausnahme von Professor Auerbach."

50. See also Martin Vialon, "Kommentar," *Trajekte* 9 (2004): 14.

51. The letter is dated June 5, 1938. Erich Auerbach, "Ein Exil-Brief Erich Auerbachs aus Istanbul an Freya Hobohm in Marburg—versehen mit einer Nachschrift von Marie Auerbach (1938), ed. by Martin Vialon," *Trajekte* 9 (2004): 11.

52. Responsible for this is, after all, Turkey's switch from the Arabic to the Roman alphabet in 1928 and the establishment of the Institute for the Turkish Language in the 1930s that promoted the "purification" of the Turkish language, thereby replacing Arabic and Persian words with Turkish vocabulary. The Arabic script ceased to be taught in schools.

53. Erich Auerbach, *Gesammelte Aufsätze zur Romanischen Philologie*, 305.

54. "was ich für die Wahrheit halte, könnte ich nicht öffentlich äußern." Martin Vialon, ed., *Erich Auerbachs Briefe an Martin Hellweg (1939–1950)*, 78. The letter is dated May 16, 1947.

55. "Ich bin doch sehr liberalistisch, die von den Umständen mir verliehene Lage hat diese Neigung noch verstärkt; ich geniesse hier die grösste Freiheit des ne pas conclure. Ich konnte mich hier wie nirgends sonst von jeder Bindung freihalten; gerade meine Haltung als nirgends Hingehöriger, grundsätzlich und unassimilier-

bar Fremder ist das, was man von mir wünscht und von mir erwartet. aber, wo Sie mich hinhaben wollen, erwartet man eine 'Grundbereitschaft.'" Auerbach's letter to Werner Krauss is dated August 27, 1946: Erich Auerbach and Werner Krauss, "Eine unveröffentlichte Korrespondenz," *Beiträge zur Romanischen Philologie* 26(2) (1987): 317. I have slightly changed Gumbrecht's translation of this passage in Hans Ulrich Gumbrecht, "'Pathos of the Earthly Progress': Erich Auerbach's Everydays," in *Literary History and the Challenge of Philology: The Legacy of Erich Auerbach*, ed. Seth Lerer, 32.

56. Translated from a letter to Werner Krauss dated October 27, 1946, archived in the Literaturarchiv Marbach.

57. "Türken sind wir nicht geworden, nicht einmal rechtlich, jetzt sind wir wieder passlose Deutsche, alles ist provisorisch." Vialon, ed., *Erich Auerbachs Briefe an Martin Hellweg (1939–1950)*, 70. The letter is dated May 16, 1947. In a 1946 letter, Auerbach complained to Werner Krauss about the impossibility of moving, since he did not have a passport. Karlheinz Barck, "Eine unveröffentlichte Korrespondenz: Erich Auerbach/Werner Krauss," *Beiträge zur Romanischen Philologie* 26(2) (1987): 316.

58. Emir Kıvırcık, *Büyükelçi*, 10.

59. According to Nazi records, 3,042 Turkish Jews lived in Paris alone in 1942: Politisches Archiv des Auswärtigen Amts, "R 100889, Akte Judenfrage in der Türkei 1942–1944, Inland II g 207." A telegram from Paris, dated February 12, 1943, reports that the Turkish general consul presented Nazi authorities with a list of 631 Turkish Jews whose citizenship he had cleared. A memorandum dated February 17, 1943, states the estimated figure of Turkish Jews living in the Western occupied territories as 3,000. Another report dated March 12, 1943, refers to the departure of 121 Turkish Jews in mid-March. The same record refers to a list of 5,000 Turkish Jews, which has not been archived. All documents are located in Politisches Archiv des Auswärtigen Amts, "Judenfrage in der Türkei, R 99446 1938–1943, Inland II A/B." In *Turkey and the Holocaust*, Stanford Shaw evaluated a different set of archival sources. For a novel dealing with Turkish Jews in France, see Ayşe Kulin, *Nefes Nefese*.

60. Corinna Görgü Guttstadt, "Depriving Non-Muslims of Citizenship as Part of the Turkification Policy in the Early Years of the Republic: The Case of Turkish Jews and Its Consequences during the Holocaust," in *Turkey Beyond Nationalism: Towards Post-Nationalist Identities*, ed. Hans-Lukas Kieser, 56.

61. See, for example, a report from Paris to the Foreign Office Berlin, June 23, 1943: "Mündlich hat der hiesige türkische Generalkonsul durchblicken lassen, daß die Türkische Regierung auf diese Anfrage keine Antwort erteilen könne, weil sie offiziell einen Unterschied zwischen türkischen Staatsangehörigen jüdischer und anderer Rasse nicht mache." Politisches Archiv des Auswärtigen Amts, "Judenfrage in der Türkei, R 99446 1938–1943, Inland II A/B."

62. Memorandum of von Thadden, dated September 22, 1943. Koç, the representative of the Turkish embassy in Berlin, informed von Thadden of the Turkish government's decision: "die türkischen Konsularvertretungen mit der Weisung zu

versehen, alle rückkehrwilligen Juden türkischer Staatsangehörigkeit nach Prüfung jedes Einzelfalles in der Türkei zu übernehmen. Hierbei solle davon ausgegangen werden, daß eine Masseneinwanderung von Juden in die Türkei zu verhindern sei, insbesondere von solchen Juden, die zwar ordnungsgemäß türkische Papiere hätten, aber bereits seit Jahrzehnten mit der Türkei keinerlei Kontakt mehr hätten." Ibid.

63. Isaak Behar's autobiographical account of his life as a Turkish Jew in Nazi Germany tells a tragic story. Behar writes that in April 1939, the Turkish government asked his family to verify their citizenship. After handing over their Turkish passports to German authorities, however, the Behar family was left unprotected and eventually declared stateless. Isaak Behar survived by going underground; his parents and two sisters were deported and killed in death camps: Isaak Behar, *Versprich mir, dass Du am Leben bleibst: Ein jüdisches Schicksal*, 73–74.

64. At the time, it was not known that the Soviets sank the *Struma*. Tuvia Friling, *Between Friendly and Hostile Neutrality: Turkey and the Jews during World War II*, vol. 2, 331 ff. For other accounts of the *Struma* tragedy see Ergun Hiçyılmaz and Meral Altındal, *Büyük Sığınak: Türk Yahudilerinin 500 Yıllık Serüveninden Sayfalar*. For the most comprehensive account see Frantz and Collins, *Death on the Black Sea*.

65. Bali, *Cumhuriyet Yıllarında Türkiye Yahudileri*, 361.

66. Frantz and Collins, *Death on the Black Sea*, 217. See also Bali, *Cumhuriyet Yıllarında Türkiye Yahudileri*, 361.

67. On October 14, 1942, the German embassy provided the Foreign Office Berlin with a detailed report on the "State of the Jewish Problem in Turkey." The report by Julius Seiler showed that there was an increase in anti-Semitism in Turkey—evidenced by tax measures, Saydam's response to Jewish refugees, and labor camps: Politisches Archiv des Auswärtigen Amts, "Judenfrage in der Türkei, R 99446 1938–1943, Inland II A/B."

68. Rıfat N. Bali, *The "Varlık Vergisi" Affair: A Study of Its Legacy—Selected Documents*, 55

69. For a discussion of the discriminatory nature of the capital tax, see Rıfat Bali's study, which includes original documents from various national archives. All in all, between the years 1942 and 1943, 1,443 members of minorities were sent to the Aşkale labor camp and were released by December 1943. Ibid., 99.

70. Sule Toktas, "Citizenship and Minorities: A Historical Overview of Turkey's Jewish Minority," *Journal of Historical Sociology* 18(4) (2005): 404.

71. Küçük, *Dönmeler (Sabatayistler) Tarihi*, 43, 438. A renewed interest in the religious practices of *dönme* is also evident in publications from the war period. İbrahim Alaettin Gövsa suggested in 1940 that twelve thousand Sabbataian families lived in Turkey. See İbrahim Alaettin Gövsa, *Sabatay Sevi: İzmirli Meşhur Sahte Mesih Hakkında Tarihî ve İçtimaî Tetkik Tecrübesi*.

72. See the collection of cartoons in *Yahudi Fıkraları*.

73. Nadir Nadi, *Cumhuriyet*, January 23, 1943. Nadi's article is summarized in Bali, *Varlık Vergisi*, 266.

74. Public Record Office, FO371/37470/R5698, "Report by H. Knatchbull-Hugessen to the Right Honorouble Anthony Eden, M.C., M.P., No. 254 (779/3/43) British Embassy, Ankara. 21st June, 1943." Quoted in Bali, *Varlık Vergisi*, 278. I assume that the insertion in brackets "[450 years ago!]" stems from Knatchbull-Hugessen.

75. Moltke went to Istanbul in July and December 1943, where he also met Paul Leverkuehn, who directed the Istanbul branch of the German intelligence service, and the German ambassador Franz von Papen. Moltke unsuccessfully tried to "dissuade the Allies from the demand of unconditional surrender on the part of the Germans." Freya von Moltke, *Memories of Kreisau and the German Resistance*, trans. Julie M. Winter, 38. See also Klemens von Klemperer, *German Resistance Against Hitler: The Search for Allies Abroad, 1938–1945*, 331.

76. The document can be viewed at http://germanhistorydocs.ghi-dc.org/sub_document.cfm?document_id=1517 (accessed December 1, 2007). For a detailed overview of Moltke's and Rüstow's efforts in Istanbul see Michael Balfour and Julian Frisby, *Helmuth von Moltke: A Leader Against Hitler*, 270–281.

77. The original letter was published in Helmuth James von Moltke, *Briefe an Freya 1939–1945*, 504. I have slightly changed the translation of the letter in Helmuth James von Moltke, *Letters to Freya: 1939–1945*, trans. Beate Ruhm von Appen, 319. The letter is dated July 7, 1943.

78. Translated from a letter published in Vialon, ed., *Erich Auerbachs Briefe an Martin Hellweg (1939–1950)*, 69–70.

79. In March 1944 the capital tax debts were released. Bali, *Varlık Vergisi*, 55.

80. Nurullah Ataç, *Diyelim*, 98–99.

81. Orhan Pamuk, "The Two Souls of Turkey," *New Perspectives Quarterly* 24(3) (2007): 10.

WORKS CITED

Aslandaş, Alper Sedat, and Baskın Bıçakçı. *Popüler Siyasi Deyimler Sözlüğü*. Istanbul: İletişim Yayınları, 1995.

Ataç, Nurullah. *Diyelim*. Istanbul: Varlık Yayınları, 1954.

Auerbach, Erich. "Ein Exil-Brief Erich Auerbachs aus Istanbul an Freya Hobohm in Marburg—versehen mit einer Nachschrift von Marie Auerbach (1938), ed. by Martin Vialon." *Trajekte* 9 (2004).

———. *Gesammelte Aufsätze zur Romanischen Philologie*. Bern and Munich: Francke Verlag, 1967.

Baer, Marc. "The Double Bind of Race and Religion: The Conversion of the Dönme to Turkish Secular Nationalism." *Comparative Study of History and Society* 46(4) (2004): 682–708.

Balfour, Michael, and Julian Frisby. *Helmuth von Moltke: A Leader Against Hitler*. London: Macmillan, 1972.

Bali, Rıfat. *Cumhuriyet Yıllarında Türkiye Yahudileri: Bir Türkleştirme Serüveni.* Istanbul: İletişim, 1999.

———. *Sarayın ve Cumhuriyetin Dişçibaşısı Sami Günzberg.* Istanbul: Kitabevi, 2007.

———. *The "Varlık Vergisi" Affair: A Study of Its Legacy—Selected Documents.* Istanbul: Isis Press, 2005.

Barck, Karlheinz. "Eine unveröffentlichte Korrespondenz: Erich Auerbach/Werner Krauss." *Beiträge zur Romanischen Philologie* 26(2) (1987): 301–326.

"Başvekil Refik Saydam'ın gazetecilerle hasbıhali." *Vakit,* January 27, 1939.

Behar, Isaak. *Versprich mir, dass Du am Leben bleibst: Ein jüdisches Schicksal.* Berlin: Ullstein, 2002.

Benhabib, Seyla. "Traumatische Anfänge, Mythen und Experimente: Die multikulturelle Türkei im Übergang zur reifen Demokratie." *Neue Zürcher Zeitung,* November 26, 2005, 71.

Bhabha, Homi K. *The Location of Culture.* London: Routledge, 1994.

Çınar, Alev. *Modernity, Islam, and Secularism in Turkey: Bodies, Places, and Time.* Minneapolis: University of Minnesota Press, 2005.

Cremer, Jan, and Horst Przytulla. *Exil Türkei: Deutschsprachige Emigranten in der Türkei 1933–1945.* Munich: Verlag Karl M. Lipp, 1991.

Einstein, Albert. "Einstein on His Theory: Time, Space, and Gravitation." *The Times,* November 28, 1919, 13–14.

Frantz, Douglas, and Catherine Collins. *Death on the Black Sea: The Untold Story of the Struma and World War II's Holocaust at Sea.* New York: Ecco, 2003.

Friling, Tuvia. *Between Friendly and Hostile Neutrality: Turkey and the Jews during World War II.* Vol. 2. Jerusalem: Tel Aviv University, 2002.

Gövsa, İbrahim Alaettin. *Sabatay Sevi: İzmirli Meşhur Sahte Mesih Hakkında Tarihî ve İçtimaî Tetkik Tecrübesi.* Istanbul: S. Lütfi Kitabevi, 1940.

Grosz, Elizabeth. "Judaism and Exile: The Ethics of Otherness." In *Space and Place: Theories of Identity and Location,* ed. Erica Carter, James Donald, and Judith Squires, 57–72. London: Lawrence & Wishart, 1993.

Gumbrecht, Hans Ulrich. "'Pathos of the Earthly Progress': Erich Auerbach's Everydays." In *Literary History and the Challenge of Philology: The Legacy of Erich Auerbach,* ed. Seth Lerer, 13–35. Stanford, CA: Stanford University Press, 1996.

———. *Vom Leben und Sterben der großen Romanisten: Carl Vossler, Ernst Robert Curtius, Leo Spitzer, Erich Auerbach, Werner Krauss,* ed. Michael Krüger. Edition Akzente. Munich and Vienna: Carl Hanser Verlag, 2002.

Günaltay, Şemseddin. "Açış Dersi: Türklerin Ana Yurdu ve Irki Mes'elesi." In *Üniversite Konferansları 1936–1937,* I-XIV. Istanbul: Ülkü Basımevi, 1937.

Guttstadt, Corinna Görgü. "Depriving Non-Muslims of Citizenship as Part of the Turkification Policy in the Early Years of the Republic: The Case of Turkish Jews and Its Consequences during the Holocaust." In *Turkey Beyond Nationalism: Towards Post-Nationalist Identities,* ed. Hans-Lukas Kieser, 43–49. London: I.B. Tauris, 2006.

Güvenç, Duygu. "Turkey Battles Genocide Claims in Hollywood." *Turkish Daily News*, February 13, 2007. http://www.turkishdailynews.com.tr/article.php?enews id=66071 (accessed March 19, 2007).

Hasan-Rokem, Galit, and Alan Dundes. *The Wandering Jew: Essays in the Interpretation of a Christian Legend*. Bloomington: Indiana University Press, 1986.

Hiçyılmaz, Ergun, and Meral Altındal. *Büyük Sığınak: Türk Yahudilerinin 500 Yıllık Serüveninden Sayfalar*. Istanbul: Belgesel, 1992.

Istanbul University. "Chaire de Philologie Romane à la Faculté des lettres, 11.12.1936." In *Erich Auerbach Nachlaß, Zugehörige Materialien*. Literaturarchiv Marbach.

Kastoryano, Riva. "From *Millet* to Community: The Jews of Istanbul." In *Ottoman and Turkish Jewry: Community and Leadership*, ed. Aron Rodrigue, 253–277. Bloomington: Indiana University Press, 1992.

Kıvırcık, Emir. *Büyükelçi*. Istanbul: Goa, 2007.

Klemperer, Klemens von. *German Resistance Against Hitler: The Search for Allies Abroad, 1938–1945*. Oxford: Oxford University Press, 1992.

Konuk, Kader. "Erich Auerbach and the Humanist Reform to the Turkish Education System." *Comparative Literature Studies* 45(1) (2008): 74–89.

———. "Eternal Guests, Mimics, and *Dönme*: The Place of German and Turkish Jews in Modern Turkey." *New Perspectives on Turkey* 37 (2007).

Küçük, Abdurrahman. *Dönmeler (Sabatayistler) Tarihi*. Ankara: Alperen Yayınları, 2001.

Küçük, Yalçın. *İsimlerin İbranileştirilmesi:Tekelistan-Türk Yahudi İsimleri Sözlüğü*. Istanbul: Salyangoz Yayınları, 2006.

Kulin, Ayşe. *Nefes Nefese*. 15th ed. Istanbul: Remzi Kitapevi, 2007.

Levi, Avner. *Türkiye Cumhuriyeti'nde Yahudiler*. Istanbul: İletişim, 1992.

Levy, Avigdor. *The Jews of the Ottoman Empire*. Princeton, NJ: Darwin Press, 1994.

———. *The Sephardim in the Ottoman Empire*. Princeton, NJ: Darwin Press, 1992.

Lier, Thomas. "Hellmut Ritter in Istanbul 1926–1949." *Die Welt des Islams* 38(3) (1998): 334–385.

Moltke, Freya von. *Memories of Kreisau and the German Resistance*, trans. Julie M. Winter. Lincoln: University of Nebraska Press, 2005.

Moltke, Helmuth James von. *Briefe an Freya 1939–1945*. Munich: C.H. Beck, 1988.

———. *Letters to Freya: 1939–1945*, trans. Beate Ruhm von Appen. New York: Alfred A. Knopf, 1990.

Pamuk, Orhan. "The Two Souls of Turkey." *New Perspectives Quarterly* 24(3) (2007): 10–11.

Politisches Archiv des Auswärtigen Amts. "Akten des Generalkonsulats Istanbul, # 3989, Paket 28, Akte 2 Istanbul Emigranten."

———. "Auswärtiges Amt Abteilung III, Akte Deutsche [Experten ?] in der Türkei 1924–36, R 78630."

———. "Judenfrage in der Türkei, R 99446 1938–1943, Inland II A/B."

————. "Konstantinopel / Ankara, # 539, Akte Judentum 1925–1939."

————. "R 100889, Akte Judenfrage in der Türkei 1942–1944, Inland II g 207."

Reisman, Arnold. "Jewish Refugees from Nazism, Albert Einstein, and the Modernization of Higher Education in Turkey (1933–1945)." *Aleph: Historical Studies in Science and Judaism* 7 (2007): 253–281.

————. *Turkey's Modernization: Refugees from Nazism and Atatürk's Vision*. Washington, DC: New Academia Publishing, 2006.

Ritter, Karl Bernhard. *Fahrt zum Bosporus: Ein Reisetagebuch*. Leipzig: Hegner, 1941.

Schwartz, Philipp. *Notgemeinschaft: Zur Emigration deutscher Wissenschaftler nach 1933 in die Türkei*. Marburg: Metropolis-Verlag, 1995.

Schwarzenbach, Annemarie. *Winter in Vorderasien*. Basel: Lenos Verlag, 2002.

"Şehrimizdeki Alman Musevileri Almanlıktan çıkardılar." *Yeni Sabah*, August 12, 1939.

Shaw, Stanford J. *Turkey and the Holocaust: Turkey's Role in Rescuing Turkish and European Jewry from Nazi Persecution, 1933–1945*. Hampshire and London: Macmillan Press, 1993.

Timms, Edward. *The Wandering Jew: A Leitmotif in German Literature and Politics*. Brighton: University of Sussex, 1994.

Toktas, Sule. "Citizenship and Minorities: A Historical Overview of Turkey's Jewish Minority." *Journal of Historical Sociology* 18(4) (2005): 394–429.

Tunaya, Tarık Z. *Türkiyenin Siyasi Hayatında Batılılaşma Hareketleri*. Istanbul: Yedigün Matbaası, 1960.

Vialon, Martin, ed. *Erich Auerbachs Briefe an Martin Hellweg (1939–1950)*. Tübingen: A. Francke Verlag, 1997.

————. "Kommentar." *Trajekte* 9 (2004): 13–16.

*Yahudi Fıkraları*. Istanbul: Akbaba Yayını, 1943.

Yelda. *Istanbul'da, Diyarbakır'da Azalırken*. Istanbul: Belge, 1996.

Zorlu, Ilgaz. *Evet, Ben Selanikliyim: Türkiye Sabetaycılığı*. Istanbul: Belge Yayınları, 1998.

# CHAPTER NINE

# Experiment Mars, Turkish Migration, and the Future of Europe

*Imaginative Ethnoscapes in Contemporary German Literature*

LESLIE A. ADELSON

Contemporary literatures of migration do not always serve the preservationist agendas that reading publics and literary critics may expect of them. Azade Seyhan, for example, stresses the importance of "discovering forgotten idioms" and "restoring neglected individual and collective stories to literary history" in her widely cited account of "writing outside the nation" late in the twentieth century (Seyhan 2001, 13). By contrast, this essay marks an initial foray into what I am inclined to call the new futurism in contemporary German literature. As I have argued elsewhere, Seyla Benhabib's call for a "'disaggregated' approach to changing social practices of citizenship" and social membership in Europe today should also be complemented by a "disaggregated" approach to the cultural labor that migration literature performs (Benhabib 2002, 168–169; Adelson 2005, 8, 124). That is to say, we should as readers cultivate an open-ended curiosity about what is culturally at stake when literature engages the phenomenon of migration. An a priori answer to this question is no real answer at all. Some literary practices may indeed serve the recuperation of lost archives or the preservation of neglected memories, disenfranchised communities, and established identities, while others will not. This experimental essay entertains the possibility that an imaginative engagement with futurity rather than tradition may help to produce new modes of affiliation for a changing public sphere in Europe.

A focus on futurity in literature written on the cusp of a new century departs from a longstanding emphasis on the past in both German literature after 1945 and the transnational migration literature that began to appear in Germany in the 1970s.[1] Even much of the prose fiction signaling the cultural influence of Turkish migration on German literature of the 1980s and 1990s arguably entails imaginative reworkings of a German past in the main—as associated with twentieth-century genocide and the Cold War, for example—en route to a shared multicultural future in Europe (see Adelson 2005 on "the Turkish turn"). Because literatures of migration and their cultural arenas of engagement are constantly changing in our age of globalization, however, literary conceits of futurity may speak to many different functions accruing to the literary imagination more broadly today. This may apply in particular where labor migration is at play, but we would be misguided to associate such labor effects with immigrant populations alone (Turks in Germany, for example). For this reason the analytical project abbreviated here as "experiment Mars" uses the lens of futurity to conjoin the experimental prose of Alexander Kluge, on the one hand, and a poetic trilogy by Berkan Karpat and Zafer Şenocak, on the other. These authors are unlikely co-conspirators in futuristic time travel to a famously red planet.[2] They would generally not be considered together under the rubric of ethnicity in today's Europe, and Kluge could easily not appear at all in a volume devoted to contemporary manifestations of "ethnicity." Only when we consider their literary production through the lens of futurity does a certain resonance emerge between their aesthetic projects, and only then does the comparison appear consequential for a new approach to the meaning of *ethnos* in Europe today. This essay is a speculative experiment that aims to grasp imaginative and social ties in Europe on the cusp of a new era. Although the literary texts in question are not yet widely read by a European readership (this is less true for Kluge, whose prose works are generally better known both in and outside Germany), reading them with an eye to futurity underscores their potential importance for thinking about contemporary literature as a social phenomenon.

Widely known and celebrated in Germany since the 1960s as an innovative filmmaker, social theorist, legal expert, experimental fiction writer, and—since the 1980s—for his so-called cultural windows in television programming, Alexander Kluge might best be considered a multimedial conceptual artist of extraordinary imaginative range.[3] First published in 1973, his "theory-fiction" titled *Lernprozesse mit tödlichem Ausgang* was republished in 2000 as part of a two-volume "chronicle of feelings" including both old and new experimental prose, much of it influenced by the rich German tradition of critical theory (Scherpe 2001).[4] Only the first chapter of these "learning processes with a deadly outcome" will be discussed here, since it revolves around the loss of earthly territory on a planetary scale and quirky reflections from Mars on what is *"übrig"* [left over] in the human wake of Earth's demise. "Der Verlust des Planeten" [The loss of the planet], as this inaugural chapter is called, will culminate in the year 2103 in what the text comes to call *"Die Avantgarde im Sektor Morgenröte"* [The avant-garde in Sector Rosy Dawn] (Kluge 2000, 918). The military connotations of the term avant-garde are hardly coincidental in this work or the oeuvre of an author long concerned with the production of both war and hope in human history. Mars also denotes an ancient god of war.

If Kluge's imaginative conjurings of a Martian avant-garde prompt us to contemplate learning something new, as the book's original title and narrative trajectory suggest, so does a so-called futurist epilogue coauthored by Berkan Karpat and Zafer Şenocak, whose multimedial collaborations of the late 1990s may even inaugurate a Turkish-German avant-garde of a different sort.[5] Best known in Germany for his journalistic commentary in print, radio, and television media on Turks in relation to European culture and democracy since 1989, Şenocak is also a poet and novelist whose literary production to date has been most enthusiastically received outside Germany, notably in North America, Great Britain, France, Italy, and Turkey.[6] By contrast, Karpat's installation art, which foregrounds performance, sculpture, and sound in public spaces in Munich (and more recently in Düsseldorf), does not seem to have found much resonance as yet beyond the Bavarian capital.[7] While the "futurist epilogue" on which Karpat and Şenocak collaborated consists of three independently published texts—and may also be said to include several of Karpat's sound sculptures and installations, especially those incorporating coauthored textual material—this essay will focus on the first published installment of the so-called epilogue—*nâzım hikmet: auf dem schiff zum mars.*

This installment first appeared in 1998 with the publishing house of Babel in the form of twelve short poetic segments. The recurring trope of a rocket ship en route to Mars lends itself to juxtaposition with Kluge's "avant-garde" fiction, though other elements of the "futurist epilogue" more readily recall the actual historical phenomenon of the futurist avant-garde in Europe, especially in the Soviet Union. After all, the second installment of Karpat and Şenocak's collaborative labors—*Tanzende der Elektrik: szenisches Poem,* which followed in 1999—directly invokes the spirit of Russian Futurism in punning allusions to Velimir Khlebnikov, whom Roman Jakobson once called "the greatest world poet of our century." Today, however, the Russian Futurist known in the 1920s for his so-called transrational "invention of new words based purely on sound" (as opposed to semantics, syntax, or morphology, for example) remains largely undiscovered in the West despite an English translation of his collected works in 1997 (Perloff 2003, xxix, 121; see also Folejewski 1980). Yet to say that Khlebnikov's ghost figures in playful bits and pieces in *Tanzende der Elektrik*—as it does in the coinage *"sprachchlebtomane"* or "language khlebtomaniac," for example—is not to say that Karpat and Şenocak mimic the historical Futurist's aesthetic practice. One might say instead that bits and pieces of historical and cultural matter circulate in all parts of the "futurist epilogue" without ever yielding an intelligible whole. One is reminded here of a line in conversation in Kluge's "Verlust des Planeten" chapter, where legal and medical experts wonder how they should think about humanity's material leftovers on Mars after human society on Earth has been destroyed and few interplanetary travelers escape attacks on their spaceships intact. Uneasy with the situation even though he himself has not been physically harmed, one of the conversationalists describes the mood that unsettles him: *"Ich fühle mich oft ganz zerstückelt"* [I often feel all in pieces] (Kluge 2000, 839–840). The voice of the past is notably *"ganz zerstückelt"* [all in pieces] in both texts under examination here.

As will become evident in reference to *nâzım hikmet: auf dem schiff zum mars,* however, even the most seemingly nostalgic of the textual components in Karpat and Şenocak's "futurist epilogue" warrants reading against the obvious grain. Resurrecting the ghost of Nâzım Hikmet (1902–63), modern Turkey's best-loved people's poet, who spent years in Turkish prisons for his communist and pacifist beliefs and then died in Soviet exile not long after the Berlin Wall went up, turns out to be more about *Zerstückelung* than *Entfremdung* [social alienation]—and more about being all in pieces than wanting to make things whole again.[8] The notion that this bespeaks some type of futurism rather than despair in postsocialist Europe may well seem far-fetched. Jean Améry, who survived torture at the hands of Nazis at a Belgian concentration camp, but hardly intact, once characterized the future as "*die eigentlich menschliche Dimension*" [the authentically human dimension] (Améry 2002, 128). If the matter of human life appears "all in pieces" in Kluge's "learning processes" and Karpat and Şenocak's "futurist epilogue," what is there to learn about a futurism that would not merely lament, repeat, or forget an inhumane past?[9]

The question as to such a futurism is fundamentally related, I propose, to changing functions of both ethnicity and literature in our time. Addressing the late twentieth-century "Turkish turn" in German literature, I have argued elsewhere that cultural constellations of *ethnos* today can be incompatible with discrete and continuous ethnic identities as multiculturalism often conceives them (Adelson 2005, 169–170 et passim). Seyla Benhabib's critique of what she calls "strong contextualism" and "mosaic multiculturalism" in political theories of membership in contemporary Europe reminds us that cultures do not function socially in the age of globalization as "seamless wholes" (Benhabib 2002, 7–8, 25). This is one reason why the conceptual language of a "runaway world" (Giddens 2003), interactive "networks," and proliferating "-scapes" circulates with ever more frequency across the disciplines. Such rhetoric bespeaks the analytical need for alternative models of sociability and context when older container-models of community and belonging fail us.[10] As recently as 2003, Alexander Kluge even explicitly characterized books as "*Netzwerke*" [networks] that are "*notwendiges Überlebensmittel*" [necessary means of survival] (Kluge 2003). The trope of survival here clearly echoes Kluge's fictional concerns with what is "left over" when earthly contexts are destroyed, but the trope of survival may also conjure—for some—more holistically oriented associations with tradition, legacy, and continuity rather than change. Such associations underwrite many assumptions—normative as well as descriptive—about the function of ethnicity, even in dramatically changing worlds on planet Earth. For that reason, it is important to note that Kluge's fictional tale of a Martian "avant-garde" circles around the question of what is "left over" in bits—and decidedly not "what remains" in any holistic representational sense.[11] Much will pivot on this distinction.

In the life of academe an attachment to territories and communities thought to cohere in their ideal form loses more and more analytical purchase as global and local phenomena become increasingly enmeshed.[12] This shifting ground of analysis manifests itself in various ways in scholarship on ethnicity in particular. Commenting on "the nature of ethnicity in the project of migration," for example, John Rex (2003, 274) observes:

> Although much of the theoretical writing about ethnicity has been concerned with the attachment of an ethnic group to a territory, in fact ethnic communities are often concerned precisely with their detachment from a territory, that it is to say with the business of international migration.[13]

Rex pointedly uncouples ethnicity and nationalism by challenging the ostensible primacy of continuous territorial homelands for migrant communities. Could the primacy of continuous human communities cohering as cultural blocs be similarly challenged if *ethnos* were no longer defined by ethnicity for nonmigrating groups too? Could it be that detachment from received forms of communal embodiment serves new forms of social affiliation for which tradition- and legacy-based models of ethnicity can no longer account? The suggestion may not be as bold as years of identity politics lead us to believe. Writing in 1914—just around the time that Futurist fervor was seizing many European intellectuals[14]—Max Weber defined the lived principle of *ethnos* in terms that are not bound to continuity of blood or even custom:

> We shall call "ethnic groups" those human groups that entertain a subjective belief in their common descent because of similarities of physical type or of customs or both, or because of memories of colonization and migration; this belief must be important for the propagation of group formation; conversely, it does not matter whether or not an objective blood relationship exists [as cited in Guibernau and Rex 2003, 18–19].[15]

Weber underscores the constitutive importance of subjective perceptions, not physical facts or cultural traits as such, for the formation of *ethnos* as a social phenomenon (Guibernau and Rex 2003, 2).[16] According to Weber, once purposive modes of affiliation turn into personal relationships, the subjective perception of "common ethnicity" may follow—not precede—such relationships (Guibernau and Rex 2003, 19).[17] If contemporary literature mobilizes or enables modes of affiliation in newly imaginative ways, perhaps it can be said that this literature, in some respects, also contributes to a reworking of *ethnos* as a social phenomenon today. Beyond the "imagined communities" of national modernities, about which so much has been said in the last twenty-five years (see especially Anderson 1991), what new forms of imagined communities are possible when the very notion of community either collapses or proliferates in bits and pieces of its former self? The language of networks lends itself to this type of analytical question especially but not only in relationship to media studies. What additional avenues of analytical inquiry might the literary experiments of conceptual artists such as Kluge, Karpat, and Şenocak suggest? Attention to functions of futurity in their work will help us think about this question.

In countless public debates about immigration and in many scholarly venues too, cultural and ethnic communities are often presumed to cohere on the basis of shared remembrances of shared pasts. This focus on the past is also evident in Weber's definition of ethnic groups cited above, even as this influential sociologist highlights subjective beliefs rather than objective histories for collective ties that bind. Yet what would it mean to conceive of ethnoscapes predicated, not on tradition and heritage—not even as subjectively affirmed—but on fictional futures instead? What if some of the ties that bind in the new Europe begin to turn on precisely this distinction? When Arjun Appadurai coined the term "ethnoscape" in his seminal study of global diasporas and changing modernities at the end of the twentieth century, he defined the concept metaphorically—in contradistinction to container-models of ethnicity—as "the landscape of persons who constitute the shifting world in which we live" (Appadurai 1996, 33). For the renowned anthropologist, the social labor of imagination at this juncture becomes "the key component of the new global order" (Appadurai 1996, 31). Bespeaking an exaggerated and optimistic claim difficult to sustain amidst widespread concerns with terrorism, war, and security today, Appadurai's bold assertion a decade ago should nonetheless give us pause to consider two questions that he does not raise. What new cultural functions accrue to the literary imagination at the turn of the twenty-first century? And what facets of this imaginative phenomenon come into view when literary ethnoscapes become oriented to the future rather than the past?

At this point one might venture a tentative definition of a new futurism in German literature as a literary form of labor concerned with the production of the future out of recycled bits and pieces of the past. According to one review of Kluge's *Chronik der Gefühle*, the "*Wiederauferstehung der Toten*" [resurrection of the dead] is the author's central motif (Schulte 2001, 347). Yet the voice of the past manifests only as bits and pieces in both *Lernprozesse* and *nâzım hikmet: auf dem schiff zum mars*, as we have already noted. In some ways this recalls Sigrid Weigel's reflections on the "*Stimme der Toten*" [voice of the dead] as the sine qua non for the "*Lesbarkeit der Kultur*" [readability of culture] in literature (Weigel 2002, 76).[18] Even when conceptualizing this as a conversation with the dead rather than about them, however, Weigel is at pains to argue that the voice of the dead in literature is never "*identisch mit der Stimme derjenigen, die einst gelebt haben*" [identical with the voice of those who once lived]. She speaks, not of a "*Nachhall*" [echo] of the past but of a "*Widerhall*" [resonance] with the past that emanates from the present of those who read (Weigel 2002, 79).[19] Weigel is not concerned with the production of futures in her account of culture's voice, and in Kluge's extraordinary voyage to Mars the voice of the past does not speak in the voice of the dead at all but in the rarefied voices of those who survive catastrophic human histories writ large. *Lernprozesse* might then be said to revolve around the production of the intangible stuff of future histories in literary form.

This pivot point for Kluge's experimental prose resonates with an interest in historical leftovers in the collaborative projects of Berkan Karpat and Zafer Şenocak, but their "futurist epilogue" is far less concerned with historical narrative as such. "*Da wo ich herkomme*," Şenocak once wrote contrasting Turkey with Germany, "*liest man die Zukunft. Hierzulande vertieft man sich in die Vergangenheit, als hätte man sie gar nicht erlebt, als müsse man sie erraten, als könne man sie gestalten*" [Where I come from, one reads the future. Here one immerses oneself in the past, as if one hadn't experienced it, as if one had to surmise it, as if one could still give it form] (Şenocak 2006, 205). This sounds like an apt description of Kluge's futuristic engagement with the past in *Lernprozesse*. Karpat and Şenocak's own "futurist epilogue," by contrast, has less to do with the forging of future histories from human catastrophe than with the reworking of *ethnos* in a newly expanded European framework, in which Turkish histories also circulate, albeit without being retold. Where Kluge's diction gives us a thickening of human substance in the alchemy of "long-distance" historical process (compare Negt and Kluge 1981, 597), Karpat and Şenocak's futurist poetics might be said to thin or stretch the ties that used to bind instead. Elements of the Cold War and the Soviet avant-garde form pieces of this framing puzzle here too. Though hardly an adequate template for textual analysis, the lived trajectory of Nâzım Hikmet—the Turkish poet, playwright, and novelist to whose memory *auf dem schiff zum mars* is ostensibly dedicated— suggests as much.

Born into the Ottoman elite in 1902, Hikmet supported the Turkish war of independence against the Allied occupation following the First World War before embarking on his first trip to Moscow in 1922. While studying in the Soviet Union between 1922 and 1928, the writer joined the Turkish Communist Party from a distance, developed friendships with Vladimir Mayakovsky and other Russian Futurists, and immersed himself in Soviet theater as well.[20] According to an anecdote widely recounted in Hikmet scholarship, the author was inspired to write the first free verse in Turkish poetry in 1922 ("Açların Gözbebekleri") by the broken typography of a Mayakovsky poem that he spotted in a Russian newspaper without being able to read it.[21] And if one recalls Aleksei Gastev's labor-based interest in the 1920s in "integrating the nervous system of the human body with the electrical networks of machines" (Fore 2006, 109), one's mind easily jumps to a series of public "*Schlafaktionen*" [sleep actions] that Berkan Karpat conceived to celebrate the one hundreth anniversary of Hikmet's birth in 2002. In varying configurations involving the historical Hikmet's recorded voice, electrodes and loudspeakers attached near sleepers' hearts, and in one instance, spaceship capsules provided for public dreaming, Karpat envisioned sleepers who would experience Hikmet's "*Sehnsucht nach einer besseren Welt*" [longing for a better world] as a resonance in their bodies, as a physical "*Vibration*" [vibration].[22] Like a compact disc adaptation of Hikmet's voice produced by Karpat and Peer Quednau in 1998, these "sleep actions" also resonate with Karpat and Şenocak's "futurist epilogue" and may be understood as companion pieces to *auf dem schiff zum mars* in particular.

As Karin Yeşilada observes in her discussion of the compact disc, archival recordings of Hikmet reciting his own verse were long held in the Soviet Union and not accessible to the public until the 1990s. The original sounds of the author's voice are rendered in Karpat and Quednau's appropriation, however, as Yeşilada astutely remarks, only in "*Tonfetzen*" [scraps of sound], "*als Flüstern quasi*" [almost a whisper], "*Wortfetzen*" [scraps of words], and "*dann wieder nur ein Rauschen, bis die nächste Welle der Sprachfragmente zu uns gelangt*" [then again only a rustling on the wind, until the next wave of language fragments reaches us] (Yeşilada 2002, 191, 203–204). The twelve poetic segments authored by Karpat and Şenocak and published independent of sleep actions and compact disc under the title *nâzım hikmet: auf dem schiff zum mars* are themselves introduced by a list of "*Stimmen*" [voices]—as if to suggest a theatrical cast of characters—along with due notice that the "*Stück*" [play or piece] takes place "*auf einem Schiff*" [on a ship]. In the numbered segments, Yeşilada rightly notes, characters appear at best "*nur als Stimmen*" [only as voices] (Yeşilada 2005, 485), including a reel-to-reel tape recorder that seems to appear in a voice of its own. Segment 5, for example, consists only of the following: "*bandgeschwindigkeit 9.5 cm/sec//15 umdrehungen lang: stille*" [tape speed 9.5 cm/sec//15 rotations: silence].[23] Other "voices" listed include an unidentified "*Sprecher*" [speaker], a group of "*fünfzehn Kinder*" [fifteen children], a "*Toningenieur*" [sound engineer], and a "*Derwisch-Engel*" [dervish-angel]. Notably absent from this list is Hikmet's own voice, though the lyrical conceit "*ich nâzım*" [i nâzım] figures at various points in lowercase letters, as do multiple nâzıms in the third person, including one associated with Stalin and Lenin and another associated with the beloved Mevlana Jalal al-Din Rumi, a thirteenth-century mystic. The only tagged invocation of the historical voice of Nâzım Hikmet comes at the end of segment 1, which is also where the sole Turkish words in the text coincide with a named reference to Mars. Segment 1 follows in its entirety here, first in the original and then all but the last line in English translation:

> heute nacht trinke ich sonne
> heute nacht auf diesem schiff
> die sonne aus den adern der maschine
> der literarischen maschine
> dem maschinenraum
> aus dem maschinenraum der henker
> der literarischen maschine nâzım
> trinke ich die stimme der sonne
> die sonne aus den adern der tonbänder

trinke ich şemseddin
zwei mal zwei meter dunkelraum
dreht sich in meinen adern
den adern der tonbänder
die maschine nâzım
träumt

Technoider Schiffsmaschinenklang,
*darin verwoben*
*Nâzıms Stimme:*
*"merihe giden kosmos gemisinde turistler . . ."*

tonight i am drinking sun
tonight on this ship
the sun from the arteries of the engine
the literary engine
the engine room
from the engine room of the executioners
of the literary engine nâzım
i am drinking the voice of the sun
the sun from the arteries of the reels of tape
i am drinking şemseddin
two by two metres of darkspace
whirls in my arteries
in the arteries of the reels of tape
the engine nâzım
dreams

Technoid ship's engine noise,
*and woven into it*
*Nâzım's voice:*
*"merihe giden kosmos gemisinde turistler . . ."*

The final line in Turkish in this segment is a marked recitation of only the first line of Hikmet's poetic response to the space race launched with Sputnik I in 1957, a line that gives us, not the survival experts we encountered in Kluge but "tourists traveling on a space ship to Mars."[24] By Yeşilada's account, *auf dem schiff zum mars* is riddled with unmarked Hikmet quotations as well, and the ship to Mars metaphorically encodes elements from the poet's confinement in prison, his escape into exile, and his early futuristic sound poetry, inspired by machines. In her analysis travel to Mars ultimately becomes a metaphor for the "*Reise zum Herzen der Poesie*" [travel to the heart of poetry] by radically reclaiming Hikmet's artistic legacy in the name of lyrical mysticism from a reception overdetermined by communist ideology. With mystical motifs—whirling dervishes and spiritual desire, for example—the text's homage to Hikmet's poetic language "*überwindet*" [overcomes] "*die technoide Maschinensprache*" [the technoid language of machines] in this view (Yeşilada 2005, 488).[25]

The analytical approach that I pursue to the strains of spirit and matter in the "segments" takes a different tack, though Yeşilada is undoubtedly correct in identifying this basic tension in the text. To the limited degree that Hikmet's historical voice can be said to accompany *auf dem schiff zum mars* acoustically, it appears distorted—broken, partial, and distant—reminiscent perhaps of those electromagnetic transmissions from radio and television that continue to emanate into outer space long after earthly frameworks for their intended audiences have dissolved. In Karpat and Şenocak's text, Hikmet's historical voice is not rendered acoustically but manifests only in partial quotations—leftovers, one might say. The breaking points may themselves be telling. The tourists traveling to Mars in Hikmet's poem of 1959, which we read in the original, for example, "*yeryüzünde yazılmış şiirler okuyacak*" [will read poems written on the face of the earth] while the tourists travel, through language, into the future (Hikmet 1976a, 37). As in Kluge's *Lernprozesse*, however, the face of the Earth seems to have fallen away in *auf dem schiff zum mars*, and no world survives whole here either. The many conceits of physical violence (including execution, torture, and open wounds) that circulate in the segmented text may even remind us of the violent histories and recycled body parts that figure in Kluge's prose. Hikmet himself reportedly considered poetry "'the bloodiest of the arts'" (see Edward Hirsch's foreword, Hikmet 2002, viii). Yet the voice of human suffering in Karpat and Şenocak's Martian experiment registers not as memory but as something akin to scrap material. Abstract processes of reforging the leftover bits and pieces of human history are at stake here too, despite the absence of conceptual narrative. Another example of broken quotation supports this.

Segment 9 ends with an unmarked citation from the nondiegetic beginning and subsequent refrain of Hikmet's poem of 1923 entitled

"Makinalaşmak" [To become a machine]: "*trrrum/trrrum/trrrum!/trak/tiki/ tak!*" (Hikmet 1976b, 179–180).[26] While these "scraps of sound" mimic the sounds a working machine might make, the missing pieces of the Hikmet poem give us a poetic persona that explicitly expresses its desire to "become a machine," to find its flesh, skeleton, veins, and tongue transformed into the dynamism of machines. Asım Bezirci remarks both the Russian Futurist influence on this piece and Hikmet's stated preference for propellers and such as poetic symbols into the 1930s (Hikmet 1976b, 318). Two things are especially worth noting here. First, the "*Makinalaşmak / istiyorum!*" [I want / to become a machine!] of Hikmet's diction falls away in Karpat and Şenocak's rendition because their lyrical conceit of "nâzım" as a multiply refracted "i" already signals a network of social and material production, a literary "machine"—*maschine* in Karpat and Şenocak's writing—rather than a discrete human being or even a symbol of one. Tom Cheesman's translation of "*die maschine nâzım*" as "the engine nâzım" is thus not entirely felicitous, since it obscures a resonance here with Soviet factography as a making in language of social things (see Fore 2006).[27] Second, the "arteries" of the literary machine and "the arteries of the reels of tape" in segment 1 do not symbolize human life so much as recycle the stuff of which it is made. The repetitive reeling of tape and whirling of dervishes on a spaceship to Mars can be grasped analogously in this sense. Even the repetition of words and sounds in segment 1 (especially the word "*maschine*" and its component sounds) mimics acoustically the mechanized reeling of tape. The circulation of tape does not symbolize the circulation of blood in this poetic diction. The two forms of circulation manifest in the text in analogy to each other instead, and the analogy gestures toward some form of lived future in the making. One is reminded here of a passage in Kluge's *Lernprozesse* where recycled body parts tied to each other in Martian orbit represent "*noch irgendwie einen Kreislauf*" [still a circulatory system somehow] (Kluge 2000, 838). The material residue of human pasts is recycled and restructured—but not simply repeated—in both texts.

If *Lernprozesse* interrogates the stuff and alchemy of human history writ large, *nâzım hikmet: auf dem schiff zum mars* engages changing trajectories of cultural affiliation instead. Beyond the worlds that nation-states, ethnic communities, or even cosmopolitan networks are often thought to be, the circulatory analogy discussed above resonates with another futurism that once moved Europe in new directions. Readers familiar with F. T. Marinetti's founding manifesto of Italian Futurism in 1909 may already have suspected some vibrating aftereffects in Karpat and Şenocak's multimedial homage to Hikmet. The opening paragraph of Marinetti's manifesto (his first among many) speaks of "the prisoned radiance of electric hearts" shining in Milan amidst "rich oriental rugs" and "hanging mosque lamps."[28] In his "Technical Manifesto of Futurist Literature" (1912) Marinetti explicitly celebrated analogy—in his understanding, a radical juxtaposition of nouns without mediating punctuation or syntax—and for one particular reason. "Analogy is nothing else but profound love which binds together distant and apparently alien things" (Marinetti 1972, 84–89; see also Folejewski 1980, 26). This seems close indeed to the radiant "hearts" and other bits and pieces of dematerialized life reeling in resonance en route to a distant planet. We also know that some of the most common verbs and themes in Hikmet's own poetry concern love.[29] Yet in many other important ways, *auf dem schiff zum mars* has no stylistic or affective affinity to what Marinetti demanded of futurist poetry prior to the First World War. The Italian Futurist's well-known infatuation with "the punch and the slap," "the love of danger," and "the beauty of speed"—or even radical beginnings—is nowhere to be found here. Karpat and Şenocak do not aim to "destroy syntax," "glorify war," or celebrate "violence, cruelty, and injustice" in art, as Marinetti did.[30] The turning and reeling in their own poetic diction seems downright languorous in comparison. The twelfth segment, labeled "epilogue," is almost but not quite wistful in tone as it turns on variations of a refrain. The German original is cited here, followed by my English translation, which deviates from Cheesman's (2001):

> das meiste von nâzım verging
> und nur weniges blieb . . .
> [ . . . ]
> das meiste von mir vergeht
> und nur weniges bleibt . . .
> [ . . . ]
> das meiste verging
> und nur weniges blieb . . .
>
> was kümmert es mich

most of nâzım was lost
and only a little remained . . .
[ . . . ]
most of me is lost
and only a little remains . . .
[ . . . ]
most was lost
and only a little remained . . .

what is it to me[31]

This is not the "language of rupture" (Perloff 2003) that characterized Futurism for many in Europe nearly a century ago, though it is a language of partial loss. Out of leftover bits and pieces comes a language of analogy and connection, albeit without continuous worlds that would render this social and historical matter continuously meaningful. Unworlded Turkish, Soviet, and German leftovers—east and west—circulate in *auf dem schiff zum mars* as a newly but diffusely European project in this sense. Ironically perhaps, despite significant differences in experiment and style, the futurist Martian ventures by Kluge, Karpat, and Şenocak discussed here may highlight the importance of contemporary German literature for understanding some structural shifts in world literature today. The making of future histories and the remaking of *ethnos* are among them.

NOTES

This is an abbreviated and modified version of an article first published as "Experiment Mars" in *Über Gegenwartsliteratur: Interpretationen—Kritiken—Interventionen*, ed. Mark W. Rectanus (Bielefeld: Aisthesis, 2008): 23–49. The author retains the copyright.

1. The focus on futurity in this piece departs too from the celebration of new beginnings since 1989.

2. For an analysis of realism and utopia in a science-fiction trilogy that gives us the planet in red, green, and blue variations, see Jameson 2005, 393–416.

3. In April 2008 the German Film Academy recognized Kluge for a lifetime of distinguished achievement. For a brief overview of related accomplishments, see Davidson 2005. Many of Kluge's theoretical insights have been coauthored with the sociologist Oskar Negt (see especially Negt and Kluge 1972; 1981; 1993). *New German Critique* devoted a special issue to Alexander Kluge in 1990 (vol. 49). See also

Lutze 1998. The German-language scholarship on Kluge is too voluminous to be listed here.

4. The *Lernprozesse* cited here will be from *Chronik der Gefühle* (Kluge 2000). Claudia Rosenkranz (1988) uses the term "theory-fiction" to characterize Kluge's *Lernprozesse* in particular.

5. Coined by the authors but not originally included in their published work, the term "*Futuristenepilog*" is documented in an unpublished conversation conducted with Karpat and Şenocak and recorded by Karin E. Yeşilada in Munich on November 15, 2002. In her pioneering study of lyric poetry by second-generation Turkish immigrants in Germany, Yeşilada notes that Karpat and Şenocak's "futurist epilogue" represents a fundamentally new topographical field in both migration literature and recent German poetry (Yeşilada 2005, 503). The three collaborative publications that together comprise the "futurist epilogue" include: Karpat and Şenocak 1998; 1999; and 2000. All three texts plus some new material will be included in a new book scheduled for publication by Babel Verlag. To the best of my knowledge, Yeşilada is to date the only scholar to have published analyses of the "futurist epilogue" (Yeşilada 2002, 2005). She also discusses a compact disc produced in 1998 (Karpat and Quednau 1998) as a companion piece in sound to the text *nâzım hikmet* (Yeşilada 2002, 203–206). If the work advanced by Karpat and Şenocak can be understood as a Turkish-German avant-garde, it cannot be grasped in the same vein as what Feridun Zaimoğlu has termed an "*Ethno-Avantgarde.*" Interviewed on German television on May 13, 2007, he applied this phrase in the spirit of cultural identity politics to characterize young Muslim women in Germany who wear headscarves by choice.

6. While Şenocak's language of literary production has long been German in the main, he has recently begun to write poetry and novels in Turkish too. For the latter, see especially Şenocak 2007. On Şenocak more generally, see especially Cheesman and Yeşilada 2003 and Yeşilada's (2006) entry on Şenocak in the periodically updated *Kritisches Lexikon zur deutschsprachigen Gegenwartsliteratur*.

7. On Karpat, see: Yeşilada 2005, 479–480; 2002, 191–194; and Hübener 2002. A recent publication on avant-garde art in post-Wall Germany includes important installation art by Kutluğ Ataman, a sound-and-sight innovator whose international reputation was first established by his multilingual film production in Germany (*Lola und Bilidikid*, 1998), but no mention of Karpat, who actually lives in Germany (Eckmann 2007, 34–36). The Ataman piece included is "It's a Vicious Circle," in which sound becomes a key sculptural element. Karpat might be compared with Ataman on this count.

8. For overviews of Hikmet's biography and analyses of his work, see: Carbe and Riemann 2002; Kraft 1983; and Gronau 1991. As Yeşilada notes, UNESCO devoted its World Poetry Day in 2002 to Hikmet (Yeşilada 2005, 480). Kraft and Gronau discuss the longstanding ban on Hikmet publications in Turkey between the mid-1930s and mid-1960s, which complicates the conception of Hikmet as a people's poet.

9. It should be noted that no endorsement of torture, dismemberment, or loss of

life in war is in any way intended in either the works under discussion here or this analysis of them.

10. The analytical conceit of networks is especially common in urban studies and media studies. Writing on recent avant-garde art in Germany, Lutz Koepnick observes in a related vein that networks represent "the dominant structure of communication, collaboration, and cultural production" today. As he puts it, this is because "the exchange of immaterial goods—of information, knowledge, and ideas" predominates, and the principally "open form of the network" is able to elude "material form, finality, and closure" (Koepnick 2007, 105). Arjun Appadurai's anthropological study of changing diasporas first discussed "global cultural flows" in terms of "ethnoscapes," "mediascapes," "technoscapes," "financescapes," and "ideoscapes" (Appadurai 1996, 33–34 et passim). Negt and Kluge's frequent rhetorical and analytical recourse to *Zusammenhänge* in situations where nothing quite "hangs together" to present a whole might be considered in this historical connection too.

11. The figure of "what remains" informs Christa Wolf's (1990) eponymous reflections on life in the German Democratic Republic, which were published after its demise.

12. The term "glocalization" was coined in Japanese business practices in the 1980s and subsequently adopted for scholarly analysis by Roland Robertson at a conference on globalization and indigeneity (Nobutaka 1997). Critical reflections on interactive global and local spheres are now widespread.

13. See Axel 2002 for related theoretical interventions.

14. Perloff dates the height of "the Futurist Moment" to the six months prior to the First World War, though she also discusses Italian Futurism prior to 1914 as well as Russian Futurism of the 1920s and notes that Vladimir Mayakovsky gave his Futurist lectures in Moscow in 1912 (Perloff 2003, xxi, xxiv, 116–160).

15. Originally published in German in 1922 for inclusion in Weber's *Wirtschaft und Gesellschaft: Grundriss der verstehenden Soziologie*, Weber's remarks on ethnic groups are reprinted in *The Ethnicity Reader*, in English translation from Weber 1978.

16. Guibernau and Rex's editorial introduction to their anthology on ethnicity also points out that the category has become "increasingly crucial in the social sciences" since the 1960s—because of phenomena associated with political decolonization, postcolonial nation-building, and transnational labor migration to Europe—and again since the 1990s, when so-called ethnic cleansing wrought havoc in post-socialist Europe (Guibernau and Rex 2003, 1).

17. If the late nineteenth and early twentieth centuries are often seen as a period of modernity when wholeness ceases to characterize social life—as Nietzsche famously observed—perhaps ethnicity has become rather than remained a compensatory category of presumed wholeness over the course of the last century. Weber's formulation is useful for revisiting this presumption.

18. Weigel's point of departure for reading voice in literature through the combined lenses of historical philosophy and cultural studies (*Kulturwissenschaft*)

is Heinrich Heine. For other histories of voice and sound, see Alter and Koepnick, who remark an "unprecedented proliferation of sound production technologies" today (Alter and Koepnick 2004, 3).

19. Weigel uses both "*Wider*hall" and "*Resonanz*" for resonance in contrast to "*Nach*hall" for echo. Like Schulte, however, Weigel uses the language of resurrection even though her differentiated discussion of voice as a cultural phenomenon might be said to preclude it.

20. Kraft provides an especially detailed yet succinct overview of the poet's life and work, on which I rely. Some of this information circulates in other scholarship as well. The volume edited by Carbe and Riemann is also helpful in this regard and additionally includes Zafer Şenocak's essay, "Meine drei Begegnungen mit Nâzım Hikmet" (Carbe and Riemann 2002, 84–89).

21. Hikmet could not read Russian at the time (Kraft 1983, 3). Credited with inaugurating free verse in Turkish—against the many formal conventions of classical Ottoman poetry—Hikmet later aspired to "'put dialectical materialism into the rubaiyat form'" (Blasing and Konuk 1994, 241).

22. For these and other details, see http://www.karpat.de, accessed March 20, 2007. Karpat was creating "sleep actions" with Hikmet in mind as early as the late 1990s (Brembeck 1998).

23. Most of the translations provided here are drawn from Tom Cheesman's (2001) translation, posted electronically since 2001. Alternative translations that make a difference for interpretation will be noted. Neither the German original nor Cheesman's English translation is paginated; quotations will be referenced by segment number only.

24. The untitled poem was written in December 1959 (Hikmet 1976a, 37–38).

25. See also Yeşilada 2002, 195–198. Yeşilada further notes that Şenocak, a poet and published translator of such figures as Yunus Emre and Pir Sultan Abdal, knows the Turkish mystic, *divan*, and folk traditions extremely well (Yeşilada 2005, 484).

26. The English translation used here is mine. Karpat and Şenocak deviate from Hikmet's typography.

27. One might also consider Friedrich Kittler's (1990) account of media technologies, discourse networks, and reading "machines" here.

28. The manifesto was originally published in French. The English translation is cited here from F. T. Marinetti, "The Founding and Manifesto of Futurism" (Marinetti 1972, 39–44, here 39). Yeşilada argues that Karpat and Şenocak's "futurist epilogue" represents a "*dritten Ort*" [third space] independent of any established communities (Yeşilada 2005, 483).

29. See especially segments 3 and 8 for Karpat and Şenocak's "heart" conceits. A line in segment 8 features a nâzım-persona declaring, "*auch ich hatte etwas über die liebe zu sagen*" [I too had something to say about love].

30. Most of these formulations are taken from Marinetti's manifesto of 1909. The imperative to "destroy syntax" is part of the literary manifesto of 1912.

31. Yeşilada claims this segment resembles a ghazel in its form and universal theme of mortality (Yeşilada 2002, 202).

## WORKS CITED

Adelson, Leslie A. 2005. *The Turkish Turn in Contemporary German Literature: Toward a New Critical Grammar of Migration.* New York: Palgrave Macmillan.

Alter, Nora M., and Lutz Koepnick, eds. 2004. *Sound Matters: Essays on the Acoustics of Modern German Culture.* New York: Berghahn.

Améry, Jean. 2002. *Jean Améry: Werke,* ed. Irene Heidelberger-Leonard. Vol. 2, ed. Gerhard Scheit. Stuttgart: Klett-Cotta.

Anderson, Benedict. 1991. *Imagined Communities: Reflections on the Origin and Spread of Nationalism.* Rev. ed. London: Verso.

Appadurai, Arjun. 1996. *Modernity at Large: Cultural Dimensions of Globalization.* Minneapolis: University of Minnesota.

Axel, Brian. 2002. "The Diasporic Imaginary." *Public Culture* 12(2): 411–428.

Benhabib, Seyla. 2002. *The Claims of Culture: Equality and Diversity in the Global Era.* Princeton, NJ: Princeton University Press.

Blasing, Randy, and Mutlu Konuk, trans. 1994. *Poems of Nâzim Hikmet.* New York: Persea.

Brembeck, Reinhard J. 1998. "Ein Mensch, der nicht aufgibt." *Süddeutsche Zeitung,* October 15.

Carbe, Monika, and Wolfgang Riemann, eds. 2002. *Hundert Jahre Nâzım Hikmet, 1902–1963.* Hildesheim: Georg Olms.

Cheesman, Tom, trans. 2001. Berkan Karpat and Zafer Şenocak, *Nâzım Hikmet: On the Ship to Mars.* http://www.swan.ac.uk/german/cheesman/senocak/nazim .htm

Cheesman, Tom, and Karin E. Yeşilada, eds. 2003. *Zafer Şenocak.* Cardiff: University of Wales.

Davidson, John E. 2005. "Alexander Kluge." In *Encyclopedia of Literature and Politics: Censorship, Revolution, and Writing,* ed. M. Keith Booker, 400–401. Westport, CT: Greenwood.

Eckmann, Sabine, ed. 2007. *Reality Bites: Making Avant-garde Art in Post-Wall Germany/Kunst nach dem Mauerfall.* Ostfildern: Hatje Cantz.

Folejewski, Zbigniew. 1980. *Futurism and Its Place in the Development of Modern Poetry: A Comparative Study and Anthology.* Ottawa: University of Ottawa.

Fore, Devin Alden. 2005. *All the Graphs: Soviet and Weimar Documentary Between the Wars.* Doctoral thesis, Columbia University.

———. 2006. "The Operative Word in Soviet Factography." *October* 118: 95–131.

Giddens, Anthony. 2003. *Runaway World: How Globalisation Is Reshaping Our Lives.* New York: Routledge.

Gronau, Dietrich. 1991. *Nâzım Hikmet. Eine Biografie.* Reinbek bei Hamburg: Rowohlt.

Guibernau, Montserrat, and John Rex, eds. 2003. *The Ethnicity Reader: Nationalism, Multiculturalism, and Migration*. Oxford: Blackwell.

Hikmet, Nâzım. 2002. *Human Landscapes from My Country: An Epic Novel in Verse*, trans. Randy Blasing and Mutlu Konuk. New York: Persea.

———. 1976a. *Son Şiirleri*. 7th ed. Istanbul: Habora Kitabevi.

———. 1976b. *Tüm Eserleri I, Şiirler 3 [İlk Şiirler, 835 Satır, Sesini Kaybeden Şehir]*, ed. Şerif Hulûsi and Asım Bezirci. 2nd ed. Istanbul: Cem.

Hübener, Fabienne. 2002. "Schatzsuche im kunstfreien Raum—Der Installationskünstler Berkan Karpat." *Die Zeit*, October 18. http://www.karpat.de/pag/1/BerkanKarpat.php

Jameson, Fredric. 2005. *Archaeologies of the Future: The Desire Called Utopia and Other Science Fictions*. London: Verso.

Karpat, Berkan, and Peer Quednau. 1998. *nâzım hikmet. im garten der flüsterpupillen*. Munich: Babel-Bibliothek Intermedia.

Karpat, Berkan, and Zafer Şenocak. 1998. *nâzım hikmet. auf dem schiff zum mars*. Munich: Babel.

———. 1999. *Tanzende der Elektrik: Szenisches Poem*. Munich, Berlin, and Cambridge [USA]: Verlag im Gleisbau.

———. 2000. "wie den vater nicht töten. Ein Sprechlabyrinth." In *Morgen Land: Neueste deutsche Literatur*, ed. Jamal Tuschick, 179–190. Frankfurt am Main: Fischer.

Kittler, Friedrich A. 1990. *Discourse Networks, 1800/1900*, trans. Michael Metteer, with Chris Cullens. Foreword by David E. Wellbery. Stanford, CA: Stanford University Press.

Kluge, Alexander. 2003. "Büchner-Preis-2003 Rede." Section 2. http://www.kluge-alexander.de/presse_dankrede_buechnerpreis-2003.shtml

———. 2000. *Lernprozesse mit tödlichem Ausgang*. In *Chronik der Gefühle*, vol. 2, 827–920. Frankfurt am Main: Suhrkamp.

Koepnick, Lutz. 2007. "Bits and Pieces: Art in the Age of Global Networks." In *Reality Bites: Making Avant-garde Art in Post-Wall Germany/Kunst nach dem Mauerfall*, ed. Sabine Eckmann, 103–149. Ostfildern: Hatje Cantz.

Kraft, Gisela. 1983. "Nâzım Hikmet." In *Kritisches Lexikon zur fremdsprachigen Gegenwartsliteratur*, ed. Heinz Ludwig Arnold, vol. 5 [no pagination]. Munich: edition text+kritik.

Lutze, Peter. 1998. *Alexander Kluge: The Last Modernist*. Detroit: Wayne State University Press.

Marinetti, F. T. 1972. *Marinetti: Selected Writings*, ed. R. W. Flint, trans. R. W. Flint and Arthur A. Coppotelli. New York: Farrar, Straus and Giroux.

Negt, Oskar, and Alexander Kluge. 1981. *Geschichte und Eigensinn: Geschichtliche Organisation der Arbeitsvermögen, Deutschland als Produktionsöffentlichkeit, Gewalt des Zusammenhangs*. Frankfurt am Main: Zweitausendeins.

————. 1972. *Öffentlichkeit und Erfahrung: Zur Organisationsanalyse von bürgerlicher und proletarischer Öffentlichkeit*. Frankfurt am Main: Suhrkamp.

————. 1993. *Public Sphere and Experience: Toward an Analysis of the Bourgeois and Proletarian Public Sphere*, trans. Peter Labanyi et al. Minneapolis: University of Minnesota.

Nobutaka, Inoue, ed. 1997. *Globalization and Indigenous Culture*. Tokyo: Institute for Japanese Culture and Classics, Kokugakuin University.

Perloff, Marjorie. 2003. *The Futurist Moment: Avant-Garde, Avant Guerre, and the Language of Rupture*. With a new preface. Chicago: University of Chicago Press.

Rex, John. 2003. "The Nature of Ethnicity in the Project of Migration." In *The Ethnicity Reader: Nationalism, Multiculturalism, and Migration*, ed. Montserrat Guibernau and John Rex, 269–283. Oxford: Blackwell.

Rosenkranz, Claudia. 1988. *Ambivalenzen aufklärerischer Literatur am Beispiel einer Text- und Rezeptionsanalyse von Alexander Kluges 'Lernprozesse mit tödlichem Ausgang'*. Trier: Wissenschaftlicher Verlag Trier.

Scherpe, Klaus. 2001. "Die Entdramatisierung der Kritischen Theorie in der Literatur: Hans Magnus Enzensberger und Alexander Kluge." *Cultura Tedesca* 18: 141–160.

Schulte, Christian. 2001. "Die Lust aufs Unwahrscheinliche. Alexander Kluges 'Chronik der Gefühle'." *Merkur. Deutsche Zeitschrift für europäisches Denken* 55(4): 344–350.

Şenocak, Zafer. 2007. *Alman Terbiyesi*. Istanbul: Alef.

————. 2006. "Rückkehr auf die Insel." In *Das Land hinter den Buchstaben: Deutschland und der Islam im Umbruch*, 205–208. Munich: Babel.

Seyhan, Azade. 2001. *Writing Outside the Nation*. Princeton, NJ, and Oxford: Princeton University Press.

Weber, Max. 1978. *Economy and Society: An Outline of Interpretive Sociology*, ed. Guenther Roth and Claus Wittich, trans. Ephraim Fischoff et al. Berkeley: University of California Press.

Weigel, Sigrid. 2002. "Die Stimme der Toten: Schnittpunkte zwischen Mythos, Literatur und Kulturwissenschaft." In *Zwischen Rauschen und Offenbarung: Zur Kultur- und Mediengeschichte der Stimme*, ed. Friedrich Kittler, Thomas Macho, and Sigrid Weigel, 73–92. Berlin: Akademie.

Wolf, Christa. 1990. *Was bleibt: Erzählung*. Frankfurt am Main: Luchterhand.

Yeşilada, Karin E. 2002. "Nâzıms Enkel schreiben weiter." In *Hundert Jahre Nâzım Hikmet, 1902–1963*, ed. Monika Carbe and Wolfgang Riemann, 180–211. Hildesheim: Georg Olms.

————. 2005. "Poesie der dritten Sprache. Die deutsch-türkische Migrationslyrik der zweiten Generation." Dissertation, Phillips-Universität Marburg.

————. 2006. "Zafer Şenocak." In *Kritisches Lexikon zur deutschsprachigen Gegenwartsliteratur*, ed. Heinz Ludwig Arnold [no pagination]. Munich: text+kritik.

# CHAPTER TEN

## Jews in Contemporary Europe

CAROLE FINK

It is not that some societies distinguish between fiction and history and others do not. Rather the difference is in the range of narratives that specific collectivities must put to their own tests of historical credibility because of the stakes involved in these narratives.[1]

— MICHEL-ROLF TROUILLOT

What times are these, where
A conversation about trees is almost a crime
Because it contains silence about so many atrocities![2]

— BERTOLT BRECHT

The great upheavals since 1989 have affected European Jews in several significant ways. First of all, the external political conditions have changed dramatically. In the East, the end of communist rule brought new religious, political, and personal freedom, including the right to emigrate. In the West, the decision to expand the European Union, first to three former neutrals and subsequently to ten former people's democracies, has created a giant political, economic, and legal entity in which European Jews now reside. Since 2001, however, the European project has slowed down; and after the terrorist attacks on New York and Washington, Madrid and London, the continent has been rent by religious, ethnic, regional, and political divisions, which threaten the small, still loosely organized, extremely diverse Jews of Europe.

Second, with the end of the Cold War, within Europe's burgeoning memory culture there has been a marked renewal of interest in the Holocaust. Spurred by the questions surrounding German unification and by the bloody war in the Balkans, there has been an intense reexamination of hitherto unchallenged national myths. When the Vatican recognized Israel in 1995 and opened a dialogue with the Jews, many questions regarding Christian-Jewish relations were also reopened. Moreover, the past has been alive in the courts; the 1990s witnessed highly publicized trials in France, Britain, and Austria not only against long-sheltered war criminals but also involving Holocaust deniers. Victims and their descendents made claims against banks, insurance companies, industrial firms, museums, and art galleries that had profited from the destruction of European Jewry. The European Union has officially recognized the spoliation, deportation, and murder of European Jewry as a pan-European phenomenon, an intrinsic element of the continent's history; and after many years of debate, in April 2007 it voted to outlaw Holocaust denial in its twenty-seven member countries.

On the other hand, the extremely volatile conditions in the Middle East—a region adjoining Europe, a major trading partner, and the principal source of its oil supply—have also affected European Jews. Increasingly, the European Union, individual European governments, and a growing segment of the European public have expressed strong opposition to Israel's policies over the still unresolved Palestinian question. And from the Gulf War (1991), to the Second Intifada (2000), to Israel's wars in Lebanon (2006) and in Gaza (2008–9), European Jews who support Israel have been placed in a thorny position.

Finally, post-1989 Europe has witnessed a dramatic revival of anti-Semitism in words, images, and violent deeds. Fueled by a combination of religious prejudice, anti-Israeli sentiments, and old-fashioned hooliganism, this virulent movement spans the entire continent, forming a grim counterpart to Europe's earnest efforts to come to terms with its past.

Technology has played an important role. The Internet revolution of the 1990s along with the advent of satellite television, mobile telephones, and text-messaging have all effaced time and distance, while the widespread use of English has connected former enemies and strangers. Instantaneous communication has linked distant groups, reinforcing fears and prejudice.

Sensationalist texts and images, including numerous anti-Semitic blogs as well as the ubiquitous anti-Semitic placards and graffiti have undoubtedly added to the vulnerability of European Jews.[3]

In this chapter I shall examine the impact of the dramatic political, social, and cultural changes since 1989 on the European Jewish community. But first some qualifications and details. To be sure, the term "community"—either in supranational, national, or local terms—is shorthand. Europe's Jews are not simply a religious, ethnic, or national group; they speak dozens of languages and observe widely different forms of the Jewish religion, and many practice none at all. They include descendents of Sephardic, Ashkenazic, and Mizrahi Jews coming from places all over the world. They range from members (active and inactive) of informal or well-established official organizations—some with elaborate educational, social, and cultural components—to the vast majority without any religious or cultural affiliation with the Jewish people. They also include some who, although not fitting under the Halakic definition, count themselves in spirit and mentality as Jews. Let us thus simply refer to Europe's Jews as a group who in some way, through family, history, belief, or culture, identify themselves as Jews.[4]

Although imprecise, the most recent figures are significant in several ways. Between 1.5 and 2 million Jews reside in Europe, spread over a continent now numbering some 729 million people. The largest numbers reside in five countries: France (500,000), the United Kingdom (300,000), Russia (265,000), Germany (150,000), and Ukraine (100,000), but there are Jews in every European state, including the tiny 100-strong communities in Macedonia, Slovenia, and Andorra and the fewer than 50 remaining in Albania.[5]

The highest concentration of Jews are in Western Europe, where they comprise 8 percent of the total population; the largest national percentages are in France (4 percent), the United Kingdom (2 percent), and Germany (1.5 percent). In Eastern Europe, Jews make up about 7 percent of the population, with the highest percentages in European Russia (5 percent) and Ukraine (1 percent). This is still a highly urbanized population, almost a third of which resides in the three metropolises of Paris (310,000), London (195,000), and Moscow (150,000); indeed, two-thirds of Serbia's 1,200 Jews reside in the cities of Belgrade and Novi Sad.[6]

As a result of the Holocaust and the postwar migrations to Israel and elsewhere, and the more recent population movements from the East to the West, there are virtually no ancient Jewish communities left in Europe. Before 1939, more than 60 percent of world Jewry resided in Europe, primarily in Eastern Europe; today that figure is 15 percent. The total Jewish population represents a precipitous drop from the 9.5 million in 1938 to the 3.5 million in 1950, which stayed steady until 1980 but then fell dramatically to 2.6 million in 1990 and continues to plunge. In Ukraine, for example, whose overall population has been reduced by 2 million since 1991, the Jewish population has fallen by 33 percent because of a 13:1 death-to-birthrate ratio, emigration, and intermarriage.[7]

It is nonetheless clear that we are not dealing with a pale relic of Hitler's extermination project or—as in some stereotypes—with a small, aging, endangered species inhabiting a graveyard far from the large, vibrant centers of Jewish life in the United States and in Israel. Indeed, the demographic drop would have been greater without immigration from several directions. Since the 1960s, the decolonization of Europe's empires and the establishment of new, nationalistic states brought an influx of Jews from northern and southern Africa, the Middle East, and Asia. France's Jewish community was almost completely transformed by the arrival of 150,000 Jews from North Africa. In the 1980s, political turmoil in Latin America brought scores of Jews to post-Franco Spain and post-Salazar Portugal. Since the 1990s, more than 200,000 Jews from the former Soviet Union have migrated westward, primarily to Germany, which has also been a significant destination for thousands of Israelis.[8]

To be sure, the Jewish situation has also been affected by the arrival of millions of other immigrants from Eastern Europe, Africa, the Middle East, and Asia. No longer a unique diasporic people, Europe's Jews now live alongside far larger non-Christian immigrant communities; and they are no longer the continent's only victims, which also include the Sinti and Roma and the hundreds of thousands of refugees, asylum seekers, and illegal aliens from other continents.

There is one additional point: Even within these reduced numbers we are dealing with three distinctive generations.[9] Those now in their mid-sixties to mid-eighties, who were born in Europe between 1920 and 1945, have endured fascism, the Second World War, the militarization of the continent in the Cold War (and in post-1945 Eastern Europe the waves of anti-Semitism unleashed by Stalin and his successors), and the great changes since 1989. Those born elsewhere experienced colonial rule, world war, the postwar national revolutions, and the shock and losses of displacement.

This older generation, which was largely urbanized, well educated, and politically active, which generally shed its parents' religious practices and was lukewarm toward Zionism, dedicated itself either to integrating into the dominant nation or meliorating it through various forms of socialism. After the Holocaust, as members of decimated communities, they attempted to reclaim their maimed citizenship by proclaiming loyalty to the state or to humankind, linking their Jewishness with justice and human rights. In the political realm, this includes two exemplary figures: the recently deceased Polish historian and statesman Bronisław Geremek, and the French lawyer and politician Simone Veil. There are also the East European literary giants Imre Kertész, György Konrád, Ivan Klíma, Jurek Becker, Hanna Krall, and Henryk Grynberg, and their Western counterparts—in France, the film directors Claude Lanzmann and Marcel Ophuls, the philosopher Robert Misrahi, the doctor-turned-activist and diplomat Bernard Kouchner, and the historian Pierre Nora; and in Germany the brilliant director Peter Zadek—who have woven the Jewish imagination and Jewish ethical values into their public lives and work.[10]

Then came the middle generation of European Jews, born between 1945 and 1970, many in places far from their ancestral homeland, who grew up in the shadow of the Holocaust and on the fault lines of the Cold War, decolonization, and the Arab-Israeli conflict. Witnesses to the Eichmann and Auschwitz trials and to the ferment of the 1960s, a few emulated their parents' activism. In the East, Wolf Biermann and Adam Michnik called for a humane socialism; and in the West, Daniel Cohn-Bendit agitated for a more humane capitalism and the end of war, racism, gender discrimination, and the destruction of the environment.[11]

On the other hand, under the impact of the 1967 war, some in this generation recovered their Jewish identity. Barbara Honigmann, for example, one of the German Democratic Republic's foremost theater directors, suddenly in the early 1980s declared her adherence to Judaism and, in powerful autobiographical fiction, has described her dislocation as a child of exiles who had returned to Germany.[12] From her Jewish and feminist perspective, the Swiss graphic artist Miriam Cahn has detailed the horrors of war. The Bulgarian-born musician Moni Ovadia, with his satirical klezmer sounds, connects the exhilarating present with a destroyed Jewish world. In their novels and stories, the Argentinean-born Reina Roffé, now living in Spain, evokes her Sephardic ancestors, and the Algerian-born Marlène Amar, her vanished North African birthplace.[13]

After the *Wende* in 1989–90, a new generation moved into the spotlight. Those born after 1970 either under a listless communism or an expanding and increasingly prosperous European community came of age when Jewishness had attained a political and cultural status unknown to their parents and grandparents but had also attracted new strains of hostility. From them have come the bold initiatives not only against traditional religious practices, gender roles, and communal life but also against the very tenor of Jewish art, intellectual life, and politics in today's Europe.[14]

One apt example is the young Russian writer Lena Gorelik. Born in 1981 in Leningrad, at age 11 she journeyed with her family to Germany during the first great wave of postunification migration. In her tough autobiographical fiction Gorelik details the Russians' arduous struggle to obtain a Jewish identity in the homeland of the Holocaust, and their difficulties in dealing with Germans *and* Jews as well as with earlier Soviet immigrants.[15]

Yet despite the external changes since 1989 and the differences among generations, there is also an element of continuity in the lives of all European Jews: a common memory of a complicated past in Europe or elsewhere of accomplishments, destruction, and displacement. Practically all European Jews have ties with the far larger, more active Jewish communities abroad, especially with Israel. And most, given their relatively small numbers and the highly charged political atmosphere since 1989, acknowledge a fear of discrimination, exclusion, anti-Semitism, and personal violence.

## Coping with Europe's New Pluralist Societies

European Jews are distinctive in several ways. Unlike American Jews with their philanthropic tradition and munificent benefactors, and the Israelis with their state-supported religious, educational, and cultural institutions, European Jewish communal organizations rely on a mixture of modest dues, state support, and foreign contributors. For example, in 1993, the Jewish Agency spent $10 million in the former Soviet Union; rabbis have been sent to congregations in Eastern Europe and Russia by Israeli, American, and Australian congregations; and the most visible participants, in the ultra-orthodox Lubavitch movement, have been active on their own. Renewing Judaism with foreign funds, people, and ideas has rekindled the synagogue, but it has also stirred controversy among locals, and between locals and patrons.[16]

No doubt the greatest challenge to resurrecting Jewish life in Eastern Europe has been the revival of Jewish education, which had disappeared for decades under communist rule. Again, the stimulus and the moral, material, and personnel support have come primarily from outside: from ORT, a global Jewish charity based in Switzerland, which has projects all over the former Soviet Union; from the Ronald S. Lauder Foundation, which subsidizes schools and summer camps in sixteen Eastern European countries; and from the government and private agencies in Israel.[17]

Jewish education in Eastern Europe is still in flux. Although the donors have generally allowed communities to choose and shape their schools, there have been continuing disputes between givers and given over staffing, curriculum, and access to modern technology. The state also plays a role. Because Polish government regulations prohibit the exclusion of any child, one third of the 250 children in Warsaw's only Jewish school are Christians, who study Hebrew and English and learn Jewish history and religion. And all over Europe, from Great Britain to the Caucasus, Jewish educators are engaged in a delicate balancing act between resurrecting a distinctive Jewish identity and inculcating the rights and responsibilities of citizenship in their increasingly multicultural societies.[18]

Jewish communal structures, particularly in the former communist world, are not yet robust or representative. Until recently the local and national organizations were dominated by a coterie of aged citizens; but more recently, younger, more liberal Jews have contested their elders and moved into leadership positions. Across the continent, the political experience and skill of Jewish leaders vary greatly as do their size, resources, and local traditions.[19]

In the transnational realm, European Jewry is also weakly organized. The newest body, the European Council of Jewish Communities, which was founded in 1990 to train a new generation of leaders, is heavily subsidized from outside and has yet to manifest much vitality. The European Jewish Congress (EJC), founded in 1986, has established an ambitious agenda of promoting Holocaust memory, combating anti-Semitism, and improving relations between Europe and Israel; but the EJC, plagued by internecine rivalries, has yet to make its influence felt in Brussels and Strasbourg. Indeed, pan-European Jewish causes are more likely to be taken up by non-Jewish notables, by nonaffiliated Jews, or by the government of Israel.[20]

## Living in Jewish Space

In the words of historian Diana Pinto an astonishing thing has happened:

> Sixty years after post-war Europe relegated the Shoah to the realm of private suffering or buried it publicly in a sea of anti-fascist rhetoric, Jewish themes, references, and life now occupy center stage in ways that seemed unimaginable even twenty years ago. Across Europe, it has become impossible to open a newspaper without reading about some aspect either of the Jewish past or, increasingly, the Jewish present.[21]

Jewish space, born in the 1980s and greatly expanded in the past twenty years, is a complex phenomenon comprising social, cultural, and artistic elements as well as an undoubted political dimension.[22] Indeed, the liveliest elements exist in countries where Jewish life was almost extinguished, in Spain, Germany, and Poland. In these countries golden ages have been celebrated, tragic endings reassessed, and synagogues and cemeteries have been restored, not only for tourists but also as part of the national heritage.[23]

All over Europe there is a thriving academic field of Jewish studies, which includes university chairs, institutes, language training, scholarly conferences, journals, and ambitious publication projects, as well as close ties with institutions in Israel. In Vilnius there are programs not only in Jewish history but also in Yiddish language and literature. In Germany there are now thirty professorships in Jewish studies, one third of which were established in the past ten years. In Saint Petersburg, Moscow, and Budapest and in all the important state archives in Central and Eastern Europe long-hidden manuscripts on Jewish subjects have been opened to researchers.[24]

This burgeoning scholarly establishment, generously subsidized from abroad and staffed mainly by non-Jews and Israelis, has a uniquely European flavor. Because of its indispensable partnership with non-Jews, European Jewish studies will, by nature, be broad and comparative. Certain topics, such as biblical studies, archaeology, and languages as well as European national histories predominate; significantly, the history and culture of American Jewry and of Israel are largely absent from the curricula, despite the size of these communities and the influence they exert. On the other hand, the European Association for Jewish Studies has become a modestly successful international project drawing Jewish and non-Jewish scholars from abroad to its meetings.[25]

Another remarkable feature of Jewish space is the cult of klezmer music, particularly in Germany and Poland. First introduced by American bands in the 1980s, klezmer is now a permanent fixture at European festivals as distant as Bari in Italy, Göteborg in Sweden, and the tiny town of Coutances in Normandy. Viewed as quintessentially Jewish expression but played largely by non-Jewish European musicians before hip, liberal, and primarily non-Jewish audiences, klezmer's sudden popularity has raised several problems for Jews. Older Jews fret over the dilution of a central European art form into a world folk music and cringe at vulgar forms of representation.[26]

Moreover, "Jewish tourism," now attracting large numbers of Europeans and overseas visitors, has also raised concern. The mass-produced memorabilia—from the kitschy Einstein and Kafka T-shirts sold in Prague to the hideous Jewish wooden figures formerly on display in Warsaw souvenir stands—have stirred shock and fear among Holocaust survivors. With themes and itineraries emphasizing persecution, death, and absence, it ignores or stereotypes the living of today.[27]

The proliferation of Jewish museums and monuments, seen as Europe's answer to forgetfulness and prejudice, also raises questions. Almost every one of these has kindled controversy in the press and in local and national governments over cost, size, location, concept, and even contents. German Jews were at odds over the Berlin memorial: some were appalled by the scale and grimness; others questioned whether stones could enlighten; and still others feared a display of Jewish victimization in the glittering German capital. Although Daniel Liebeskind's Jewish Museum and Peter Eisenmann's Monument to the Murdered Jews of Europe have become major tourist attractions, it is clear that their message is not primarily for Jews.[28] These powerful sites of commemoration and instruction create almost no links among the successors of the sufferers, the perpetrators, and the bystanders.[29]

The Jewish experience has also entered hallowed national institutions. Thus in 2000 Queen Elizabeth II opened a long-delayed, much-contested, and carefully constructed exhibition in the Imperial War Museum—which for fifty-five years had ignored the Holocaust—on the liberation of Bergen-Belsen.[30] European museums and galleries now regularly include exhibitions of Jewish art, and not only the works of Pissarro, Modigliani, and Chagall but also of Samuel Bak, R. B. Kitaj, and Chaim Soutine. European concert halls regularly feature the compositions of Kurt Weill, Ernst Bloch, Erich Korngold, Paul Dessau, and Hanns Eisler. Although some Jews welcome these signs of attention, others see them as a form of cultural tokenism. Indeed, some have questioned the whole idea of defining, no less choosing, a "Jewish" artist. Does Lucien Freud "count"; or did Marcel Marceau?[31]

Jewish space also extends to the European commemorative calendar. Throughout Europe, January 27 (the day that Soviet troops liberated Auschwitz) has been designated a day of remembrance for the victims of racism and murder.[32] And on September 2, 2007, thirty countries in Europe marked a Day of Jewish Culture that included exhibitions, concerts, lectures, and food. In Milan, for example, thousands of people gathered for readings, discussions, and testimonies. A moment of silence was followed by a solemn procession and a sumptuous banquet.[33]

Again, among the older generation there is considerable skepticism over this expansive Jewish space, which has been appropriated by non-Jews for their own historical, cultural, and creative needs. Will all this exposure strengthen or weaken Jewish life in Europe? Does the shared commemoration in Germany of the November 1938 pogrom relegate Jews to objects? Indeed, does the Jewish space risk being turned into something of a Jewish zoo?[34]

Diana Pinto, who is based in Paris, welcomes it all: from the interfaith dialogues to the Israeli folk-dancing courses, from the university programs to the ubiquitous bagel, from Jewish websites to the annual name-readings of Shoah victims, from heritage tourism even to kitschy artifacts.[35]

However, the Jewish social scientists and activists Ian Leveson and Sandra Lustig, both based in Berlin, take a more pessimistic view. They point out that Europe's Jews have little control over Jewish space, over decisions on its content and boundaries, or even over who profits. Not only is there insufficient weight given to their opinions, but it is still unclear who arbitrates disputes between majority and minority. Packaging and selling a culture involves selecting and reducing a people into a digestible buffet of food, music, decorations, cinema, and festivals—which can be easily consumed by the majority. But what happens to the project when the market inevitably dries up? Will any more understanding have been achieved?[36]

Because cultural interaction is driven by power, Leveson and Lustig also insist that Jewish space is an inadequate substitute—if not a dangerous diversion—from the quest for a fundamental improvement in Jewish–non-Jewish relations. Until a fully developed civil society and all the legal prerequisites are in place all over Europe, the Jews' civic rights remain precarious and their persons remain vulnerable. Indeed, Leveson and Lustig question whether it will ever be possible for Europe's Jews and non-Jews to commemorate the past together, because they occupy two separate memory worlds, one remembering persecution, the other mixing the imposed obligation of shame and guilt with their own memories of suffering.[37]

## The Specter of Anti-Semitism

The grim counterpart to the expansion of Jewish space is the expansion of European anti-Semitism. In the passionate words of the UK's chief rabbi Jonathan Sacks:

> Anti-Semitism is alive, active and virulent . . . after more than a half century of Holocaust education, interfaith dialogue, UN declarations, dozens of museums and memorials, hundreds of films, thousands of courses, and tens of thousands of books exposing its evils; after the Stockholm Conference of January 2000, after the creation of a National Holocaust Memorial Day, after 2,000 religious leaders came together in the UN to fight hatred and engender mutual respect.[38]

There is an uncanny connection between Europe's preoccupation with the Shoah and the current rise of anti-Semitism. In Sweden, for example, which organized a global Holocaust Conference in 2000, public anti-Semitism is the highest in its history. Along with native Swedish anti-Jewish sentiments—manifested in the ban on kosher slaughtering and the up-to-now unsuccessful efforts to outlaw circumcision—there is the Lutheran church, which refers continually to Christ-killers; the media, which frequently mentions "Jewish power"; and a government that still refuses to open certain Second World War records and to prosecute war criminals.[39]

Sweden is not alone. The catechisms in France, Italy, and Spain continue to deny Christ's Jewishness, ignore the Holocaust, and take a negative attitude towards the idea of a "chosen people."[40] Recent learned tomes on national history in Spain and Greece contain coded anti-Semitic language, and popular literature in Bulgaria still purveys anti-Semitic myths.[41]

European politics still includes anti-Jewish rhetoric.[42] It is not unusual for someone to refer to his opponent's Jewish ancestry. Right-wing politicians in Germany regularly complain over payments to Holocaust survivors and accuse the Jews of unleashing bolshevism on the world. Further east, where skinhead movements flourish and right-wing parties have reemerged, not only has every former communist country dragged its feet over prosecuting war criminals and over restitution claims—leaning on the term "Judeo-bolshevism" to link Jewish victims with the horrors of communism—but in countries such as Serbia and Romania there have been strong movements to elevate former national fascist leaders, and in Lithuania to prosecute Jewish partisans.[43] Western Europe also has its share of thuggishness and violence against Jews.[44]

The European right still claims a Jewish conspiracy to dominate the world, most recently by instigating the events of 9/11. In an Anti-Defamation League (ADL) poll conducted in twelve countries in May 2005, 20 percent of all respondents still believed that the Jews were responsible for the death of Christ, 30 percent that Jews dominated the business world and international finance, and 40 percent that Jews "talked too much about the Holocaust."[45] A year earlier, on the eve of Holocaust Day, 20 percent of Britons considered a Jewish prime minister less acceptable than a non-Jewish one, and 15 percent thought the scale of the Holocaust had been exaggerated.[46] Indeed, "Holocaust fatigue"—and a growing resentment against the Jews—has spread from the halls of European politics and academia to cafes, beer halls, and kitchen tables.[47]

European anti-Semitism has been fueled by anti-Israel sentiments, which began in 1967, rose in 1982, and have reached massive proportions after 2000.[48] The European media are alive with ancient anti-Semitic stereotypes (deicide, child murder, and blood lust) merged with Nazi iconography (jack-boots, swastikas, and Hitler salutes) in portraying Israel as the perpetrator of genocide against the Palestinians. The staged footage by state-owned France 2 television of the death of Muhammad al-Dura in Gaza on September 20, 2001, instantly became a global image of Israeli brutality; the European press and television labeled the house-to-house combat six months later between the Israeli Defense Forces (IDF) and armed Palestinian militants the "Jenin massacre" and portrayed the April 2002 IDF siege of the Church of Nativity in Bethlehem as a classic anti-Semitic narrative of deicide.[49] Another power-ful stimulus to the new anti-Semitism is the growing anti-Americanism, in which Jews and Israel are viewed as coagents with Washington in the pursuit of colonialism, globalization, and military aggression.[50]

Anti-Israel attitudes have spread across Europe's political spectrum, from the conservative German politician who has referred to Israel's *Vernichtungs-krieg* (War of Annihilation) against the Palestinians, to left-wing activists who assemble lists of Israel's human rights violations, even to centrist figures who support EU trade boycotts and international censure. Israeli Apartheid Week, now in its fifth year, was commemorated March 1–8, 2009, in twenty-five cities around the world, among them Copenhagen, London, Madrid, Oxford, and Pisa.[51] European governments regularly vote against Israel in international forums; and recent polls indicate that a majority of Europeans consider Israel a greater threat to world peace than any other country.[52]

Moreover, Israel's critics have tarred every Jew living in the Diaspora as accomplices to Israeli crimes.[53] Thus the 2001 UN conference held in Dur-ban, specifically excluded anti-Semitism from the global struggle against racism. In 2002, six months after his visit to Ramallah, the Portuguese Nobel Prize-winning author José Saramago compared Israel's treatment of the Palestinians with conditions at Auschwitz; because of these sins, he has asserted, the Jewish people no longer deserve sympathy for the suffer-ing they endured during the Holocaust.[54] According to the 2005 ADL poll, more than 50 percent of the respondents in Germany, Italy, Poland, and Spain believed that their Jewish compatriots were more loyal to Israel than to their own country.[55]

Another major element in this explosive mixture has been the expansion of Muslim space in Europe. There are now some fifteen million Muslims in the countries comprised in the European Union, ranging from recent arrivals to the descendents of migrants a half century ago, and who, over the past ten years, have grown more visible, more politically active, and more numerous, now comprising 9 percent of the population of France, 6 percent of the Netherlands, 4 percent of Belgium, 3 percent of Germany, Sweden, and the United Kingdom, and 2.5 percent of Spain.[56] Much of this population holds not only anti-Zionist and pro-Palestinian sentiments kindled by Arab satellite television and websites, by sermons in the mosques, and by the local and international Arab press, but also negative feelings towards their Jewish neighbors, who appear to exceed them in wealth and political influence. Among the youth, high rates of unemployment, social marginalization, and incendiary messages from abroad have added to this explosive mixture.[57]

It is thus not surprising that the largest outbreaks of anti-Jewish violence in Europe following the 2000 intifada occurred in France, Belgium, and Britain, and not in Eastern Europe. In France alone the four hundred documented anti-Semitic incidents in 2001 were mostly perpetrated by Muslim youth of North African origin. In 2006 the abduction, torture, and murder of Ilan Halimi by an extortionist gang of African youths placed a spotlight on the targeting of Jewish individuals, which has spread throughout Western Europe.

Jewish responses to the rise of anti-Semitism have been diverse, depending on age, gender, status, means, and country of residence. Some, especially in the older generation, have simply retreated from the public sphere, while others have decided to emigrate; some hide outward signs of Jewishness, while others display them proudly; some have called for unified Jewish action, while others have worked closely with private and public organizations.[58] The Center for Research on Anti-Semitism at Berlin's Technical University monitors television broadcasts, websites, blogs, and public exhibitions and has issued the strongest, best-documented reports on the recent violence against European Jews.

In the absence of strong transnational European Jewish organizations, the Israeli government and American Jews have stepped in. Spurred by the Anti-Defamation League, the fifty-five-member Organization for Security and Cooperation in Europe (OSCE) has convened major conferences on European Anti-Semitism in 2003 (Vienna), 2004 (Berlin), 2005 (Córdoba), and 2007 (Bucharest) and has set up new monitoring mechanisms and consultation procedures. While it is too early to gauge the effectiveness of these initiatives, they signal an increased international awareness of the dangers to European Jewry.

. . .

To some, European Jewry is now an endangered people. There are those who consider the Jews' survival in Europe, rather than a positive phenomenon simply proof of their inability to learn the lessons of history. Responding to the wave of violence in 2003, the Israeli prime minister Ariel Sharon publicly implored his French coreligionists to leave before it was "too late." Others fear that Europe's Jews will disappear because of the attractions of assimilation and the removal of all Jewish religious content from European life.[59]

Diana Pinto, on the other hand, believes that the Jews of Europe are capable of making an audacious wager—to "end the finished exile." From Portugal to the Urals, indeed from Malta to Istanbul, Pinto believes they can now choose to be Jews without compromising their identity, their safety, their civic responsibilities, and their religious needs, thus forging a creative symbiosis with a transforming Europe. They have an opportunity to share in cultural, political, social, and humanitarian projects within the world's wealthiest, more politically stable continents.[60]

Are multiple identities the way to safety and survival? In Sweden, with one of Europe's most established and affluent Jewish communities, polls indicate that 84 percent of Jews attend a Seder, 50 percent have their children circumcised, 47 percent fast on Yom Kippur, and 10 percent avoid driving on the Sabbath; but 70 percent want female equality in the synagogue and a prompt solution to the Israeli-Palestinian question.[61] For a skeptic such as Bernard Wasserstein, this growing smorgasbord of selective loyalties and practices, combined with a rising anti-Semitism, bodes darkly for the survival of European Jewry.[62]

Jews inside and outside Europe have long had an ambivalent relationship to this continent, the place of a very long (but not the longest) Diaspora, the home of the Enlightenment, slow and uneven emancipation, and singular achievements, but also of exclusion, persecution, and the Shoah.[63] After 1945, the shrunken Jewish life in a divided Europe stood in strong contrast with the growing, self-confident Jewry of Israel, America, Canada, and Australia; and since 1990, when new hopes were kindled, there have been gains in some places, setbacks in others.[64]

There are nonetheless hopeful signs in unexpected places. There is the European project, although fuzzy and politically stalled, which now exerts considerable attraction to the young generation. In a 2000 poll of sixteen-to-twenty–year-old Austrian Jews who had studied in the United States and Israel, an overwhelming number planned to spend their lives in Austria or anywhere else in Europe but definitely not abroad.[65]

In Central Europe there is a growing movement among Jewish women to revitalize and democratize the home and the synagogue.[66] In Germany there is a small renaissance of Jewish culture.[67] And in Hungary today there is a community of some 120,000 Jews, primarily in Budapest, in which 30 percent of those between the ages of eighteen and fifty-four adhere to religious tradition.[68] Despite the lachrymose message in István Szabó's film *Sunshine* and the newly energized Hungarian radical right, which periodically creates public anti-Semitic incidents, this is a growing Jewish community that still wants to make its history within Hungary and Europe.[69]

To return to the topic of generations, György Konrád, in an autobiographical story set during Chanukah in 1995, joyously anticipated the birth of his granddaughter:

> Now is the beginning of winter. . . . At this season the self-conscious person tortures himself (if not others) thinking he has neglected something that can no longer be set right, because what happened, after all, *cannot* be set right; it is frozen into time's vault, filed away in the storehouse of the cosmos. Today or tomorrow you can do good—but not yesterday.
>
> At times like this it is common, too, to await the arrival of the one who might know what we still do not, the one who will set us on a new road, mark a new beginning for the grand experiment. . . . Our hope is that someone else will do it—that the next generation will do it for our own.
>
> Perhaps they will be more humane than we, more clear-sighted, more courageous, kinder—in a word, more perfect. . . . *This* person, still zero years of age, will surely set us right . . . she will acquit us of enormous charges, even as she sews unforeseen stitches into the great family carpet.
>
> So many messiahs! I say to myself as I peer through the fence of the kindergarten, so many exceptional anointed persons, designed by fate to be undying candle flames for those around them. . . . We await a little woman whose soul will dominate over fatigue, which means that even if she has nothing, she will be rich.[70]

The most beloved Jewish prayer, *l'dor v'dor* [from generation to genera-tion], calls for the preservation of memory, of the bad and the good, the suffering and survival, and even in the worst of times, for the struggle to preserve humanity. Today, however, for most of Europe's Jews—whose daily thoughts and recollections remain distant from their neighbors—the task of continuation is still daunting.

NOTES

I thank Sarah Kernan of The Ohio State University for her research assistance.

1. Michel-Rolf Trouillot, *Silencing the Past: Power and the Production of History*, 13–14.

2. Bertolt Brecht, "An die Nachgeborenen" [To posterity], *Svendborger Gedichte*, 60.

3. Katarzyna Marciniak, "New Europe: Eyes Wide Shut," *Social Identities* 12(5) (2006): 615–633.

4. Useful discussions in: Jonathan Webber, "Jews and Judaism in Contemporary Europe: Religion or Ethnic Group?" *Ethnic and Racial Studies* 20(2) (1997): 257–279; Valeriy Chervyakov, Zvi Gitelman, and Vladimir Shapiro, "Religion and Ethnicity: Judaism in the Ethnic Consciousness of Contemporary Russian Jews," *Ethnic and Racial Studies* 20(2) (1997): 280–305.

5. "The Jewish Population of the World" (2006), http://www.jewishvirtuallibrary .org/jsource/Judaism/jewpop.html; cf. Sergio Della Pergola and Amos Gilboa, *The Jewish People Policy Planning Institute Annual Assessment, 2004–2005*, 299–368; Sergio Della Pergola, "World Jewish Population 2002," *American Jewish Year Book* (2002), http://www.jafi.org.il/education/100/concepts/democragraphy/demtables.html.

6. Urban figures in Della Pergola, "World Jewish Population," p. 8.

7. Bernard Wasserstein, *Vanishing Diaspora: The Jews in Europe Since 1945*, viii; also "Jewish Population of Europe in 1945," U.S. Holocaust Memorial Museum, http://www.ushmm.org/wlc/article.php?land=en&moduleId=10005687.

8. Oliver Bradley, "Soviet Jews Flooding Germany," *European Jewish Press*, October 25, 2007, http://www.ejpress.org/article/in_deptch/1969; cf. Wasserstein, *Vanishing Diaspora*, 180–205.

9. An important element in Mark Kurlansky, *A Chosen Few: The Resurrection of European Jewry*, which follows a half century of Jewish personal histories in Paris, Antwerp, Budapest, Prague, Warsaw, Berlin, and Amsterdam.

10. *Rok 1989: Bronisław Geremek opowiada, Jacek Żakowski pyta*; Maurice Szafran, *Simone Veil: Destin*; Louise O. Vasvári and Steven Tötösy de Zepetnek, *Imre Kertész and Holocaust Literature*; György Konrád, *A Guest in My Own Country: A Hungarian Life*, trans. Jim Tucker; Ivan Klíma, *My Golden Trades*, trans. Paul Wilson; Hanna Krall, *To Steal a March on God*, trans. Jadwiga Kosicka; Henryk Grynberg, *Drohobycz*,

*Drohobycz and other Stories*, trans. Alicia Nitecki; Stuart Liebman, ed., *Claude Lanzmann's* Shoah: *Key Essays*; Robert Misrahi, *Un juif laïque en France*; Bernard Kouchner, *Deux ou trois choses que je sais de nous*; Jacques Le Goff and Pierre Nora, *Faire de l'histoire*, 3 vols.; Klaus Dermutz, *Peter Zadek: His Way*.

11. Wolf Biermann, *Für meine Genossen: Hetzlieder, Balladen, Gedichte*; Adam Michnik, *Letters from Prison and Other Essays*, trans. Maya Latyński; Daniel Cohn-Bendit, *Obsolete Communism: The Left-Wing Alternative*, trans. Arnold Pomerans.

12. Barbara Honigmann, *Das Gesicht wiederfinden: Über Schreiben, Schriftsteller und Judentum*; also Christine Guenther, "Exile and the Construction of Identity in Barbara Honigmann's Trilogy of Diaspora," *Comparative Literature Studies* 40(2) (2003): 215–231.

13. See esp.: Miriam Cahn, *Arbeiten, 1979–1983*; Moni Ovadia, *L'ebreo che ride: l'umorismo ebraico in otto lezioni e duecento storielle*; Reina Roffe, *Conversaciones americanas*; Marlène Amar, *Des Gens infréquentables*.

14. Larissa Remennick, "Idealists Headed to Israel, Pragmatics Chose Europe: Identity Dilemmas and Social Incorporation among Former Soviet Jews who Migrated to Germany," *Immigrants and Minorities* 23(1) (2005): 30–58; Sander Gilman, "Becoming a Jew by Becoming a German: The Newest Jewish Writing from the 'East,'" *Shofar* 26(1) (2006): 16–32.

15. Lena Gorelik, *Meine weissen Nächte*; also *Hochzeit in Jerusalem*.

16. Clive A. Lawton, "European Models of Community: Can Ambiguity Help?" in *Turning the Kaleidoscope*, ed. Lustig and Leveson, 41–62.

17. The Ronald S. Lauder Foundation, "Our Work in Central and Eastern Europe," n.d., http://www.rslfoundation.org/html/ourwork/ourwork.htm.

18. Jan Velinger, "Jewish Education in Czech Republic Sees Tenth Anniversary," April 9, 2007, Radio Prague website, http://www.radio.cz/en/article/95099; also: Dinah Spritzer, "Jewish Schools Flourish in Central Europe," *New Jersey Jewish Standard*, March 16, 2006; Dinah Spritzer, "Foundation Helps Jewish Schools Thrive in Central, Eastern Europe," *Jewish News Weekly of Northern California*, July 29, 2008, http://www.jewishsf.com/content/2-0-/module/displaystory/story_id/29885/edition_id/56.

19. See, for example, "Der Zentralrat der Juden in Deutschland," June 7, 2006, http://www.tagesschau.de/inland/meldung113942.html.

20. On the ECJC, see "Introduction," *Turning the Kaleidoscope*, ed. Lustig and Leveson, 14–15; EJC website, http://www.eurojewcong.org/ejc/index.php. Also Michael White, "International Organizations: Combating Anti-Semitism in Europe," *Jewish Political Studies Review* 16(3–4) (2004), http://www.jcpa.org/phas/phas-whine-f04.htm.

21. Diana Pinto, "The Jewish Space in Europe," in *Turning the Kaleidoscope*, ed. Lustig and Leveson, 179–186 (quotation on p. 179).

22. Miriam Sivan, "Jewish Spaces in the European Theater: European Performing Arts Forum, Prague 14–16 June 2003," http://www.jewishcultureineurope.org/theatre_summing_up.htm.

23. Ruth Ellen Gruber, *Virtually Jewish: Reinventing Jewish Culture in Europe*.

24. Albert Van der Heide and Irene E. Zwiep, eds., *Jewish Studies and the European Academic World: Plenary Lectures Read at the VIIth Congress of the European Association for Jewish Studies (EAJS), Amsterdam, July 2002*.

25. Diana Pinto, "Jewish Studies at the European Cross-Roads," in ibid., 153–162.

26. For example, on the fifty-third anniversary of the *Kristallnacht* in 1991 a German concert poster contained the stock image of a stooped, hooked-nosed East European man watching the musicians, rubbing his hands, and exhibiting the sly, sexually lewd Jewish male.

On the complexities of klezmer, see Gruber, *Virtually Jewish*, 183–204; also Elizabeth Loentz, "Yiddish, *Kanak Sprak*, Klezmer, and HipHop: Ethnolect, Minority Culture, Multiculturalism, and Stereotype in Germany," *Shofar* 25(1) (2006): 33–62.

27. Gruber, *Virtually Jewish*, recounts her discomfort "as I experienced so vividly during my *Schindler's List* tour of Kraków, the clashes among Jews and 'virtual Jews,' current realities and the past, commercial representation and collective memory, frequently remain fraught with perplexity and contradiction," 154.

28. See esp. Katharina Von Ankum, "German Memorial Culture: The Berlin Holocaust Monument Debate," *Response* 68 (Fall 1997/Winter 1998): 41–48.

29. Gerd Knischewski and Ulla Spittler, "Remembering in the Berlin Republic: The Debate about the Central Holocaust Memorial in Berlin," *Debatte* 13(1) (2005): 25–43.

30. Suzanne Bardgett, "The Depiction of the Holocaust at the Imperial War Museum since 1961," *Journal of Israeli History* 23(1) (2004): 151–156.

31. See Ruth Ellen Gruber, "Budapest Jewish Exhibit Tackles Question of Art and Identity," *Jewish Heritage Report* 1(3–4) (Winter 1997–98), http://www.isjm.org/jhr/no3-4/buda.htm.

32. Robert S.C. Gordon, "The Holocaust in Italian Collective Memory: *Il giorno della memoria*, 27 January 2001," *Modern Italy* 11(2) (2006): 167–188.

33. "European Day of Jewish Culture," February 2, 2007, http://www.jewish-theatre.com/visitor/article_display.aspx?articleID=2378.

34. Y. Michal Bodemann, "Reconstructions of History: From Jewish Memory to Nationalized Commemoration of Kristallnacht in Germany," in *Jews, Germans, Memory, Reconstructions of Jewish Life in Germany*, ed. Y. M. Bodemann, 179–223.

35. Diana Pinto, "A New Role for Jews in Europe: Challenges and Responsibilities," in *Turning the Kaleidoscope*, ed. Lustig and Leveson, 27–40.

36. Ian Leveson and Sandra Lustig, "Caught Between Civil Society and the Cultural Market: Jewry and the Jewish Space in Europe: A Response to Diana Pinto," in *Turning the Kaleidoscope*, ed. Lustig and Leveson, 187–204.

37. Sandra Lustig, "'The Germans Will Never Forgive the Jews for Auschwitz': When Things Go Wrong in the Jewish Space: The Case of the Walser-Bubis Debate," in ibid., 205–222. On the issue of modern European memory and the current

conflict of "aggrieved memories," see Tony Judt, *Postwar: A History of Europe Since 1945*, 803–831.

38. "The New Anti-Semitism," *Ha'aretz*, September 8, 2002.

39. David Titelman, Mikael Enckell, and Henrik Bachner, "Antisemitism in Sweden and Finland," *Scandinavian Psychoanalytic Review* 17 (2004): 52–57.

40. Maria Brutti, "Jews and Judaism in Catholic Religious Textbooks" (1988–2006), http://www.unigre.it/pugjudaicstudies/doc/SpecialProjectBrutti.pdf; Brutti, "Catechesis-Jews-Judaism," October 2006, http://www.unigre.it/pub/judaicstudies/doc.SpecialProjectBruttiCathechesis.pdf.

41. Vladimir Paounovsky, "Anti-Semitism in Bulgaria—Yesterday, Today, and Tomorrow," in *Jews and Slavs*, ed. Wolf Moskovich, Oto Luthar, and Irena Šumi, 75–76.

42. David I. Kertzer, ed., *Old Demons, New Debates: Anti-Semitism in the West*; also: John Rosenthal, "Anti-Semitism and Ethnicity in Europe," *Policy Review* (2003): 17–38; Roger Eatwell, "Why Are Fascism and Racism Reviving in Western Europe?" *Political Quarterly* 65(3) (1994): 313–325.

43. André W.M. Gerrits, "Jüdischer Kommunismus: Der Mythos, die Juden, die Partei," *Jahrbuch für Antisemitismusforschung* 14 (2005): 243–264; Cas Mudde, "Racist Extremism in Central and Eastern Europe," *East European Politics and Societies* 19(2) (2005): 161–184; also "Jews and Anti-Semitism in the Balkans," in *Jews and Slavs*, ed. Moskovich, Luthar, and Šumi, vol. 12: 7–147; cf. Jovan Byford, "Distinguishing 'Anti-Judaism' from 'Antisemitism': Recent Championing of Serbian Bishop Nikolaj Velimirović," *Religion, State and Society* 34(1) (2006): 7–31; Tim Whewell, "Reopening Lithuania's Old Wounds," *BBC News*, July 21, 2008, http://news.bbc.co.uk/2/hi/programmes/crossing_continents/7508375.stm.

44. Paul Iganski and Barry Kosmin, "Antisémite ou antisocial? Le 'nouvel antisémitisme' de rue en Grande-Bretagne," in *Les habits neufs de l'antisémitisme en Europe*, ed. Manfred Gerstenfeld and Shmuel Trigano, 199–209.

45. Anti-Defamation League, *Attitudes Towards Jews in Twelve European Countries*.

46. *The Guardian*, January 23, 2004.

47. David Cesarani, "Holocaust Controversies in the 1990s: The Revenge of History or the History of Revenge?" *Journal of Israel History* 23(1) (2004): 78–90; Tony Kushner, "Too Little, Too Late? Reflections on Britain's Holocaust Memorial Day," ibid., 116–129; Carolyn J. Dean, "Recent French Discourses on Stalinism, Nazism, and 'Exorbitant' Jewish Memory," *History and Memory* 18 (2006): 43–85; Efraim Zuroff, "Eastern Europe: Anti-Semitism in the Wake of Holocaust Related Issues," *Jewish Political Studies Review* 17(1–2) (2005): 63–80.

48. Edward H. Kaplan and Charles A. Small, "Anti-Israel Sentiment Predicts Anti-Semitism in Europe," *Journal of Conflict Resolution* 50(4) (2006): 548–561; also these important articles: Robert Wistrich, "Anti-Zionism and Anti-Semitism," *Jewish Political Studies Review* 16(3–4) (2004): 27–32; Siegfried Jäger, "Zur diskursiven

Dynamik des Redens über Antisemitismus," *Tel Aviver Jahrbuch für Deutsche Geschichte* 33 (2005): 110–139; Juliane Wetzel, "Antisemitismus in Europe: Zwischen Tradition und Einwanderung—neue Tendenzen und alte Diskussion," in *Gerüchte über die Juden. Antisemitismus, Philosemitismus und aktuelle Verschwörungstheorien*, ed. Hanno Lowy, 27–45; Helga Embacher, "Neuer Antisemitismus in Europa?" *Kirche und Israel* 19(1) (2004): 68–80; Andreas Zick and Beate Küpper, "Antisemitismus in Deutschland und Europa," *Aus Politik und Zeitgeschichte* 31 (2007): 12–19.

49. Detailed in Manfred Gerstenfeld, "The Deep Roots of Anti-Semitism in European Society," *Jewish Political Studies Review* 17(1) (2005): 3–46.

50. Andrei S. Markovits, "An Inseparable Tandem of European Identity? Anti-Americanism and Anti-Semitism in the Short and Long Run," *Journal of Israeli History* 25(1) (2006): 85–105.

51. Israeli Apartheid Week 2009, http://apartheidweek.org/.

52. Manfred Gerstenfeld, "Anti-Semitism in European Society," *Jewish Political Studies Review* 17(3–4) (2005): 22–29; Manfred Gerstenfeld, "European Politics: Double Standards Toward Israel," http://www.jcpa.org/phas/phas-gerstenfeld-1-f05.htm.

53. Jonathan Sacks in *Ha'aretz*, September 8, 2002: "What we are witnessing today is . . . a mutation so ingenious, demonic and evil that it paralyzes the immune systems the West built up over the past half-century . . . The worst crimes of anti-Semites in the past—racism, ethnic cleansing, attempted genocide, crimes against humanity—are now attributed to Jews and to the State of Israel"; also Monique Eckmann, "Antisemitismus im Namen der Menschenrechte?" in *Gerüchte über die Juden*, ed. Loewy, 101–120.

54. *The Guardian*, December 28, 2002.

55. ADL, *Attitudes Towards Jews in Twelve European Countries* (May 2005), 5, 18, 20, 21. More than a third of those surveyed in Switzerland, Spain, Austria, and Denmark viewed Jews differently as a result of the actions taken by Israel, p. 10; and 69 percent of respondents in Spain, 63 percent in Belgium, and 62 percent in the Netherlands acknowledged that they were likely to view Jews more negatively as a result of the actions taken by the State of Israel, p. 11.

56. *BBC News*, "Muslims in Europe," December 23, 2005, http://news/Bbc.co.uk/2/hi/Europe/4385768.stm; Omar Taspinar, "Europe's Muslim Street," *Brookings Institution Report*, March/April 2003, http://www.brookings.edu/opinions//2003/03/middleeast_taspinar.aspx.

57. Detailed in "Exporting Islamic Violence to Western Democracies," Raphael Israeli, in *War, Peace and Terror in the Middle East*, 159–173; Suzanne Wirtz, "Antisemitismus in Europa," *Tribune* (2007): 123–134.

58. Website of the Zentrum für Antisemitismusforschung, the only such institution outside of Israel: http://www2.tu-berlin.de/zfa/.

59. Wasserstein, *Vanishing Diaspora*, 253–279.

60. Diana Pinto, "The Wager: Europe, the Jews, and Israel," in *Jüdische Lebenswelt Schweitz/Vie et culture juives en Suisse*, 344–351; also "Are There Jewish Answers to Europe's Questions?" *European Judaism* 39(2) (2006): 47–57.

61. Lars Dencik, "'Homo Zappiens': A European Jewish Way of Life in the Era of Globalisation," in *Turning the Kaleidoscope*, ed. Lustig and Leveson, esp. 89–90 ("Typical but Special? Swedish Jewry").

62. Wasserstein, *Vanishing Diaspora*, 280–290.

63. Jacob Katz, *From Prejudice to Destruction: Anti-Semitism, 1700–1933*; and esp. Jacob Talmon, *The Origins of Totalitarian Democracy*.

64. David Weinberg, "Between America and Israel: The Quest for a Distinct European Jewish Identity in the Post-War Era," *Jewish Culture and History* 5(1) (2002): 91–120.

65. Matti Bunzl, "Austrian Zionism and the Jews of the New Europe," *Project Muse*, 154–173, http://muse.jhu.edu.

66. Lara Dämmig, and Elisa Klapheck, "Debora's Disciplines: A Women's Movement as an Expression of Renewing Jewish Life in Europe," trans. Sandra Lustig, in *Turning the Kaleidoscope*, ed. Lustig and Leveson, 147–163.

67. Y. Michal Bodemann, "A Jewish Cultural Renascence in Germany?" in ibid., 164–175.

68. Kati Vörös, "How Jewish Is Jewish Budapest?" *Jewish Social Studies* 8(1) (2001): 88–125; cf. András Kovács, "Jewish Groups and Identity Strategies in Post-Communist Hungary: Beyond the Concept of Assimilation," in *Haskala* 26(2), ed. Moses Mendelssohn Zentrum für europäisch-jüdische Studien, 611–629.

69. Susan R. Suleiman, "Jewish Assimilation in Hungary, the Holocaust, and Epic Film: Reflections on István Szabó's *Sunshine*," *Yale Journal of Criticism* 14(1) (2001): 233–252.

70. György Konrád, "Expectations," trans. James A. Tucker, in *Here I Am: Contemporary Jewish Stories from Around the World*, ed. Marsha L. Berkman and Elaine M. Starkman, 277–279.

WORKS CITED

Amar, Marlène. *Des Gens infréquentables*. Paris: Gallimard, 1996.

Anti-Defamation League (ADL). *Attitudes Towards Jews in Twelve European Countries*. New York: ADL, May 2005.

Bardgett, Suzanne. "The Depiction of the Holocaust at the Imperial War Museum since 1961." *Journal of Israeli History* 23(1) (2004): 151–156.

BBC News. "Muslims in Europe." December 23, 2005. http://news/Bbc.co.uk/2/hi/Europe/4385768.stm (accessed October 28, 2007).

Biermann, Wolf. *Für meine Genossen: Hetzlieder, Balladen, Gedichte*. Berlin: Wagenbach, 1972.

Bodemann, Y. Michal. "A Jewish Cultural Renascence in Germany?" In *Turning the*

*Kaleidoscope: Perspectives on European Jewry*, ed. Sandra Lustig and Ian Leveson, 164–175. New York and Oxford: Berghahn, 2006.

———. "Reconstructions of History: From Jewish Memory to Nationalized Commemoration of Kristallnacht in Germany." In *Jews, Germans, Memory, Reconstructions of Jewish Life in Germany*, ed. Y. M. Bodemann, 179–223. Ann Arbor: University of Michigan Press, 1996.

Bradley, Oliver. "Soviet Jews Flooding Germany." *European Jewish Press*, October 25, 2007. http://www.ejpress.org/article/in_depth/1969 (accessed October 25, 2007).

Brecht, Bertolt. "An die Nachgeborenen" [To posterity]. *Svendborger Gedichte*. London: Malik-Verlag, 1939.

Brutti, Maria. "Cathechesis-Jews-Judaism." October 2006. http://www.unigre.it/pub/judaicstudies/doc.SpecialProjectBruttiCathechesis.pdf (accessed March 24, 2008).

———. "Jews and Judaism in Catholic Religious Textbooks." 1988–2006. http://www.unigre.it/pugjudaicstudies/doc/SpecialProjectBrutti.pdf (accessed March 24, 2008).

Bunzl, Matti. "Austrian Zionism and the Jews of the New Europe." *Project Muse*, http://muse.jhu.edu, 154–173.

Byford, Jovan. "Distinguishing 'Anti-Judaism' from 'Antisemitism': Recent Championing of Serbian Bishop Nikolaj Velimirović." *Religion, State and Society* 34(1) (2006): 7–31.

Cahn, Miriam. *Arbeiten, 1979–1983*. Basel: Basler Kunstverein, 1983.

Cesarani, David. "Holocaust Controversies in the 1990s: The Revenge of History or the History of Revenge?" *Journal of Israel History* 23(1) (2004): 78–90.

Chervyakov, Valeriy, Zvi Gitelman, and Vladimir Shapiro. "Religion and Ethnicity: Judaism in the Ethnic Consciousness of Contemporary Russian Jews." *Ethnic and Racial Studies* 20(2) (1997): 280–305.

Cohn-Bendit, Daniel. *Obsolete Communism: The Left-Wing Alternative*, trans. Arnold Pomerans. New York: McGraw-Hill, 1968.

Dämmig, Lara, and Elisa Klapheck. "Debora's Disciplines: A Women's Movement as an Expression of Renewing Jewish Life in Europe," trans. Sandra Lustig. In *Turning the Kaleidoscope: Perspectives on European Jewry*, ed. Sandra Lustig and Ian Leveson, 147–163. New York and Oxford: Berghahn, 2006.

Dean, Carolyn J. "Recent French Discourses on Stalinism, Nazism, and 'Exorbitant' Jewish Memory." *History and Memory* 18 (2006): 43–85.

Della Pergola, Sergio. "World Jewish Population 2002." *American Jewish Year Book* (2002). http://www.jafi.org.il/education/100/concepts/democragraphy/demtables.html (accessed March 19, 2008).

Della Pergola, Sergio, and Amos Gilboa. *The Jewish People Policy Planning Institute Annual Assessment, 2004–2005*, 299–368. Jerusalem: FPPPI, 2005.

Dencik, Lars. "'Homo Zappiens': A European Jewish Way of Life in the Era of Globalisation." In *Turning the Kaleidoscope: Perspectives on European Jewry*, ed. Sandra Lustig and Ian Leveson, 79–105. New York and Oxford: Berghahn, 2006.

Dermutz, Klaus. *Peter Zadek: His Way*. Berlin: Henschel, 2006.

Eatwell, Roger. "Why Are Fascism and Racism Reviving in Western Europe?" *Political Quarterly* 65(3) (1994): 313–325.

Eckmann, Monique. "Antisemitismus im Namen der Menschenrechte?" In *Gerüchte über die Juden. Antisemitismus, Philosemitismus und aktuelle Verschwörungstheorien*, ed. Hanno Loewy, 101–120. Essen: Klartext Verlag, 2005.

Embacher, Helga. "Neuer Antisemitismus in Europa?" *Kirche und Israel* 19(1) (2004): 68–80.

"European Day of Jewish Culture." February 2, 2007. http://www.jewish-theatre. com/visitor/article_display.aspx?articleID=2378 (accessed October 18, 2007).

Gerrits, André W.M. "Jüdischer Kommunismus: Der Mythos, die Juden, die Partei." *Jahrbuch für Antisemitismusforschung* 14 (2005): 243–264.

Gerstenfeld, Manfred. "Anti-Semitism in European Society." *Jewish Political Studies Review* 17(3–4) (Fall 2005): 17–22.

———. "The Deep Roots of Anti-Semitism in European Society." *Jewish Political Studies Review* 17(1) (2005): 3–46.

"European Politics: Double Standards Toward Israel." http://www.jcpa.org/phas/ phas-gerstenfeld-1-f05.htm (accessed October 16, 2007).

Gilman, Sander. "Becoming a Jew by Becoming a German: The Newest Jewish Writing from the 'East'." *Shofar* 26(1) (2006): 16–32.

Gordon, Robert S.C. "The Holocaust in Italian Collective Memory: *Il giorno della memoria*, 27 January 2001." *Modern Italy* 11(2) (2006): 167–188.

Gorelik, Lena. *Hochzeit in Jerusalem*. Munich: SchirmerGraf, 2007.

———. *Meine weissen Nächte*. Munich: SchirmerGraf, 2004.

Gruber, Ruth Ellen. "Budapest Jewish Exhibit Tackles Question of Art and Identity." *Jewish Heritage Report* 1(3–4) (Winter 1997–98). http://www.isjm.org/jhr/nos3-4/ buda.htm (accessed October 10, 2007).

———. *Virtually Jewish: Reinventing Jewish Culture in Europe*. Berkeley, Los Angeles and London: University of California Press, 2002.

Grynberg, Henryk. *Drohobycz, Drohobycz and Other Stories*, trans. Alicia Nitecki. New York: Penguin Books, 2002.

Guenther, Christine. "Exile and the Construction of Identity in Barbara Honigmann's Trilogy of Diaspora." *Comparative Literature Studies* 40(2) (2003): 215–231.

Honigmann, Barbara. *Das Gesicht wiederfinden: Über Schreiben, Schriftsteller und Judentum*. Munich: C. Hanswer, 2006.

Iganski, Paul, and Barry Kosmin. "Antisémite ou antisocial? Le 'nouvel antisémitisme' de rue en Grande-Bretagne." In *Les habits neufs de l'antisémitisme en Europe*, ed. Manfred Gerstenfeld and Shmuel Trigano, 199–209. Paris: Éditions Café Noir, 2004.

Israeli, Raphael. *War, Peace and Terror in the Middle East*, 159–173. London and Portland, OR: Frank Cass, 2003.

Jäger, Siegfried. "Zur diskursiven Dynamik des Redens über Antisemitismus." *Tel Aviver Jahrbuch für Deutsche Geschichte* 33 (2005): 110–139.

"Jewish Population of Europe in 1945." U.S. Holocaust Memorial Museum. http://www.ushmm.org/wlc/article.php?land=en&moduleId=10005687 (accessed March 19, 2008).

"The Jewish Population of the World." 2006. http://www.jewishvirtuallibrary.org/jsource/Judaism/jewpop.html (accessed March 19, 2008).

Judt, Tony. *Postwar: A History of Europe since 1945*. New York: Penguin, 2005.

Kaplan, Edward H., and Charles A. Small. "Anti-Israel Sentiment Predicts Anti-Semitism in Europe." *Journal of Conflict Resolution* 50(4) (2006): 548–561.

Katz, Jacob. *From Prejudice to Destruction: Anti-Semitism, 1700–1933*. Cambridge, MA: Harvard University Press, 1980.

Kertzer, David I., ed. *Old Demons, New Debates: Anti-Semitism in the West*. Teaneck, NJ: Holmes & Meier, 2005.

Klíma, Ivan. *My Golden Trades*, trans. Paul Wilson. New York: Scribner, 1994.

Knischewski, Gerd, and Ulla Spittler. "Remembering in the Berlin Republic: The Debate about the Central Holocaust Memorial in Berlin." *Debatte* 13(1) (2005): 25–43.

Konrád, György. "Expectations," trans. James A. Tucker. In *Here I Am: Contemporary Jewish Stories from Around the World*, ed. Marsha L. Berkman and Elaine M. Starkman, 277–279. Philadelphia and Jerusalem: Jewish Publication Society, 1998/5758.

———. *A Guest in My Own Country: A Hungarian Life*, trans. Jim Tucker. New York: Other Press, 2007.

Kouchner, Bernard. *Deux ou trois choses que je sais de nous*. Paris: Laffont, 2006.

Kovács, András. "Jewish Groups and Identity Strategies in Post-Communist Hungary: Beyond the Concept of Assimilation." In *Haskala* 26(2), ed. Moses Mendelssohn Zentrum für europäisch-jüdische Studien, 611–629. Hildesheim, Zurich, and New York: Georg Olms, 2002.

Krall, Hanna. *To Steal a March on God*, trans. Jadwiga Kosicka. Amsterdam: Harwood, 1996.

Kurlansky, Mark. *A Chosen Few: The Resurrection of European Jewry*. Reading, MA: Addison-Wesley, 1995.

Kushner, Tony. "Too Little, Too Late? Reflections on Britain's Holocaust Memorial Day." *Journal of Israel History* 23(1) (2004): 116–129.

Lawton, Clive A. "European Models of Community: Can Ambiguity Help?" In *Turning the Kaleidoscope: Perspectives on European Jewry*, ed. Sandra Lustig and Ian Leveson, 41–62. New York and Oxford: Berghahn, 2006.

Le Goff, Jacques, and Pierre Nora. *Faire de l'histoire*. 3 vols. Paris: Gallimard, 1974.

Leveson, Ian, and Sandra Lustig. "Caught Between Civil Society and the Cultural Market: Jewry and the Jewish Space in Europe. A Response to Diana Pinto." In *Turning the Kaleidoscope: Perspectives on European Jewry*, ed. Sandra Lustig and Ian Leveson, 187–204. New York and Oxford: Berghahn, 2006.

Liebman, Stuart, ed. *Claude Lanzmann's Shoah: Key Essays*. Oxford and New York: Oxford University Press, 2007.

Loentz, Elizabeth. "Yiddish, *Kanak Sprak*, Klezmer, and HipHop: Ethnolect, Minority Culture, Multiculturalism, and Stereotype in Germany." *Shofar* 25(1) (2006): 33–62.

Lustig, Sandra. "'The Germans Will Never Forgive the Jews for Auschwitz': When Things Go Wrong in the Jewish Space: The Case of the Walser-Bubis Debate." In *Turning the Kaleidoscope: Perspectives on European Jewry*, ed. Sandra Lustig and Ian Leveson, 205–222. New York and Oxford: Berghahn, 2006.

Lustig, Sandra, and Ian Leveson. "Introduction." *Turning the Kaleidoscope: Perspectives on European Jewry*, 14–15. New York and Oxford: Berghahn, 2006.

Marciniak, Katarzyna. "New Europe: Eyes Wide Shut," *Social Identities* 12(5) (2006): 615–633.

Markovits, Andrei S. "An Inseparable Tandem of European Identity? Anti-Americanism and Anti-Semitism in the Short and Long Run." *Journal of Israeli History* 25(1) (2006): 85–105.

Michnik, Adam. *Letters from Prison and Other Essays*, trans. Maya Latyński. Berkeley: University of California Press, 1985.

Misrahi, Robert. *Un juif laïque en France*. Paris: Entrelacs, 2004.

Mudde, Cas. "Jews and Anti-Semitism in the Balkans." In *Jews and Slavs*, ed. Wolf Moskovich, Oto Luthar, and Irena Šumi, vol. 12, 7–147. Jerusalem and Ljubljana: Slovenian Academy of Sciences, 2004.

———. "Racist Extremism in Central and Eastern Europe." *East European Politics and Societies* 19(2) (2005): 161–184.

Ovadia, Moni. *L'ebreo che ride: l'umorismo ebraico in otto lezioni e duecento storielle*. Turin: Einaudi, 1998.

Paounovsky, Vladimir. "Anti-Semitism in Bulgaria—Yesterday, Today, and Tomorrow." In *Jews and Slavs*, ed. Wolf Moskovich, Oto Luthar, and Irena Šumi, vol. 12, 75–76. Jerusalem and Ljubljana: Slovenian Academy of Sciences, 2004.

Pinto, Diana. "Are There Jewish Answers to Europe's Questions?" *European Judaism* 39(2) (2006): 47–57.

———. "A New Role for Jews in Europe: Challenges and Responsibilities." In *Turning the Kaleidoscope: Perspectives on European Jewry*, ed. Sandra Lustig and Ian Leveson, 27–40. New York and Oxford: Berghahn, 2006.

———. "The Jewish Space in Europe." In *Turning the Kaleidoscope: Perspectives on European Jewry*, ed. Sandra Lustig and Ian Leveson, 179–186. New York and Oxford: Berghahn, 2006.

———. "Jewish Studies at the European Cross-Roads." In *Jewish Studies and the European Academic World: Plenary Lectures Read at the VIIth Congress of the European Association for Jewish Studies (EAJS), Amsterdam, July 2002*, ed. Albert Van der Heide and Irene E. Zwiep, 153–162. Paris, Louvain, and Dudley, MA: Peeters, 2005.

———. "The Wager: Europe, the Jews, and Israel." In *Jüdische Lebenswelt Schweitz/ Vie et culture juives en Suisse*, 344–351. Zurich: Chronos, 2004.

Remennick, Larissa. "Idealists Headed to Israel, Pragmatics Chose Europe: Identity Dilemmas and Social Incorporation among Former Soviet Jews Who Migrated to Germany." *Immigrants and Minorities* 23(1) (2005): 30–58.

Roffe, Reina. *Conversaciones americanas.* Madrid: Páginas de Espuma, 2001.

*Rok 1989: Bronisław Geremek opowiada, Jacek Żakowski pyta.* Warsaw: Plejada, 1990.

Rosenthal, John. "Anti-Semitism and Ethnicity in Europe," *Policy Review* (2003): 17–38.

Sivan, Miriam. "Jewish Spaces in the European Theater: European Performing Arts Forum, Prague 14–16 June 2003." http://www.jewishcultureineurope.org/theatre_summing_up.htm (accessed October 10, 2007).

Spritzer, Dinah. "Foundation Helps Jewish Schools Thrive in Central, Eastern Europe." *Jewish News Weekly of Northern California,* July 29, 2008. http://www.jewishsf.com/content/2-0-/module/displaystory/story_id/29885/edition_id/56 (accessed October 22, 2007).

———. "Jewish Schools Flourish in Central Europe." *New Jersey Jewish Standard,* March 16, 2006.

Suleiman, Susan R. "Jewish Assimilation in Hungary, the Holocaust, and Epic Film: Reflections on István Szabó's *Sunshine.*" *Yale Journal of Criticism* 14(1) (2001): 233–252.

Szafran, Maurice. *Simone Veil: Destin.* Paris: Flammarion, 1994.

Talmon, Jacob. *The Origins of Totalitarian Democracy.* London: Secker & Warburg, 1955.

Taspinar, Omar. "Europe's Muslim Street." *Brookings Institution Report* (March/April 2003). http://www.brookings.edu/opinions//2003/03/middleeast_taspinar.aspx (accessed Oct. 28, 2007).

Titelman, David, Mikael Enckell, and Henrik Bachner. "Antisemitism in Sweden and Finland." *Scandinavian Psychoanalytic Review* 17 (2004): 52–57.

Trouillot, Michel-Rolf. *Silencing the Past: Power and the Production of History.* Boston: Beacon Press, 1995.

Van der Heide, Albert, and Irene E. Zwiep, eds. *Jewish Studies and the European Academic World: Plenary Lectures read at the VIIth Congress of the European Association for Jewish Studies (EAJS), Amsterdam, July 2002.* Paris, Louvain, and Dudley, MA: Peeters, 2005.

Vasvári, Louise O., and Steven Tötösy de Zepetnek. *Imre Kertész and Holocaust Literature.* West Lafayette, IN: Purdue University Press, 2005.

Velinger, Jan. "Jewish Education in Czech Republic Sees Tenth Anniversary." April 9, 2007. *Radio Prague.* http://www.radio.cz/en/article/95099 (accessed October 22, 2007).

Von Ankum, Katharina. "German Memorial Culture: The Berlin Holocaust Monument Debate." *Response* 68 (Fall 1997/Winter 1998): 41–48.

Vörös, Kati. "How Jewish Is Jewish Budapest?" *Jewish Social Studies* 8(1) (2001): 88–125.

Wasserstein, Bernard. *Vanishing Diaspora: The Jews in Europe since 1945*. Cambridge, MA: Harvard University Press, 1996.

Webber, Jonathan. "Jews and Judaism in Contemporary Europe: Religion or Ethnic Group?" *Ethnic and Racial Studies* 20(2) (1997): 257–279.

Weinberg, David. "Between America and Israel: The Quest for a Distinct European Jewish Identity in the Post-War Era." *Jewish Culture and History* 5(1) (2002): 91–120.

Wetzel, Juliane. "Antisemitismus in Europe: Zwischen Tradition und Einwanderung—neue Tendenzen und alte Diskussion." In *Gerüchte über die Juden: Antisemitismus, Philosemitismus und aktuelle Verschwörungstheorien*, ed. Hanno Lowy, 27–45. Essen: Klartext Verlag, 2005.

Whewell, Tim. "Reopening Lithuania's Old Wounds." *BBC News*, July 21, 2008. http://news.bbc.co.uk/2/hi/programmes/crossing_continents/7508375.stm (accessed March 28, 2009).

White, S. Michael. "International Organizations: Combating Anti-Semitism in Europe." *Jewish Political Studies Review* 16(3–4) (2004). http://www.jcpa.org/phas/phas-whine-f04.htm (accessed October 16, 2007).

Wirtz, Suzanne. "Antisemitismus in Europa." *Tribune* (2007): 123–134.

Wistrich, Robert. "Anti-Zionism and Anti-Semitism." *Jewish Political Studies Review* 16(3–4) (2004): 27–32.

Zick, Andreas, and Beate Küpper. "Antisemitismus in Deutschland und Europa." *Aus Politik und Zeitgeschichte* 31 (2007): 12–19.

Zuroff, Efraim. "Eastern Europe: Anti-Semitism in the Wake of Holocaust Related Issues." *Jewish Political Studies Review* 17(1–2) (2005): 63–80.

NEWSPAPERS

*The Guardian*

*Ha'aretz*


WEBSITES

European Jewish Congress. http://www.eurojewcong.org/ejc/index.php (accessed March 23, 2008)

Israeli Apartheid Week 2009. http://apartheidweek.org/ (accessed March 28, 2009)

Ronald S. Lauder Foundation. http://www.rslfoundation.org/html/ourwork/ourwork.htm (accessed October 22, 2007)

Der Zentralrat der Juden in Deutschland. http://www.tagesschau.de/inland/meldung113942.html (accessed October 25, 2007)

Zentrum für Antisemitismusforschung. http://www2.tu-berlin.de/zfa/ (accessed March 23, 2008)

# Index